LOST
BUILDINGS

THIS IS A GOODMAN BOOK

First published in 2008 by Goodman
An imprint of the Carlton Publishing Group
20 Mortimer Street
London W1T 3JW

10 9 8 7 6 5 4 3 2 1

Text © Jonathan Glancey 2008
Design © Carlton Books Limited 2008

A catalogue record for this book is available from the British Library.

ISBN 978 1 84796 001 6

Publishing Manager: Penny Craig
Art Director: Gülen Shevki-Taylor
Designer: Anna Pow
Picture Researcher: Claire Gouldstone
Picture Manager: Steve Behan

Printed and bound in China.

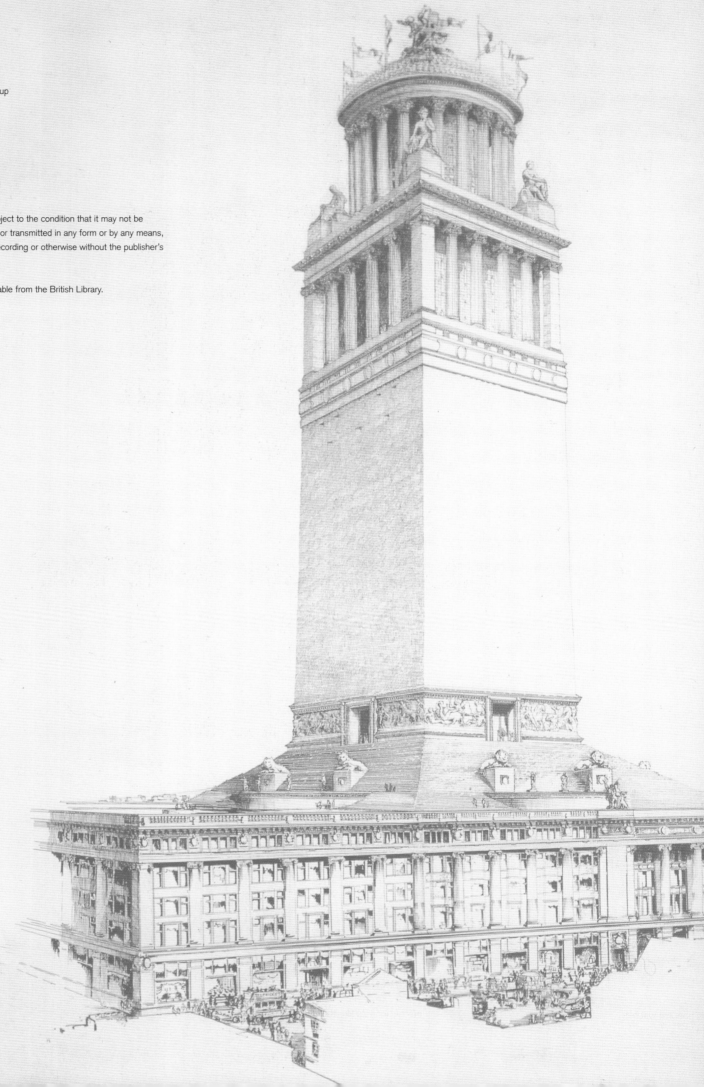

Previous page La Ville
Contemporaine, see p.241.

Right Selfridge's Tower, see p.235.

LOST BUILDINGS

DEMOLISHED   DESTROYED   IMAGINED   REBORN

JONATHAN GLANCEY

GOODMAN

CONTENTS

Opposite The Grand Staircase,
Carlton House, see pp.62–63.

Right Pennsylvania Station, New York, see pp.100–104.

INTRODUCTION

Buildings are big things and you might be forgiven for thinking that it must be all but impossible to lose them. They are not exactly the kind of everyday objects – like umbrellas, sunglasses and mobile phones – that you might mislay on a bus or train and turn up, hoping to find at a lost property office. They do not fall out of holes in pockets or drop through cracks in floorboards. They will never be found, unless they are toys or models, under a bed or down the back of a sofa. This might sound a little obvious and yet throughout history and around the world, humankind has made something of a habit of losing buildings as if these were nothing more substantial than a copper coin, a hairpin or a set of car keys. Even with our greatest and most celebrated monuments we have been, to say the least, careless.

How on earth, for example, did we manage to lose not one but six of the original Seven Wonders of the World? How have we lost not only so many of the great temples of ancient Greece and Rome, but entire cities from antiquity, which tourists would throng to see today? Who, in their right mind, would ever have destroyed so much of Georgian Dublin, or demolished the Euston Arch in London (p.154)? And why, in an age where we talk so much of energy conservation, are perfectly usable and even brand new buildings so promiscuously pulled down as if we had no thought for environmental concerns?

There are, as this book hopes to explain, several key reasons and a host of minor ones why we have lost many of the most interesting buildings of all time and why we continue to knock down buildings as if we were petulant children and architecture was nothing more than a pile of wooden bricks in a nursery.

It is tempting to think that ancient buildings must surely be lost to us largely because time itself is a great destroyer, a grim reaper for humans and architecture alike, but this is not necessarily true. Think of a great building, still more or less with us, which has been regarded as a ruin ever since it came back to world attention in the mid-eighteenth century: the Parthenon, built 447–432 BC (architects Itkinos and Kallikrates, with the sculptor Phidias). This is, quite simply, one of the two or three most important buildings in the history of the world. It is easy to think how lucky we are to be able to see it at all and what else should we expect after 2,500 years? Actually, we should expect a lot more than we see today. Beautifully and solidly built, the Parthenon, the greatest of all the ancient Greek temples, survived largely intact until as late as 1687 when it was hit by a mortar-bomb fired by Venetian soldiers during the Great Turkish War of 1683–99. At this time, the Parthenon was being used as a mosque and an Ottoman gunpowder store. Not surprisingly, it was badly damaged. Before that fateful day in the late-seventeenth century, the Parthenon had survived the transition from its status as a Greek civic temple, dedicated to the goddess Athena, to that of a Christian church – Roman Catholic in one era, Orthodox the next – before being made over into a

Right This magnificent parade of Corinthian columns announces the remains of the Antonine Baths [145–65 AD] in Carthage, a city founded by Julius Caesar to replace its Phoenician predecessor, destroyed in 146 BC. The Baths are ruins chiefly because they were looted for building materials after the fall of the Roman Empire.

mosque after Athens fell to the Ottoman Empire in 1456. A minaret was added to the building and old engravings depict an incongruous and rather funny onion dome sprouting from its noble roof. Despite so much liturgical and religious change, the Parthenon was only really damaged by politics and war.

Age itself then is not the necessarily the great destroyer of buildings. No; there have always been far more effective ways of ridding civilizations of their finest monuments, as well as everyday buildings. War aside, these are what are known as "acts of God", or storms, floods, lightning, accidental fire, earthquakes, or else the machinations of politicians, intent of getting rid of buildings they find somehow subversive or insulting. Other causes are the motivations of property developers and the ruthless workings of the free market by which architecture and buildings are viewed as commodities that can be bought and sold (and demolished) like stocks and shares. And there are many occasions, as history shows, when one regime of politicians, religious leaders and merchant princes (and modern men and women in shiny suits) have decided that the architecture around them is out of date and needs replacing with the latest designs.

This is not a new phenomenon. There are many well-documented cases of English bishops in the thirteenth century ordering the demolition of sizeable parts of Norman or Romanesque cathedrals in order to rebuild them in what was then the fashionable Gothic style. This was odd, not because bishops proved to be so worldly and ambitious, but because Gothic architecture, with its roots in the

pointed arch, had its origins in Islamic design, witnessed and admired by European knights and clergy joining the Crusades, from 1095, to "liberate" the Holy Land and to free Christians living under Muslim rule. The Norman work they so gleefully destroyed was based on the precedent of ancient Roman basilicas. As these had been the foundation for early church buildings, it is strange that they were replaced with designs adopted from Muslim precedent.

Medieval bishops might, in fact, have created new architectural wonders as they sought new styles, but in general, it is true to say that demolition is blind. Certainly our collective experience from the middle of the twentieth century to the present day, is one of fine and familiar buildings, and the streets and squares they once stood in, knocked down only to be replaced with banal, and often overbearing, office blocks, shopping malls, chain hotels and other crude junk. It is not always the case that what is lost is replaced by something worse, and yet demolition makes many of us sad because it strips away memories, childhood, old patterns and ways of life. It is for this very reason that a number of revolutionary political regimes have so energetically destroyed the architecture of previous generations. Under the rule of Joseph Stalin [1879–1953] and the Communist Party of the Soviet Union, and that of the more recent Communist dictator of Romania, Nicolae Ceausescu [1918–89], traditional architecture was wilfully destroyed because it was antithetical to the political values of their regimes and because they wanted to stamp their values, and their boots, into the facades and faces of the cities and citizens they

Above San Francisco was rocked by a massive earthquake on April 18, 1906. Although rebuilt, the Californian city is still in danger of suffering something of the same fate again, although its modern buildings are designed to withstand, as far as technically possible, such "Acts of God".

Right The Euston Arch, London, seen half-demolished on January 19, 1962. There was no need for the destruction of this much-loved and impressive Greek Revival monument of the early Railway Age; it went because business managers and politicians were in love with spurious notions of iconoclastic "modernization".

now controlled. The past was something to be erased. Even then, the actions of such tyrants were not entirely rational. As he went about destroying some of the great and well-loved monuments shaped by former rulers of Russia, Stalin insisted that Soviet architects should design and build in pseudo-traditional styles, as did Ceausescu.

Even more strangely, the real modernizers in terms of architecture and urban design in the twentieth century were often men in old-fashioned suits with cut-glass accents, who would not generally have been thought of as "modern" in any way. It was, for example, and to his eternal shame, the British Conservative Prime Minister, Harold Macmillan [1894–1986], who effectively gave the order for the demolition of the Euston Arch (p.154), one of the best-loved landmarks in central London. Macmillan thought he was being "modern", but he was simply acting like a vandal. It is hard to know exactly what went through the heads of such unlikely "modernizers", men who had been educated along Classical lines. When, as a

young Captain fighting in the Battle of the Somme during the First World War, Macmillan lay wounded and awaiting rescue in a foxhole, he spent most of the day reading the Greek writer Aeschylus – in ancient Greek, of course, not in English translation. The Euston Arch was one of the finest examples of Greek Revival architecture anywhere in Europe. Macmillan would never have consented to the burning of Aeschylus's tragedies, so why did he act so ruthlessly with the Euston Arch?

Much the same question might be asked of New York politicians: why, in the early 1960s, did they consent to the demolition of Pennsylvania Station (p.100), a superb building with its great concourses and waiting rooms modelled on the Baths of Caracalla in ancient Rome? Classical Revival architecture was immensely popular in the United States between the Declaration of Independence in 1776 and the Second World War, because it represented the ideals of republicanism and democracy that the Founding Fathers and their

successors saw in the societies and art of ancient Greece and Rome. To destroy Penn Station was to take a swipe at the very rock-bed of the United States itself. No wonder the demolition of this building was seen as an act of vandalism, and that from the day the wreckers moved in on Eighth Avenue, the architectural conservation lobby in the United States developed teeth and began to bite hard in defence of fundamental American values.

Architectural fashion is a fickle thing. The sad fate of many of the special buildings that have been lost in recent decades in cities around the world is that of being old before their time. If only such buildings as Columbia Market in East London, a Gothic fantasia of the first order, had endured a few more years, it would have been the subject of a nationwide conservation campaign and would have been as popular and as well used as St Pancras station, another Gothic Revival miracle, is today. As recently as 2005, Channel 4, the British television broadcaster, in its show *Demolition* asked viewers which buildings they would most like to see demolished. One of the buildings abused in this populist witch-hunt was Park Hill in Sheffield. Although

much run-down at the time, this once idealistic and rather fascinating local authority housing complex has since been taken on by the energetic developer Urban Splash, a company that has the knack of identifying genuinely interesting buildings and spiriting them back into useful and even fashionable life. In the past, there were times when Gothic, Baroque, Rococo and Palladian buildings were out of time and fashion; put to the popular vote, they would have been demolished, too. Architecture is the antithesis to a cruel streak in human beings, which makes them relish death and destruction. We need to nurture and protect it; it is designed, for the most part, to last.

Buildings have not only been lost through the ministries of politicians, business interests and general ignorance, but also through those of far less obvious vandals. If you live in an old timber-framed house in Britain, for example, you should keep a sharp look out for the Death Watch Beetle. You are not likely to see these secretive little brown bugs, although on a warm summer night you might hear them ticking away in the woodwork. Given a free run, it is remarkable how quickly insects like these can unsettle and even destroy a building.

Above Columbia Road Market, London, a spectacular Victorian Gothic Revival affair, met the same fate as Euston Arch; it would be a hugely popular attraction half a century on from its destruction, but the conservation lobby was not yet strong enough in the late 1950s to save it.

I was very nearly killed by an eighteenth-century building in Havana (p.217), which over many years had been eaten away by insatiably hungry tropical termites. In fact, as my Cuban architect friend, charged with the restoration of many old buildings in Havana, told me, termites go into action as soon as a building has been renovated. Unless made of coral stone or concrete or steel, buildings in such climates are always under threat from humidity and insects.

Everyday traditional buildings all around the world have tended to vanish not just because they were made of timber – some of the oldest surviving buildings in Scandinavia and Japan alike are constructed from wood – but also because they were poor structures in every way. Britain is home to some 10,000 venerable parish churches, with structures dating back to at least the tenth century; the houses that once clustered around them have long gone. This is because they were typically made of clay and wattle, or mud and straw, with some crude timber framing; as such they were susceptible to destruction by fire, storms, bugs and unscrupulous landlords and their men who could tear down, or torch, houses like these in a matter of minutes. Such acts of terror are prevalent in many parts of the world today where political regimes are spiteful, and buildings poorly made.

Buildings, though, are lost for any number of very different reasons. Some of the ones we long to see, for example, were never built in the first place. These might have got stuck on the architect's drawing board or they might have been started but never completed. They might have been the stuff of pure fiction, poetry, myths, legends and dreams. Or, over the past century, they might be creations of the cinema, radio, television and computer simulation. Even these fall into a number of categories. There are designs for buildings such as those dreamed up by Etienne-Louis Boullée (p.228) or Albert Speer (p.84), which were so overbearingly ambitious that they were destined to remain in the realm of "what ifs" and fantasy. There are buildings and even entire cities that haunt the imagination because ancient accounts give such wildly different views of them and we can never truly know whether they were magnificent or not all that special, or whether, indeed, they even existed. Among these are the Tower of Babel, Atlantis and Kublai Khan's Xanadu.

Xanadu is fascinating. We know it as the lynchpin of Samuel Taylor Coleridge's mesmerizing poem "Kubla Khan", and yet the real city of Shangdu or Yuanshangdu in what is Inner Mongolia in China, is today all but impossible to conjure. We know Xanadu was the

Below The reconstruction of Berlin after the Second World War, planned by Adolf Hitler and Albert Speer, never took place. Here is a section of Speer's 1938 model of "Germania", the new-look capital of the Third Reich, showing Runder Platz, with a fountain sculpted by Arno Breker.

summer capital of the Emperor Kublai Khan [1216–94], but although it was surrounded by walls and there must have been a number of grand buildings, the heart of the imperial enclosure might well have been a kind of tented inner-city that could be erected or dismantled as befitted the Emperor of a nomadic plains culture even though the lands he ruled stretched from Hungary to Vietnam. The mighty Khan's palace may have been a thing of fine and rare furs rather than a pile of shimmering marble. We simply don't know, and not least because the Chinese government has done little or nothing to encourage studies into Xanadu. To the Mongolians, Kublai Khan is a legendary hero, while to the Han people of China he is either a foreign devil or an honorary Chinese with Beijing as his capital. Mongolian nationalism was largely crushed by Mao Zedong during the Cultural Revolution of 1965–76, when hundreds of monasteries were destroyed, local costumes banned and the nomadic tribes were herded into collective farms. Red Guards were sent to destroy anything that remained of Xanadu, while the mere mention of the Khan's name was enough to get locals arrested. Political and cultural tensions might have eased a little since then and yet Xanadu is clearly an outcast among the world's most intriguing heritage sites. When I travelled this way, I learned much about recent Chinese and Mongolian history, but precious little about the legendary city and its buildings, if these existed.

Many buildings are lost to us because they are purely fictional, although no less special for that. From St John's description of the Heavenly City in the Book of Revelation to houses that change their form according to the moods of those living in them as evoked in J G Ballard's futuristic story, *Vermilion Sands* (1971), writers and artists have dreamed up strange and wonderful buildings and cities to set them in. However alluring, we can never step into them. Thomas Jefferson [1743–1826], principal author of the Declaration of Independence, third president of the United States and rational

Palladian architect, was highly dismissive of such dark fantasia and so much so that he cut St John, his "Revelation" and his "Heavenly City" from the edition of the Bible he edited. Jefferson referred to Revelation as "merely the ravings of a maniac, no more worthy nor capable of explanation than the incoherences of our own nightly dreams."

Sometimes as I drift into sleep I dream of walking my way through lost buildings. I love the look, for example, of William Beckford's mad "Gothick" fantasy, Fonthill Abbey, a faux-medieval abbey crowned with an unlikely 270-foot (82-metre) tower, which really did exist in the rural depths of Wiltshire in southwest England. I know the plans of this sensational building well and like to imagine myself walking up its vertiginous stairs and from room to improbable room… and disappearing into the "incoherences" of dreams.

I hope this book provides a chance to dream about some of the buildings many of us long to see or would long to see if only we knew about them, and the reason we might not know about them is that they have been demolished or otherwise destroyed. The good news is that some lost buildings have been rediscovered and with the gifts of cash and craft have been brought back to life. For many years one of my favourite houses, The Grange, home of the Gothic Revival architect, Augustus Welby Northmore Pugin [1812–52], brooded at Ramsgate on the English coast in Kent – forlorn, lonely and slowly falling into decay. In 2006 the house was reopened after a long and difficult restoration made on behalf of the Landmark Trust. Now, anyone can rent this gem and in doing so, they will find themselves stepping into the mind and soul of one of the most colourful architects of all time. What is lost can sometimes be found again and even when buildings seem to have vanished forever, at least we can find them in sketches, drawings, fragments, poems, novels, diaries, paintings, myths, legends, photographs… dreams.

Above The site of Kublai Khan's summer palace, Xanadu, in China's Hunnan province. Quite what this legendary palace looked like, we can never be certain. Today, the site is largely out of bounds. Chinese authorities, it seems, are still fearful of the power of the thirteenth-century Mongolian warlord.

Opposite This is the grandiloquent stair climbing up through the dramatic entrance lobby of Fonthill Abbey, Wiltshire. It is hard to believe that this fairy tale English country house ever really existed. It was lost for good when its lofty central tower collapsed for the final time in 1825.

1 LOST IN MYTH

If the Tower of Babel still existed, you would imagine that thousands of tourists would want to visit it. The tower was one of the most famous and haunting of all the ancient monuments that have long been lost to the world. There are, however, two reasons why the Tower of Babel might not have been such a success as a tourist attraction after all. First, it is in what, since 1921, has been Iraq, a country that few people have been able or willing to visit since the British and American-led invasion of 2003. Secondly, the precise location of the tower remains something of a mystery. Some archaeologists argue that it might not have been in Babylon itself where it is widely assumed to have been, but further south in Eridu, which may have been the world's first city.

The name Babel, which some historians translate as "confusion", is best known to us from Genesis (Chapter 11, 1–9), the first book of the Old Testament:

> "And the whole earth was of one language, and of one speech. And it came to pass, as they [the families of the sons of Noah] journeyed from the east, that they found a plain in the land of Shinar [Mesopotamia]; and they dwelt there. And they said to one another, Go to, let us make brick, and burn them thoroughly. And they had brick for stone, and slime they had for mortar. And they said, Go to, let us build us a city and a tower, whose top may reach unto heaven…"

The Lord God was not pleased. Although refraining from smiting all and sundry, He stopped construction of the tower in its tracks by making those working on it speak in different languages, so that they were unable to understand one another and could not complete the project. Clearly, the Lord had yet to visit a modern building site, where many languages are spoken and yet, as if by some miracle, the work gets done. Still, just to make sure that the tower was well and truly spiked, the Lord scattered the sons of the children of Noah "abroad from thence upon the face of all of the earth."

For generations brought up on the Bible, the Tower of Babel was always a great attraction even though its story is little more than 300 words long. What did it look like? How tall was it? Was it higher than the Great Pyramid of Cheops, taller than the spire of Salisbury Cathedral, loftier than the Empire State Building? And was it in Babylon or somewhere else in Mesopotamia and perhaps miles from this famous, and much scorned, city?

There have been hundreds of illustrations made through the ages depicting the Tower of Babel. More or less fantastic, these were always a good opportunity for artists to run wild with their imaginations without causing offence to the Church, all too willing to torture and burn those it perceived as heretics. Almost inevitably, images of the Tower of Babel reflect the artistic sensibilities of the eras they were conjured in. In a delightful illustration from an illuminated Austrian book dating from the early fifteenth century, masons are seen carving "decorated" Gothic windows for a tall, thin and battlemented stone tower, even though the Bible itself clearly says that the original was made of brick and "slime."

Right The Tower of Babel as imagined by Pieter Breughel the Elder and painted in 1563. A spiralling interpretation of the Roman Colosseum, and a symbol of overarching human vanity, the tower appears to be collapsing even as it rises. Its topmost sections vanish into the clouds.

workers and their animals, and were so spacious that these were also used as fields for growing grain to feed the humans and beasts of burden engaged on this aspirational project.

As far as reality is concerned, the Tower of Babel is often said to have been a seven-tiered ziggurat that rose from one side of ancient Babylon. It was, a guide told me in the air-conditioned comfort of Babylon's Nebuchadnezzar Museum, "91.5 metres (300 feet) high, rising from a 91.5-metre square base (305-feet square). It was designed to connect Marduk (the chief god of Babylon) to Earth and man." Babylon itself was the greatest city on earth at the time. "I built it by bitumen and bricks", said Nebuchadnezzar II [c.630–562 BC], "and by shining glazed bricks decorated with bulls and serpents. I built roofs from the trunks of the huge cedar wood and its door leaves were made of cedar. I covered them with copper sheets and made its steps from bronze, and in the gates I erected huge bronze bulls and huge serpents to… arouse the admiration of all people."

However, as Genesis was probably written somewhere between 1440 and 1400 BC, the Tower of Babel must surely have been an earlier building. And because the ziggurat at Eridu might have been the first of its kind, or at least the tallest at the time, it may indeed have been the historic Tower of Babel. It was perhaps the very first work of architecture to tower into the skies and thus, in religious terms, to threaten the majesty of God or the gods. The confusion lies in the fact that the Bible story may have its roots in the story of a real building, but its purpose is allegorical; Genesis tells us not to get too big for own boots. We are not gods and should know our place.

Mind you, God and His prophets do seem to have to have had it in for Babylon. In the Book of Jeremiah (Chapter 51, 1–2), God is as angry as ever: "Behold, I will raise up against Babylon, and against them that dwell in midst of them that rise up against me, a destroying wind; And will send unto Babylon fanners, that shall fan her, and shall empty her land…" Jeremiah had every reason to feel so sorely. He was a Jewish prophet who lived at the time of the destruction of Solomon's Temple (p.158) in 587–86 BC; this occurred during the fall of the Kingdom of Judah at the hands of… you've guessed, the Babylonians. For all its architectural and urban glories, for all the many contributions it has made to civilization, this land – Sumeria, Mesopotamia, Babylonia, Assyria… Iraq – has long been a savage battlefield.

The ziggurat at Eridu, meanwhile, may have collapsed at some time and we can never be sure whether or not this was the mythical Tower of Babel. What we do know is that this stepped pyramid was rebuilt or built over as many as 18 times. The original temple and Eridu itself, sited close to the mouth of the River Euphrates and at the time, also close to the Persian Gulf, predate the Book of Genesis by several thousand years, although it is fascinating to think that the prophet Abraham who was born and brought up in Ur, just seven miles from Eridu, would have known the ziggurats of Mesopotamia. Eridu itself, though, was long in decline even then; it seems as if this special city has lost much of its lustre by around 2000 BC and by 600 BC it had been all but abandoned.

Yet what a magical destination this place remains, even 4,000 years after the city's decline. I visited it in 2002 when Iraq was still ruled by Saddam Hussein, a tyrant who modelled himself on the

Left Just what did the Tower of Babel look like? Here, the ill-fated building is shown in medieval guise. This image, dating from 1411, is an illustration made in Austria for a fifteenth-century edition of the thirteenth-century *World Chronicle* written by the German poet Rudolf von Ems.

A famous painting by Pieter Breughel the Elder [c.1525–69] imagines the Tower of Babel as a spiralling Romanesque man-made mountain or some fantastical, high-rise representation of the Colosseum, which climbs above the passing storm clouds. This utterly compelling image, painted in 1563, hangs in the opulent Italian Renaissance-style galleries of the Kunsthistorisches Museum, Vienna [designed by Gottfried Semper, 1803–79 and Karl von Hasenauer, 1833–94].

The height of the tower, meanwhile, was the stuff of delicious fantasy. The Third Apocalypse of Baruch suggested 463 cubits (695 feet/212 metres), higher than the spire of any medieval cathedral. Writing in c.594 AD, Gregory of Tours plumped for a more modest 200 cubits. This was not enough for Giovanni Villani whose account in c.1300 says that the tower "measured eighty miles around, and it was already 4,000 paces high" (1,200 feet/366 metres) before God took umbrage and effectively cut it down to size. John Mandeville, the fourteenth-century traveller, went much further; local inhabitants told him that the tower had been 64 furlongs (8 miles/13 kilometres) high. The seventeenth-century historian Verstegan, while claiming a height of just 4¹/₂ miles (7.6 kilometres), quoted Herodotus to the effect that the tower had been wider than it was it tall and was more like a mountain than a building. I suppose that if you have never seen a building as big as, for example, the great pyramid of Cheops in Egypt, you might easily mistake that for a mountain, too. According to his sources, Verstegan said that the spiral path leading up to the top of the Tower of Babel was wide enough to shelter lodgings for building ancient kings of Mesopotamia. Saddam spent a small fortune patching up ancient monuments including the impressive remains of the ziggurat at Ur and rebuilding sizeable chunks of the legendary walled city of Babylon. Although what I saw at Eridu were ruins and little more than a hint of the ziggurat that once rose here, it was a deeply moving experience to stand on the top of this truly ancient temple in the mother of all cities.

Actually, father might be the better word. Myth has it that Eridu was created by Enki, the Sumerian god of wisdom and sweet waters. His own sweet waters were his semen; he mated with the land to make it fertile and to father what, in Sumerian legend, was without doubt the first city. The city and the religious shrine of Eridu – the most revered in ancient Mesopotamia – rose from a point where sea and land, marsh and sand, had been all but indistinguishable. According to the world's oldest written creation myth:

"A reed had not come forth, a tree had not been created. A brick had not been laid, a brick mould had not been made. A house had not been built. A city had not been built. All the lands were sea. Then Eridu was made… the holy city."

Then and only then, the gods created humankind. Here, in Eridu. In ancient Mesopotamian mythology, the city, architecture and humans rose together.

Enki was a sky god, active at the time when men began to rule the world with their machismo; abstract gods, might-is-right kings and the female Earth god or goddesses were pushed into a submissive role. This religious revolution was more or less completed, worldwide, during the Bronze Age as ideas spread around the world. Eridu itself, however, was founded well before the Bronze Age, and perhaps as long ago as 5,500 BC when the first temple was built here.

This mythical city was lost for centuries. The desert mound known as Tell Abu Shahrain was finally excavated in the late 1940s by a team led by Fuad Safar [1913–78] of the Iraqi Antiquities Department and the distinguished English archaeologist, Seton Lloyd [1902–96]. It is a shame that there is so little to see today at the site of the temple that was to spawn the Parthenon, the Pantheon, St Peter's, St Paul's, the White House and the World Trade Center, but as there are so few visitors, Enki, his temple and the city he spawned are possibly best left to themselves and the ever-shifting desert sands.

Above right The temple sanctuaries of Uruk in southern Iraq, excavated in earnest since 1954, are some of the world's very first major architectural monuments. The remains at Eridu, a possibly older city close by, although excavated at much the same time, are covered by desert sands today.

Right Remains of the ziggurat of Uruk. Last reconstructed in the third century BC, the original temple was founded thousands of years earlier. Until its excavation by German archaeologists in the twentieth century, the stepped building had been mistaken, like many lost Sumerian temples and cities, for a hill.

Ancient ruins are often wreathed in myth and cloaked in mystery, because for centuries we have known so little about them. Local people often knew no more than the first European archaeologists who came their way intent on discovering historical truths and architectural certainties. Few "lost buildings", this side of the sealed tombs of Egyptian pharaohs, have been protected by such dark myths as the ruins of the Palace of King Minos on Crete. These largely uncovered ruins were partly reconstructed by Sir Arthur Evans [1851–1941] in the 1920s, and are all that survive of a complex of Cretan palaces destroyed in two major earthquakes that occurred in *c.*1625 BC and *c.*1375 BC.

The ruins were originally discovered in the 1890s by Minos Kalokairinos, a Cretan merchant, but it was Evans, a wealthy Englishman, who bought the entire six-acre site and conducted exhaustive investigations. The Cretan just happened to share his name with the legendary King Minos, but Evans made the connection with the lost palace and the mysterious monarch.

Minos, son of the god Zeus and Europa, was the mythical king of Crete whose wife, cursed by Poseidon, god of the seas, sired a monstrous child, half-human and half-bull. This was the Minotaur. Minos had the Greek architect-inventor, Daedalus, design and construct a maze that the Minotaur could never escape from. This was the famous Labyrinth. The Minotaur fed, from time to time, on young Athenian men and women – virgins, of course – sent to Crete to appease Minos after his declaration of war on Athens. Eventually, one of the young men, Theseus, using a bit of cunning and a ball of golden thread, entered the Labyrinth, slaughtered the Minotaur and found his way out again.

When Evans uncovered around 1,300 interlocking rooms within the Palace of Knossos, he liked to believe that he had discovered the Labyrinth, or, at least, he conflated a number of Greek myths associated with Minos with the truly labyrinthine plan of the mysterious palace. When he discovered frescoes of bulls on the palace walls and found sound evidence of what seemed to have been vicious forms of bull-fighting and rituals involving human sacrifice here, he was happy

to claim that this was King Minos's Palace. In fact, it remains hard to say exactly what this vast and complex building was. It was perhaps a palace – Evans discovered a "throne room" complete with an alabaster "throne" – but it was also some sort of home for high priests, a civic centre, a store, and Minos only knows what else.

The Palace of Minos, then, although visible in parts, remains lost to us. We have yet to unveil or to understand its many secrets. We have yet to decode its most ancient language, found on clay tablets there and known as Linear A, although Michael Ventris [1922–56], a brilliant young English architect, did decode a second and younger language, Linear B, which proved to be a very early form of Greek, the Greek that Homer's heroes might have spoken over 1,000 years before the design and construction of the Parthenon in the fifth century BC when Athens was at the height of her powers.

So today we can wander through excavations and reconstructions at Knossos, knowing that there is still so much to uncover and discover. There are many other great palaces along the lines of Knossos to be found around the world, but although ruined, we can at least read their histories with greater confidence than we can with Knossos. One of the greatest of these is the Palace of Persepolis in modern-day Iran, founded by Darius I in 518 BC. The remains of the palace rise from a giant terrace overlooking countryside today, but in Darius's day it would have overlooked the grand new city of Persepolis.

These ruins are so fascinating because they display designs and forms of decoration from many different sources; the palace is an architectural tribute to the self-styled "king of kings" under whom the Achaemenid Persian Empire was never greater. An inscription at the southern end of the palace terrace reads:

"I am Darius the great king, the king of kings, the king of many countries, the son of Hystaspes, an Achaemenid.

"By the favour of Ahuramazda these are the countries which I took into my possession along with this Persian people, which felt fear of me and bore me tribute: Elam, Media, Babylonia, Arabia, Assyria, Egypt, Armenia, Cappadocia, Lydia, the Greeks who are of the mainland and those who are by the sea, and countries which are across the sea, Sargatia, Parthia, Drangiana, Aria, Bactria, Sogdia, Chorasmia, Sattagydia, Arachosia, Hindus, Gandara, Sacae, Maka."

Darius had divided his empire into 20 "satraps", or provinces, each of which was largely self-governing and allowed to nurture its own culture, unless it stepped out of line. Each of these, stretching from the Persian Gulf to India, brought their artistry and skills to work on the design and construction of Persepolis.

Substantial chunks of Persepolis survive, but not quite enough for us to get a proper grip on what Darius's great city and palace really looked and felt like to be in. Because the Persians were the enemy of the Greeks and because so much ancient western history is derived from the Greeks, the Persians and their emperors are still written about

Below A cross-sectional watercolour [Peter Connolly, 1990], demonstrates the complexity of the plan and structure of King Minos's palace. Rooms, supported by massive, inversely tapering columns, were interlocked in a complex fashion. Punctuated by courtyards and lightwells, the palace was not as dark or as horrid as legends suggest.

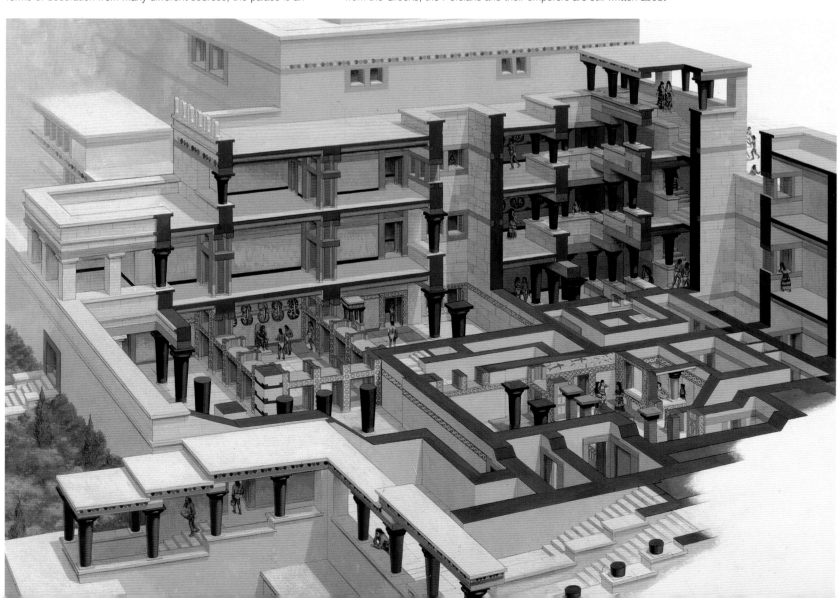

Right Caught in stone reliefs, peoples and fighting beasts drawn from across the Persian Empire climb and otherwise adorn the east staircase of the Apadana, or Audience Hall, at Persepolis. In 1933, foundation tablets excavated here proved that the building was the work of Darius the Great.

as if they were more monsters than human beings. In the curiously entertaining film, *300* (Zack Snyder, 2007), the mighty Persian army of Xerxes, son of Darius, is depicted trying to bludgeon its way through the narrow stone pass of Thermopylae (the "Hot Gates") as it attempts to invade mainland Greece. Xerxes and his hordes were heroically fought off for three days by a last-stand band of 300 Spartans led by King Leonidas. The Spartans were all but wiped out, but their delaying tactic and their sheer heroism encouraged the Greek states to unite and fight back. What is interesting about this highly stylized film, based on a startling graphic novel by Frank Miller, is that it presents Xerxes and his army of soldiers drawn from across his vast empire as terrifying and evil monsters. This was the view of the Greeks perhaps, but not the Persians. Equally, the ruins of many of the world's once great buildings are a reminder that history is written by the victors; entire cities have been lost to invading armies. In its heyday, Persepolis would have been at the heart of a thriving local as well as imperial economy, but today its ruins feel a long way from anywhere.

They remind me of the famous poem "Ozymandias" by Percy Bysshe Shelley [1792–1822]. Although there are those who claim that the great English romantic poet was writing specifically about a ruined Egyptian monument, I think he was just being fanciful, although making a profound point about how immortality defies even the grandest king or emperor:

I met a traveller from an antique land,
Who said: "Two vast and trunkless legs of stone
Stand in the desert. Near them on the sand,
Half sunk, a shatter'd visage lies, whose frown
And wrinkled lip and sneer of cold command
Tell that its sculptor well those passions read
Which yet survive, stamp'd on these lifeless things,
The hand that mock'd them and the heart that fed;
And on the pedestal these words appear:
'My name is Ozymandias, king of kings:
Look on my works, ye mighty, and despair!'
Nothing beside remains: round the decay
Of that colossal wreck, boundless and bare,
The lone and level sands stretch far away."

Left Columns rise from the ruins of Darius's palace, completed by Xerxes in 512 BC, at Persepolis. This magnificent complex was destroyed by Alexander the Great in 330 BC, although the warring Macedonian king is said to have regretted his actions when he returned this way several years later.

Below A Persian hero battles a winged lion in the doorframe of one of the great portals leading to to the palace at Persepolis. The gateways themselves were clearly influenced by Greek precedent, although both Darius and Xerxes drew their architectural inspiration from across their vast, short-lived, empire.

The greatest or certainly the biggest of all statues in the guise of a human figure must have been the long-lost Colossus of Rhodes. This was not a representation of a king or emperor, but of Helios, the Greek sun god. The bronze statue, which was around 100 feet (30.5 metres) tall, was cast by the sculptor Chares of Lindos and erected on the island of Rhodes between 292 and 280 BC. Aside from looking splendid from the sea, especially at sunrise and sunset, this heroic statue was a memorial to the lifting of the Siege of Rhodes in 305–4 BC, when the island kingdom was under mortal threat.

There is something special about giant statues, especially if they rise from ports or other city centres; they lend a surreal air to such places, confusing our sense of humanly derived proportion. Contemporary photographs recording the trial run construction of the Statue of Liberty in Paris before it was shipped to its permanent home in New York, are glorious things: the muscular arms, neck, shoulders and spiked head of the libertarian giant dwarf local streets and apartment blocks. It must have seemed, if just for a moment, that at least one old *quartier* of Paris had been transferred to Lilliput. The construction of the Colossus of Rhodes might have been similar to that of the Statue of Liberty; the bronze skin of the Colossus was most probably attached to a hidden brick or stone column; perhaps

this contained a stair and it may have been possible to climb up the statue to take in Mediterranean views and the rays of the Sun itself.

In 1903 a brass plaque was mounted inside the Statue of Liberty, which was inscribed with the famous poem by Emma Lazarus [1849–87], entitled "The New Colossus." It begins:

"Not like the brazen giant of Greek fame,
With conquering limbs astride from land to land;
Here at our sea-washed, sunset gates shall stand
A mighty woman with a torch…"

The scale of such statues as that of the Colossus of Rhodes haunted the imagination of artists of the Romantic era in France as elsewhere. The painter John Henry Fuseli [1741–1825] drew and engraved an image of himself weeping as he tries to make sense of the scale of ancient statuary. Fuseli is depicted sitting by all that is left of a giant statue of the Emperor Constantine – a huge hand and an even bigger foot. This image, made between 1778 and 1780, is entitled, "The artist in despair over the magnitude of Antique Fragments."

Sadly, there was much to despair about in Rhodes. An earthquake rocked the island in 226 BC and the statue keeled over, cracking at

Above The Colossus of Rhodes was portrayed many times by artists over the centuries. Most agreed that the giant statue straddled the harbour entrance, although none knew exactly what this sculptural behemoth really looked like. This is "The Port of Rhodes" by the Dutch artist Abraham Storck [1635–1710].

Top right Easy does it… the Colossus is shown here in a copper engraving made for the *Picture Book for Children* Vol. 1 by Friedrich Justin Bertuch, published in Weimar in 1792. The look of the statue – a naked Greek hero – reflects artistic conventions of the time.

the knees. The remains lay on the ground for some 800 years, until
the capture of Rhodes by the Arab forces of Muawiyhah I [602–80
AD], a companion of Mohammed; in 654 AD the Colossus was
broken up and sold off, according to Theophanes the Confessor, to a
merchant from Edessa who packed the fragments in pouches and had
them transported home on the backs of 900 camels.

The Colossus became the stuff of myth and legend. Had its
mighty limbs really straddled a harbour mouth as Emma Lazarus's
poem suggests and as many engravings depicted it? Probably not,
but lost buildings and monuments can be anything we want them
to be in our imaginations. Today, Mongolian, Chinese and other
archaeologists still dream of finding the hidden, mountainside tombs
of Ghengis and Kublai Khan. Who knows what treasures might be
buried in magnificent chambers cut from rock? Of course, it's possible
that these distant emperors may have chosen to be buried in humble
circumstances. Whatever the truth, it is fun to dream of what might
have been and what we have lost.

Right Exotic soldiers study the sheer scale of the Greek antiquities they
appear to have stumbled on in this engraving by Matthaus Merian [1593–1650].
The city backdrop is an improbable mix of Classical and Gothic buildings.

Not every generation has found the vast monuments of the Ancient World things of wonder. The Temple of Artemis at Selçuk, near Ephesus in present-day Turkey, is one of the Seven Wonders of the Ancient World and, from all accounts, one of the greatest of all the Classical temples, and yet it was finally destroyed not by fire, an earthquake, or even war, but by a mob in 401.

The temple was begun by Croesus of Lydia, the legendarily rich king, and completed in about 550 BC. Antipater of Sidon, who first compiled the list of the Seven Wonders, thought it the most wondrous wonder of all:

"I have set eyes on the wall of lofty Babylon on which is a road for chariots, and the statue of Zeus by the Alpheus, and the hanging gardens, and the colossus of the Sun, and the huge labour of the high pyramids, and the vast tomb of Mausolus; but when I saw the house of Artemis that mounted to the clouds, those other marvels lost their brilliancy, and I said, 'Lo, apart from Olympus, the Sun never looked on aught so grand.' "

The temple famed in legend was not the first; the site it stood on has been sacred since the Bronze Age, as excavations made in the late 1980s have confirmed. The great marble temple, the last of its line, was designed by the Cretan architect Chersiphron and his son Metagenes. We can never be sure exactly what this great religious foundation and ancient tourist attraction looked like. According to the Roman historian, soldier and natural philosopher, Pliny [23–79 AD], the colonnaded temple was three times the size of the Parthenon. The "cella" or core of the building was surrounded by no fewer than 127 Ionic columns, each 60 feet (18 metres) tall. Inside, the temple was adorned with some of the greatest sculpture of the age. Who really knows? The temple was first destroyed in 356 BC by Herostratus, who wanted, like a modern "celebrity", to be famous at all costs, perhaps even forever. Very few people have heard of Herostratus today. The temple was rebuilt by the architect, Scopas of Poras, by 323 BC, and then destroyed a second time by Goths under the leadership of Respa, Veduc and Thuruar in 262 AD.

Above left A colourful and delightfully inaccurate portrayal of the Temple of Artemis at Ephesus. This also appeared in Friedrich Justin Bertuch's *Picture Book for Children* Vol. 1, at much the same time as Prussian and Bavarian architects were working on archaeologically correct Roman and Greek Revival temples.

Left Wood engraving of a drawing by Ferdinand Knab [1834–1902] of the Temple of Artemis made for a book on the Seven Wonders of the World published in Munich in 1886. This gives a more accurate view than the illustration above of what this grand building might have looked like.

Rebuilt for a third time, the temple soldiered on until 391 AD when the Christian Roman Emperor Theodosius announced the closure of all temples. Sadly, instead of finding another use for the magnificent Temple of Artemis, where St Paul had once preached, the mob – hateful, vicious and philistine – was allowed to take it down, stone by stone. The only consolation is that with the help of a reliable guide, you can still see some of the columns from the wondrous temple reworked into the fabric of one of the greatest of all Christian churches, the Hagia Sophia – the Church of Divine Wisdom – in Istanbul. As for the original temple, its site was rediscovered after a dangerous six-year search by John Turtle Wood [1821–90], a railway architect active in Turkey and sponsored by the British Museum in 1869. There is, though, precious little to see, aside from magnificent scenery beyond the marshy field the foundations of the temple stand in. Curiously, while I was writing this book, Greek archaeologists uncovered another temple dedicated to Artemis off the southern Italian coast. It is seems that St Paul also preached there during the festival of Artemis. Perhaps he prayed for the destruction of this temple, too. If so, his prayers were answered: the ruins of the temple have been hidden under water for at least 1,500 years.

Above Ruins of the Temple of Artemis, photographed in 1980, scattered across a boggy field. What must have been a deeply impressive building was finally destroyed not by an Act of God, but by the human hands of a Christian mob. The battle for religious supremacy has long been a great destroyer.

Above left German model of Priene, the well-planned Greek city, in Turkey today, that boasted not just rational streets and fine buildings, but a comprehensive fresh water supply and sewage system.

Left Sections of fluted Ionic columns from the ruined Temple of Athena, Priene. The fourth-century city fell into rapid decline after its port – the source of its wealth – silted up.

Elsewhere in Turkey are the ruins of what was the Greek city of Priene. Once a harbour, but now some 10 miles from the sea, Priene was one of the first rationally planned cities. Laid out on a grid-iron plan in view of the sea and with a mountain backdrop, it was designed as a magnificent balance between the man-made and the natural worlds. It would be a wonder to be able to visit such a perfect "modern" ancient city neatly divided into four zones: political, cultural, religious and commercial. However, even though Alexander the Great lived there for some time, Priene declined under Roman rule and simply faded away. Excavated from the early twentieth century, Priene has revealed such important buildings as a 5,000-seat theatre, a public meeting room and political chamber, as well as remnants of

a temple dedicated to Athena Polios, a gift of Alexander the Great. The temple was designed by Pytheos, architect of the Mausoleum of Halicarnassus, another of the Seven Wonders (p.138) and was used by the Roman architect Marcus Vitruvius Pollio [c.80–25 BC] as an exemplar of the ideal Classical temple. Because Vitruvius's *The Ten Books on Architecture* became a staple of architects of the European Classical revival, from the time of the Renaissance onwards, something of the spirit and design of Priene's temple lives on in countless neoclassical buildings erected around the world ever since. The temple of Athena Polios was long lost, but in its own particular way, unforgotten. Priene was finally abandoned in the thirteenth century after an earthquake and a malaria epidemic.

Above The amphitheatre, Priene. The city was fully excavated for the first time by the German archaeologist Theodor Wiegand [1864–1936] for the Berlin Museum between 1895 and 1899.

Two other cities that seemed to have vanished without trace have haunted writers, artists and historians for many hundreds of years. Whatever, they wondered, happened to Carthage and Troy? Had they even been real or were they the stuff of legends and dreams? Both cities are quite real.

Troy is known for the story of the "Trojan Horse", for the beauty of Helen of Troy, and for the Greek–Trojan War as related in Homer's *Iliad*. The ruins of Troy are sited at Hisarlik in Anatolia, north-west Turkey. These were built over during the reign of the Roman Emperor Augustus when he founded the new town of *Iliad*. *Iliad* declined during the Byzantine era and with it, the secrets of Troy beneath its Roman feet.

Excavations made from the 1870s and led by the German archaeologist Heinrich Schliemann [1822–90] proved that Homer's Troy really had existed. Built over many times, it was only at "level seven" in the excavations that the ghosts of Helen, Paris, Agamemnon and Hector were first roused. Even then, much of what had been ancient Troy was destroyed by the crude methods employed by Schliemann and later archaeologists, many of whom were more interested in uncovering golden treasures than in preserving the fabric of the city itself. The Greeks of the Golden Age of Pericles and the Parthenon knew Troy only through legend and Homer. The Trojan War that had led to the fall of Troy took place some time between 1330 and 1184 BC, so it was an extremely remote event by the time Alexander the Great visited the site and made a sacrifice in honour of the Greek warrior, Achilles, in 334 BC.

Troy, a Bronze-Age sea port (the site is now inland) had been founded in the third millennium BC and destroyed by earthquake at least once before the Troy of our collective imagination was built at some time between the late-fourteenth and late-thirteenth century BC. We know that it was a walled city protected by stone towers 30 feet (9 metres) high and home to around 5,000 people. Even so, it is all but impossible to piece together the city we know from Homer. He probably never went to Troy, while the war he used as a literary vehicle for his magnificent story of love and vengeance, occurred some 450 years before he began writing. So although there is evidence of a city we can call Troy, we cannot know precisely where Achilles received that fateful arrow to the heel or through which gate the famous wooden horse was dragged to seal Troy's fate. Excavations continue even as tacky theme parks emerge locally to cash in our desire to get close to Troy.

Top That must be Helen, the "face that launched a thousand ships", standing on top of one of the towers of Troy as the city's finest ride out to do battle with the Greeks sailing their way. In this fifteenth-century illustration, Troy is portrayed as a medieval city.

Above In this painting from the school of the Flemish Baroque artist, Paul Bril [1554–1626], the Greeks are shown pulling the "Trojan Horse" crammed with their soldiers through the gates of the city. In Homer's *Iliad* this is how the Greeks are said to have taken Troy.

Above right Troy was settled from the early Bronze Age until the Roman era. This 1986 watercolour by Peter Connolly shows what the city might have been like at the time it featured in *The Iliad*, about 700 years before the glory days of fifth-century Athens.

Right This is the Mound of Hissarlik, Turkey, a site made famous in 1871 by Heinrich Schliemann [1822–90] the German archaeologist who discovered the remains of what he believed to be, and does indeed seem to be, the long lost city of Troy.

We know far more about Carthage. On a day trip from Tunis you can enjoy wandering around the ruins of Hannibal's city by the sea. It was definitely from here, so close to many air-conditioned modern holiday resorts, that Hannibal set out from Africa to Europe to cross the Alps with armoured elephants and to challenge the emerging might of the Roman republic.

According to legend, Carthage was founded by Queen Dido; in reality this Phoenician sea port seems to have been established

from around the end of the ninth century BC. A natural harbour, it is beautifully and intelligently sited. Unfortunately, a lack of Carthaginian art and writing means that little is known about ancient Carthage beyond a religion based on a catholic mix of regional gods and human sacrifice.

What we are sure of are the Punic Wars, an attempt over a century to wrest control of the Mediterranean from the Romans. Famously, Hannibal was defeated, at the end of the Second Punic War, on Italian soil by Roman legions in 201 BC. In the Third Punic War of 149–46 BC,

the legions of Publius Scipio Africanus sacked and destroyed Carthage.

Julius Caesar visited the historic site in 46 BC and proclaimed the building of a new city, which was eventually founded by Julius's nephew, the emperor Augustus Caesar in 29 BC. Roman Carthage, or Colonia Julia Carthago, prospered and went on to become an important centre of early Christianity. St Augustine, author of the magnificent "Confessions", came from nearby Hippo, but as a lustful young man, as he recorded himself, it was to Carthage that "I came burning".

Opposite "Dido Building Carthage, or the Rise of the Carthaginian Empire", by J.M.W. Turner, 1815. The sun rises over the water and Carthage also rises, every bit the perfect, and perfectly romantic, Classical city of legend.

Above One of the tall Roman columns that carried the lofty vaults of the Antonine Baths, Carthage. This was the third largest public baths in the Roman Empire. The city waxed rich on maritime trade.

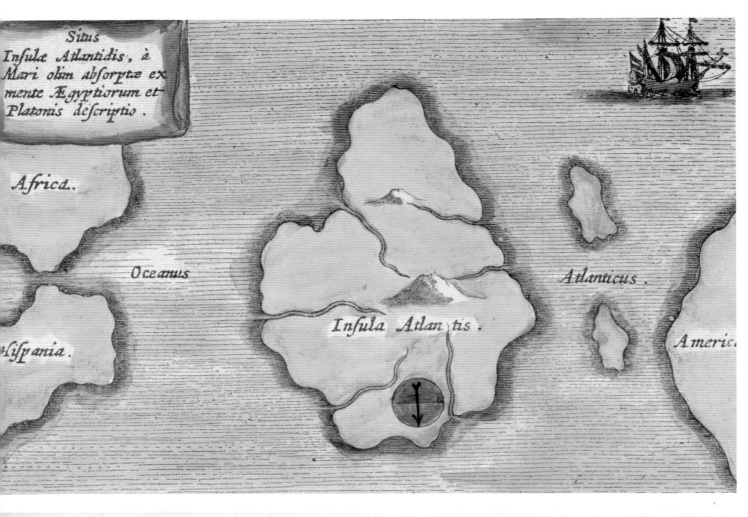

Left Set between Africa and the Americas, "the location of the sunken island Atlantis according to the Egyptians and Plato's description," is revealed in this nicely topsy-turvy engraving made for *Mundus Subterraneus*, a book by Athanasius Kircher, published in Amsterdam in 1664.

Left The capital of Atlantis, again following Plato's description, but this time in a drawing made for N Zhirov's book *Atlantis* (2001). In the spirit of Plato, the mythical city is seen as being in the Greek style, as are the ships that ply its concentric canals.

One legendary city that will probably always be lost to us is Atlantis. This underwater city was first mentioned by the Greek philosopher, Plato, in his dialogues "Timaeus" and "Critias". According to Plato, Atlantis was an ancient civilization occupying a land that lay beyond the Pillars of Heracles, in other words somewhere out in the Atlantic beyond the Rock of Gibraltar. Atlantis was a great power, but when it attempted to invade Greece thousands of years before either Plato or the mythical Greece of Homer's heroes, it literally sank overnight.

It is hard to say what Plato's story is meant to be mean. Clearly, it suggests that no civilization, no matter how powerful, should ever dare to mess with Greece, but it might also be a reworking of a number of age-old stories about countries, civilizations and indeed entire islands that had sunk without trace. Such things can and have happened. Think

of Pompeii or of South Sea islands that have been suddenly destroyed by natural forces. Plato might well have been thinking of the sudden collapse of Minoan civilization on Crete, another enemy of Greece.

Atlantis has long been a land that writers have enjoyed; it is a place where anything can happen and civilization can be whatever an author wants it to be. Atlantis became a utopian community in Francis Bacon's *The New Atlantis* (1627), while in Ignatius L Donnelly's *Atlantis: the Antediluvian World* (1882) it was the bedrock of all future civilizations. In the twentieth century, it was home to the ancestors of Nazi Aryan supermen, the stuff of science fiction and, later on, of computer games. The real Atlantis is lost to us, but the imaginary Atlantis can be anything we wish it to be, which is why its appeal is so enduring.

Above A bathing cove on the coast of Atlantis. This is a backdrop for Sir Gerald Hargreave's *Atlanta: a Story of Atlantis*, a "fantasy with music" dating from 1949. Atlantis is represented as a kind of Shangrila-on-Sea. If it ever existed, perhaps it was.

Those sailing through the Pillars of Heracles and along the Mediterranean in the ancient world, would have been thrilled by the sight of another of the Seven Wonders of the World: this was the Lighthouse of Alexandria, for hundreds of years one of the tallest buildings in the world. In fact, at around 492 feet (150 metres), it was almost as high as the Great Pyramid of Cheops, the only one of the original Seven Wonders that has survived to this day.

The lighthouse, standing on the island of Pharos (itself the Greek word for lighthouse) off the coast of Alexandria, was erected in the third century BC during the period of Greek influence in Egypt, and was originally a simple, if eye-catching, marker along the coast pointing ships in the direction of the port of Alexandria and the River Nile. Some time during the period of the Roman occupation of Egypt – probably in the first century AD – mirrors and a huge fire were installed at the top of the monument, transforming it into a fully working lighthouse. At sea, its beam could be seen from up to 35 miles (56 kilometres) away; it was certainly a wonder. Its architect was Sostratus of Cnidus.

The lighthouse was built of stone. As far as anyone can be sure of its design, a square base gave way to an octagonal shaft, although the final section up to the fire and mirrors was circular. Roman coins suggest that statues of the sea god Triton, in the guise of a merman, adorned each corner of the base, while during the Roman period, a statue of Poseidon, the great god of the sea and Triton's father, stood at the top of the tower.

The lighthouse was certainly well built. The Spanish-born Muslim poet and civil servant, Ibn Jubayr, was sent on a pilgrimage to Mecca for some misdemeanour in 1183, and on his voyage to Arabia stopped off at Alexandria. "Description of it", he wrote, "falls short, the eyes fail to comprehend it, and words are inadequate, so vast is the spectacle." Like so many travellers of his era Ibn Jubayr gives us no precise description of the building; I have long wondered why this is so. Why did Marco Polo tell us so little about the architecture and design of the court of Kublai Khan? Why was the great historian Josephus, who travelled so extensively through the ancient world so frustratingly

Above A delightful woodcut dated 1850, depicting the Lighthouse of Alexandria in the guise of a wedding-cake like Classical temple rising in ten tiers above the harbour. In all likelihood, it was a tall tower very unlike this many-sided, although compelling, ziggurat.

Left An intriguing early plan of Alexandria made for Paul Belon's *Observations de Plusiers Singularitez* (Paris, 1588), showing the principal buildings of the Mediterranean port. Curiously, the Lighthouse itself – centre foreground – appears to be rather small. Such maps, though, were not exactly the A-Zs of their day.

Above A grand and highly stylized Alexandria Lighthouse drawn by Johann Bernard Fischer von Erlach around 1700. The lighthouse is shown as a true Wonder of the World, dominating the grand neo-classical city it serves. Buildings and people are dwarfed by its commanding heights.

vague in his description of the many fascinating and magnificent buildings and cities he saw and that are lost to us? The answer might be that accurate architectural descriptions only emerged with the birth of rigorous art history and this really dates from the nineteenth century. Even today, many travellers still find it hard to describe a building they have seen in any detail.

Two earthquakes rocked the lighthouse, first in 1303 and again 20 years later. Reduced to a shadow of its former self, it seems to have disappeared by 1480. Some of its mighty stones were later incorporated into the fifteenth-century citadel of Qaitbay, the Arab fortress built by order of Sultan Al-Ashraf Sayf al-Din Qa'it Bay; others have been found on the harbour floor at Alexandria. Over the centuries, many fanciful illustrations have been made of the Lighthouse of Alexandria and although we cannot be 100 per cent sure of how it looked in its long heyday, there are a number of minarets and tombs in Arabic Egypt that were clearly influenced by its heroic design; after all it was one of the tallest buildings in the

world for hundreds of years and was only surpassed by one or two cathedrals in late medieval Europe.

We come much more down to earth with the Temple of Tara in Ireland. This is one of the country's most important archaeological sites, the seat of power of Ireland's Celtic kings. This extraordinary site, Ireland's equivalent of Stonehenge or the Egyptian pyramids, continues to spring surprises. In early 2007 construction of a new motorway, the M3, was stalled as archaeologists uncovered evidence of what appeared to be a circular timber enclosure with a round temple inside it; the date of this complex is uncertain, but the temple may well have been in use around 1000 BC.

In Ireland the government's environment minister is able to recommend the destruction of national monuments if such action is deemed to be "in the public interest". This singularly philistine legislation dates from as late as 2004. Irish politicians and businessmen who are keen on development and road building have often gone along with the destruction of Ireland's architectural and

archaeological heritage. Almost inevitably, the discovery at Tara led to a battle royal between politicians who wanted to drive their cars up a brand new motorway and, according to opinion polls, at least two-thirds of the rest of the population.

The Hill of Tara was placed on the World Monuments Fund's 2008 list of the 100 most endangered sites on the planet, while the European Union initiated legal action against the Irish government. The future of the Hill of Tara and the new excavations remains in doubt – proof that even today we are still willing to lose great art, architecture and history if we are offered fast roads, shopping malls, golf courses and, in this case, dismal new housing. Lost for centuries and now re-found, the latest temple to be uncovered at Tara should be a source of national celebration, not destruction. To the Iraqis and indeed the rest of the world, the discovery in Ireland could be compared with finding the site and even remnants of the legendary Tower of Babel. We would be mad to let such discoveries that do so much to connect us to our past, real and mythical, slip from our hands through wilful ignorance and blatant greed.

Opposite Temple hill of Tara in County Meath, Ireland, seat of the mythical High King of Ireland. This impressive Iron Age enclosure, measuring 318 by 264 metres (348 x 289 yards), was where, in myth, the king would be crowned as he touched a stone monolith set between the two circular enclosures.

Below The Mound of the Hostages at Tara is a small Neolithic passage tomb dating from around 2000 BC. During the twentieth century, the Hill of Tara was excavated British Israelites, a sect within the Church of England who believed the Irish to be a Lost Tribe and that the Ark of the Covenant was buried here.

Bottom left A stone from inside the Mound of Hostages carved with spiral and other patterns that appear to represent notions of infinity, or they might be symbols of the idea of continual rebirth – the meanings are lost and no one really knows.

Bottom right Interior of the Mound of Hostages. In several of these Irish burial mounds, sunlight strikes certain patterned stones positioned right in the heart of the structures on the morning of the solstices. Tara is, evidently, Ireland's Stonehenge and an equally mysterious place.

2 LOST IN PEACE

One of the main reasons we have lost and continue to lose so many grand old buildings is simply that they get knocked down. There are always "good reasons" for this and yet, at heart, the story is really always the same: they go because they stand in the way of what is often called progress or modernization, but in reality is a combination of ambition, greed, a lack of grace and an egotistical belief that the new is always better than the old.

Many buildings have been demolished because they have fallen out of fashion. Until very recently, it was all too easy to demolish nineteenth-century Gothic Revival buildings in Britain because they were seen as old-fashioned and ugly by a generation brought up in the twentieth century. What is ugly to one generation, however, is often a thing of beauty to the next. Although philosophers, historians, mathematicians, artists and architects have tried hard over the centuries to lay down laws of good taste, measured scientifically, this endeavour has always fallen down in practice, because people love old buildings for any number of reasons, emotionally as well as aesthetically. How can anyone fail to be excited by the magnificent, Gormenghast-like Grand Midland Hotel designed by Sir George Gilbert Scott and fronting London's St Pancras station? It might not share the Classical good manners of the Parthenon, but this great dragon of a building stirs the soul and adds greatly to our enjoyment of the London skyline. And yet this very building was under threat of demolition many times from when it ceased to be a hotel in 1935 up until its recent transformation into the new London Eurostar terminal for trains to Europe.

Certain styles of architecture that we take for granted and rightly assume to be of a very high artistic order, are still recognized by what were meant to be dismissive labels: Gothic and Baroque were words intended to deride two famous schools of great architecture. To Classical purists of the eighteenth century, such flamboyant, highly expressive and even theatrical architecture, whether with medieval spires or seventeenth-century domes, was considered vulgar.

When specific styles have fallen out of fashion, wily politicians, crafty property developers and whorish architects have had a field day, smashing down the past to make a fast buck on the new. Remarkably, high-minded architectural commentators and historians have aided such wanton destruction. Sir John Summerson [1904–92], for example, the distinguished English scholar, refused to support campaigns to save St Pancras. Being enamoured of eighteenth-century design and having been brought up in a late-flowering Victorian manner, he was only too keen to see the back of what for him was not just a neo-Gothic monstrosity, but an entire way of life he found unattractive.

In this chapter, most of my examples of buildings lost by careless or premeditated demolition are from England; these are buildings I longed to see as a boy when I first became consciously interested in architecture. Most were already long gone, while some, like Nonsuch Palace, were very nearly the stuff of myth.

Right Members of the royal family and courtiers hunting at Nonsuch Palace, Surrey, during the reign of James I. The long lost palace built by Henry VIII was a fascinating marriage of late-flowering Tudor and early-blossoming Renaissance design. This Flemish School painting belongs to the Fitzwilliam Museum, Cambridge.

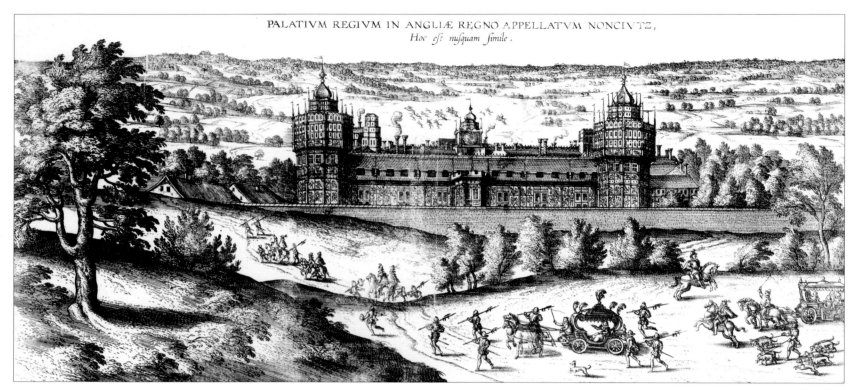

PALATIVM REGIVM IN ANGLIÆ REGNO APPELLATVM NONCIVTZ,
Hoc est nusquam simile.

Effiguaut Georgius Housnaglius Anno 1582.

Above The arrival of Elizabeth I at Nonsuch Palace in a pumpkin-like carriage in 1582. This engraving by Joris Hoefnagel [1542–1600] also depicts the social hierarchy of the palace, from ladies-in-waiting to the water bearer. Nonsuch Palace was demolished in 1682 to pay off the Duchess of Cleveland's gambling debts.

Nonsuch Palace sounds like a royal residence that never existed; the name though is derived from a quote from Queen Elizabeth I who declared, "there is none such like it." Commissioned by Henry VIII, work on Nonsuch Palace began on the site of the former manor house, church and entire village of Cuddington, near Cheam in Surrey. Work started in 1538 and although the structure of this fairy-tale palace was complete by 1541, another five years were spent on its elaborate decoration.

The palace consisted of two courtyards, the outer one made of brick and stone and entered through a turreted gatehouse. The inner courtyard was a fabulous affair, its walls adorned with stucco panels. Writing in the late 1500s, Anthony Watson, Rector of Cheam, described these as being "surrounded by huge figures of gods and goddesses gleaming white… so moulded that they seemed to be leaping off the walls… Each one stood in a golden frame that shone so brightly in the sun that it looked as though the Palace was on fire…"

The King occupied apartments on one side of the inner building, and the Queen (whichever one it was at the time who had managed to keep her head), the other. Both wings were crowned with octagonal towers.

Queen Elizabeth was clearly taken with this delightful building and it even survived the vicissitudes of the English Civil War. It all went wrong, however, when Charles II was returned to the throne in 1660. After the death in 1669 of his wife, Henrietta Maria, who had lived here, Charles gave the palace to his mistress Barbara Villiers, also known as the Countess of Castlemaine, the Duchess of Cleveland and Baroness Nonsuch. Barbara was a big-time gambler and in 1682 the King allowed her to demolish the house to sell its rich materials to pay off her debts.

This was a truly cavalier action. Not only was Nonsuch a magical building, but it was also the first in England that took real notice of contemporary developments in architectural design and decoration in Renaissance Europe. Charles did such a good wrecking job that the palace seemed to have vanished entirely without trace. To make matters worse, only three images of the palace appear to have survived. When an archaeological dig was finally carried out in 1959–60, it proved to be a hugely popular attraction; no fewer than 60,000 people visited the site. There was precious little to see, although the foundations of the banqueting hall were uncovered and a few artefacts were packed off to the care of the British Museum.

Equally fantastic, Old London Bridge is the stuff of hair-raising history and architectural wonder, remembered by the famous nursery rhyme:

"London Bridge is falling down,
Falling down, falling down.
London Bridge is falling down,
My fair lady."

There are many more verses and variations on them, and it's not clear whether or not the rhyme was concerned with even older London Bridges that had been destroyed centuries earlier than the Old London Bridge that survived until 1831.

Old London Bridge was more than 600 years old and extremely decrepit by the time it was replaced by a neoclassical design by John Rennie, which was in turn replaced in 1968 by the dull London Bridge that exists today. Old London Bridge is perhaps best known from a famous engraving of it by Claes Jansz Visscher in 1616. Here, the eccentric collection of buildings lining the bridge from end to end make it so very appealing. If only we could have a bridge like this today, and one upon which you could rent an apartment with dream-like views along the Thames. However, a closer look at the engraving reveals the severed heads of traitors, dipped in tar and stuck on long poles from the parapets of the bridge, a grim reminder that Old London Bridge belonged to a distant past that few of us would care to revisit. The first head to go on display was that of William Wallace, the Scottish leader brutally executed at Smithfield Market in 1305. St Thomas More's head was displayed on the bridge in 1535, while in 1598 a German visitor to London counted no fewer than 30

Above A wonderful winter scene, formerly attributed to Jan Wyck [1640–1700], showing a Frost Fair on the River Thames c.1685. London Bridge is in the background. Its many arches caused the flow of the river to slow, making ice likely to form in severe weather.

Above The demolition of Old London Bridge took place at the beginning of the 1830s. The scene was captured by George Pryne [1800–84], a watercolour artist and author of *Practical Rules on Drawing for the Operative Builder, and Young Student in Architecture* [1854].

Above right Old London Bridge in all its picturesque and bloody glory, with the heads of traitors impaled on the end of poles, in 1616 and before the Great Fire of London destroyed the medieval churches around it. The scene was painted by Claes Jansz Visscher [1587–1652].

heads. Charles II put an end to this practice in 1660, although public executions remained one of the most popular pastimes – and the source of much crime and money making – in London for many brutal decades to come.

Old London Bridge was commissioned during the reign of Henry II. Work began in 1176 and took 33 years to complete. Almost immediately, buildings up to seven storeys high and projecting over the parapets, rose up along the length of the new bridge. Some of these structures joined hands, as it were, over the centre of the bridge, so that walking across it, especially in the dark, felt like walking through a tunnel. Pride of place went to a grand chapel dedicated to St Thomas a Becket, complete with a river entrance for sailors and those passing by on board ships.

The bridge was equally famous, or infamous, for its 20 arches; these had the effect of slowing down the flow of water along the Thames. In winter, ice formed on the river and great fairs were held in the shadow of the bridge. When water wheels, designed by the Dutch

engineer Peter Morice, were added in 1580 to the underside of two of the arches to power a grain mill, the flow of water under the bridge became both fast and dangerous. Sometimes the depth of the water on one side of the bridge was 6 feet (1.8 metres) lower than on the other; this led to the deaths of many foolhardy or unknowing boatmen over the centuries. At the height of its architectural grandeur, or folly, the bridge was so congested that it could take up to an hour to cross it. Anyone in a hurry hailed a river taxi instead.

By the eighteenth century, as London grew to a city of a million people, Old London Bridge had outlived its usefulness. Today perhaps we might have closed such a bridge to anything other than pedestrian traffic and built a new one slightly further up or down stream, but this was not the way things were done 200 years ago and the bridge finally came tumbling down just six years before Queen Victoria ascended to the throne. Imagine what fun it would be if it had survived and been sensitively rebuilt – it would be such a popular tourist magnet, that it would still be almost impossible to cross.

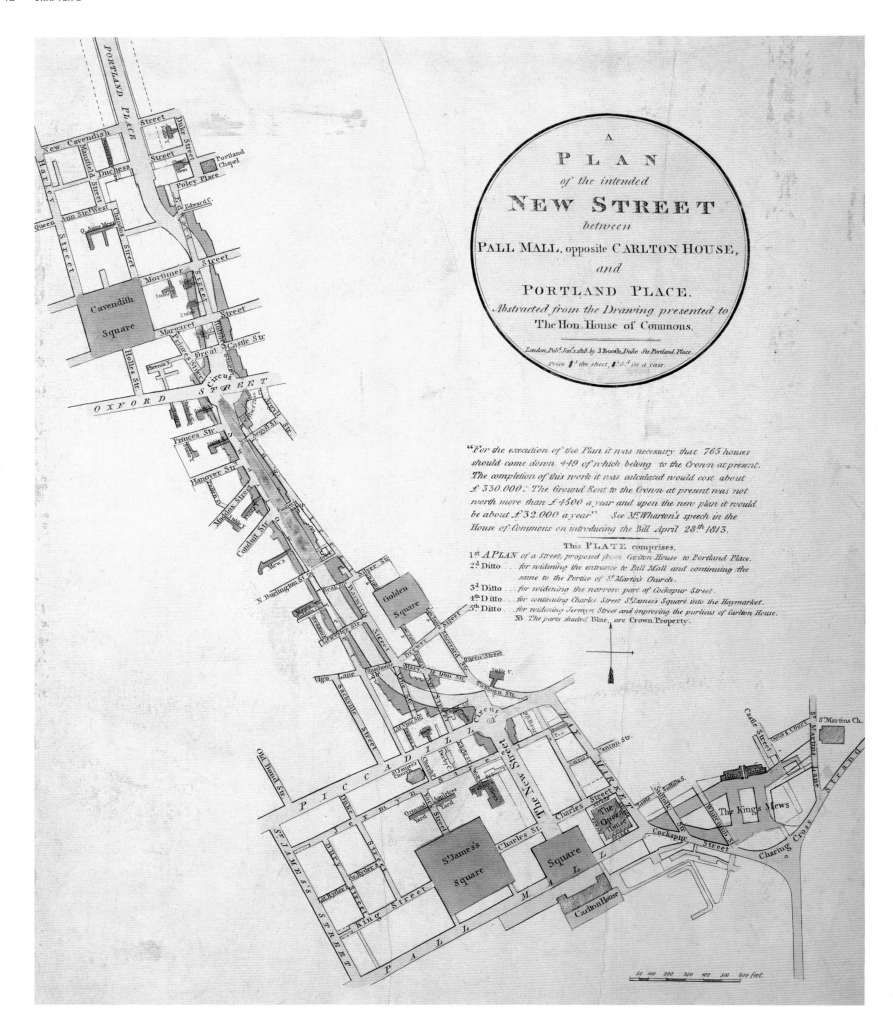

A
PLAN
of the intended
NEW STREET
between
PALL MALL, opposite CARLTON HOUSE,
and
PORTLAND PLACE.
Abstracted from the Drawing presented to
The Hon. House of Commons.

London, Pubᵈ. Janʸ. 1 1818 by J. Booth, Duke Str. Portland Place.
Price 4ˢ the sheet, 5ˢ. 6ᵈ. in a case.

"For the execution of the Plan it was necessary that 765 houses
should come down 449 of which belong to the Crown at present.
The completion of this work it was calculated would cost about
£ 330.000: The Ground Rent to the Crown at present was not
worth more than £ 4500 a year and upon the new plan it would
be about £ 32.000 a year"   See Mr Wharton's speech in the
House of Commons on introducing the Bill April 28ᵗʰ 1813.

This PLATE comprises.
1ˢᵗ A PLAN of a Street, proposed from Carlton House to Portland Place.
2ᵈ Ditto .. for widening the entrance to Pall Mall and continuing the
    same to the Portico of St Martin's Church.
3ᵈ Ditto .. for widening the narrow part of Cockspur Street.
4ᵗʰ Ditto .. for continuing Charles Street St James's Square into the Haymarket.
5ᵗʰ Ditto .. for widening Jermyn Street and improving the purlieus of Carlton House.
    ℕℬ The parts shaded Blue, are Crown Property.

Old Regent Street would be an equally popular tourist attraction, not that modern Regent is unpopular, but it is a little less classy than the original. Regent Street remains a handsome London thoroughfare even if the individual buildings are somewhat pompous and even a little dull. The grandest are those that curve at the street's southern end towards Piccadilly Circus and Lower Regent Street. They were built in the 1920s in a sombre beaux-arts Classical style designed by Sir Reginald Blomfield [1856–1942]. The project was not finally complete until 1927, by which time Regent Street was no longer a Regency street.

The original design had been very special. The new Regent Street was the backbone of the 1811 town plan for central London drawn up by the architect-developer John Nash [1752–1835] for the Prince Regent (later George IV). Nash had a genius for popular and memorable architecture, creating true grandeur from modest resources. This, though, was the cause of his Regent Street's decline and fall. Although handsome, his stucco-fronted neoclassical shops were not as well built as they might have been. The stucco had to be renewed all too frequently in a London clouded by soot and over the years these buildings proved to be far too small. Shopping habits in London changed rapidly at the beginning of the twentieth

century, especially after the arrival of the department store. The small, if perfectly formed, bespoke shops along Regent Street were increasingly a thing of the past.

There were other problems with Nash's design, although some of these were hardly the fault of the architect. Nash provided the great sweep, or Quadrant, of Regent Street with continuous colonnades. These kept the rain off the hats of Regency shoppers, but they also attracted prostitutes who found the columns choice spots from which to tout for business.

So although Regency Regent Street was probably doomed by the time Edward VII took to the throne in 1901, it is hard not to look back with nostalgia at the street that John Nash planned and styled with such verve. He created a world of popular and low-cost elegance and style, but sadly his buildings were not quite as high in the quality stakes as London's retail economy needed and wanted them to be. Sometimes even the most attractive and popular architecture is doomed when the forces of commercialism are moving at full speed. We can only look at the coloured etchings and lithographs of the street and sigh. Blomfield's Regent Street was clad in sturdy, weatherproof Portland stone, but although admirable in many ways, this is not architecture that puts a spring in our collective step.

Above The sweep of the colonnaded Quadrant in Regent Street, London, designed by John Nash. It is shown in a Regency print that looks very much like the illustrations that once adorned tins of Quality Street chocolates, commonplace sweets in fancy wrappings, which is what Nash's happily theatrical architecture here was, too.

Opposite John Nash's plan of Regent Street, as originally designed, showing how, in a very English fashion, it connected Portland Place and Pall Mall in a sequence of curves as well as continental straight lines. Engraving by J Booth, 1818.

Above Gloriously atmospheric ink and wash perspective of the internal courtyard of Newgate Gaol by John Claude Nattes [*c*.1765–1822]. Unexplained ropes, pulleys and chains add to the rather macabre feeling Nattes was evidently determined to convey. Even so, the Classical architecture is both grand and noble.

Left Newgate Gaol *c*.1900, shortly before it was sentenced to demolition and replaced by what we know as the Old Bailey, or Royal Courts of Justice, today. George Dance had created a building that was at once forbidding and yet an inspiring addition to the Georgian London streetscape.

This cannot be said for Newgate Gaol in London. Designed by George Dance the Younger [1741–1825], this powerful building was designed to imprison and execute London's wrongdoers. The prison was originally built in 1188, but was completely rebuilt after the Great Fire of London in 1666 and again by Dance in 1770–78. Within two years of its completion, it was destroyed during the anti-Catholic Gordon Riots. Dance was re-commissioned and this time he designed the gaol in a determinedly stern and even frightening manner. As a young man, Dance had been on the Grand Tour of Italy and had been particularly fascinated by the prison drawings – *Carceri d'Invenzione* (Imaginary Prisons) –by the Venetian-born artist Giovanni Piranesi [1720–78] (p.236).

The latest Newgate gaol was to be a combination of Piranesi and late English Palladianism. It was a fine, if scary building; its heavily rusticated façades hid three courtyards from view, one for male felons, another for females and a third for debtors. The prison machine ground into terrifying action as soon as the last stones had been laid. The Newgate calendar records execution after execution, as boys were hanged for first offences such as stealing letters from Post Offices, forgery or robbery. In 1820 the Cato Street Conspirators who aimed to overthrow the state, were sentenced to be hanged, drawn and quartered here. Public executions were hugely popular and continued until May 26, 1868, when Michael Barrett, the Fenian bomber, was hanged. Criminals such as Charles Scoldwell, imprisoned in Newgate in 1796, got off lightly: for stealing two ducks, a first offence, he was sentenced to transportation for life.

Newgate is where Charles Dickens imagined Fagin, head of the pickpocket gang in *Oliver Twist*, awaiting his end. Perhaps some hanging judges shed a tear when Dance's building was closed in 1902 and demolished two years later. It was replaced by the Edwardian Baroque Courts of Criminal Justice, better known as the Old Bailey, which were designed by E W Mountford. Great buildings, as the case of Newgate Gaol shows, are not always popular; if it had survived, it would have been a strange and spooky place.

Above A disturbing image of inmates at Newgate Gaol trudging around the grim exercise yard, drawn by Gustave Doré [1832–1883], the French artist who illustrated *A Christmas Carol* by Charles Dickens and helped set the tone of what we think of as Dickensian London.

Left A doorway, complete with intimidating locks, bolts and iron studs inside Newgate Gaol, shortly before its demolition in 1902. Dance has, in his own terms, very successfully translated Piranesi's famous prison drawings (pp.236–37) into a real, and frightening, building.

The Bishop's House in Birmingham, England, might also have looked a little spooky. Designed by Augustus Welby Northmore Pugin [1812–52] in what could be called a Hammer House of Horror-style Gothic manner, this was an ingeniously planned if rather spikey and craggy design dating from 1840. It was built as a house for the new Roman Catholic bishops of Birmingham. The north German Gothic-style cathedral next door, dedicated to St Chad, also designed by Pugin, was built between 1838 and 1841; this was the first new Roman Catholic cathedral built in Britain since the Reformation.

In 1959 Pugin's Gothic enclave was butchered by Birmingham's ambitious city politicians and car-crazy planners. The Bishop's House was demolished to make way for a stretch of urban ring road. At this time, Pugin, who had died young and mad, was all but forgotten and his style of architecture was considered to be dismal and vulgar. Today I hope we would be less willing to destroy work by the honorary father of the archaeologically correct Gothic Revival and the joint architect, along with Charles Barry, of the Palace of Westminster.

Above The Bishop's House, Birmingham, looking rather forlorn and not a little grim in a photograph published in *Country Life* magazine in 1960, very shortly before it was demolished to make way for a ring road. The new road also isolated Pugin's St Chad's RC Cathedral.

Right The breakfast room of the Bishop's House, photographed in February 1960 and largely unchanged from the day it was built 120 years earlier. Despite its ornate Gothic Revival decoration, the room is as trim and as well organized as a ship's cabin.

Opposite The meeting room for clergy in the Bishop's House, 1960. The Pugin table would fetch a small fortune at auction today; I wonder what happened to it? Again, this high-roofed Victorian Gothic room had hardly changed over the previous century: a time capsule unnecessarily lost.

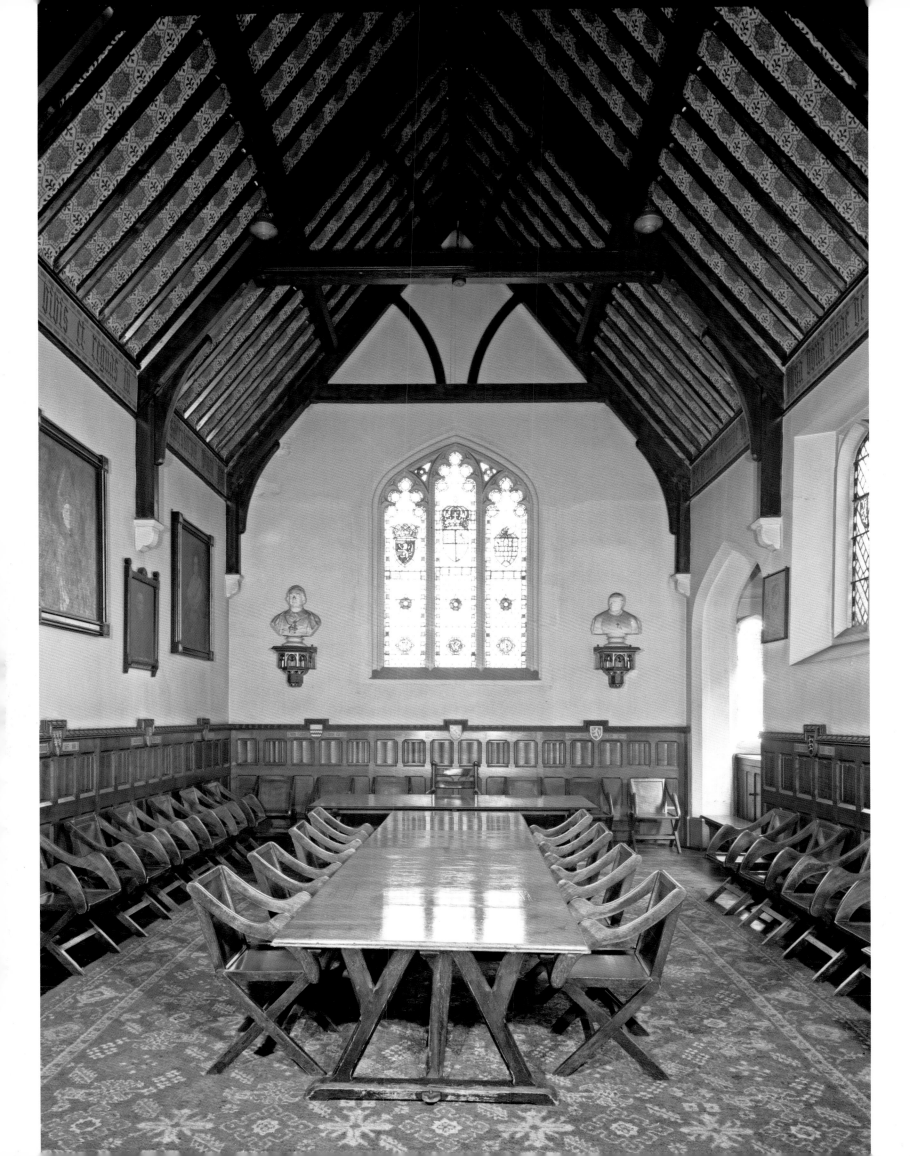

Columbia Market in Bethnal Green, east London, was a far more extreme Gothic design than the Bishop's House in Birmingham. Demolished between 1958 and 1960, it remains one of London's greatest architectural losses within living memory. Staring at photographs of this ambitious Victorian market complex, it seems almost impossible to believe that it had ever existed and heartbreaking to think that it survived the Blitz, only to face destruction by local politicians in the late 1950s.

This was a time when Britain appears to have been suffering from one of its periodic bouts of neophilia, when everything old is bad, everything new is good. At around the same time British Railways embarked on its creaking modernization programme, when the steam age and everything to do with it was to be flushed away and a "year zero", of bright new diesels and electrics, was to be initiated. The modernization of the railways did not go exactly to plan and much of value was destroyed in this managerial and political witch-hunt, in much the same way that historic buildings were razed with relish.

Columbia Market was built between 1866 and 1869 to designs by Henry Astley Darbishire [1825–99]. Along with the lofty, cathedral-like covered market with its 400 stalls, the scheme included "ideal" working-class flats set around a new square, together with a church, swimming pool, a public baths and laundry. This ambitious development was funded by the philanthropist Angela Georgina Burdett-Coutts [1814–1906]. Despite its good intentions and spectacular design, Columbia Market was not widely liked by the market traders themselves. They preferred to trade in the open air and a promised railway line aimed at bringing fish trains to the market never materialized; Columbia Market was to have been a rival to Billingsgate fish market. The covered market closed as early as 1886 and was used as a warehouse and as premises for various small businesses until its demolition. During the Second World War its cellars served as an air-raid shelter, yet Columbia Market was unable to save itself from destruction. The formation of the Victorian Society in London by Anne Rosse, with John Betjeman as its first secretary, was founded in 1958 to save just such buildings as these, but it was too late in the day to help Columbia Market.

Above A view of Columbia Market, Bethnal Green, London, showing the sheer scale, ambition and invention of this great philanthropic Victorian enterprise. It would be much prized today, but when this photograph was taken in 1958, Victorian Gothic architecture was at its critical nadir. So, down it came.

Opposite Beautifully framed, an evocative image of Columbia Market in its brief heyday. It seems hard to believe that such a poetic covered market ever existed in London. Today we like to house such things in cheap-as-chips prefabricated industrial sheds on the edge of town.

A year earlier, another impressive Gothic pile was smashed down. This was the Assize Courts [1859–64] at Strangeways, Manchester – a grand Victorian pile designed by Alfred Waterhouse [1830–1905], better known for Manchester Town Hall and the Natural History Museum in South Kensington, London. The Assize Courts was damaged by the Luftwaffe during the Second World War. It might easily have been repaired, but Manchester City Council had other, iconoclastic ideas. In 1945 the council announced a plan to continue the work of German bombers; virtually every historic landmark was to be demolished and the entire city centre rebuilt in a glum, uniform style. Although much of historic Manchester was wilfully destroyed, a long economic decline accidentally saved the very Victorian buildings that now serve as some of the most fashionable hotels, restaurants and nightclubs in a city that has successfully reinvented itself since the mid 1990s.

THE ENTRANCE HALL OF THE NEW ASSIZE COURTS AT MANCHESTER.

Above This is Manchester Assize Courts in 1886, when the ambitious Gothic Revival building was in its prime. Damaged during the Second World War, it could have been rebuilt, but its Victorian design was considered altogether too fusty by thrusting, go-ahead 1950s Mancunian councillors.

Left An engraving from *The London Illustrated News*, October 1, 1864, showing lawyers and grand members of the Manchester public investigating, and very probably admiring, the generosity and ambitious design of the brand new Assize Courts. The timber vaulting of the high-pitched roof is spectacular.

The Georgian Group was founded in 1937 by a group of influential luminaries in order to stop the wanton destruction of Georgian architecture. The event that triggered the Georgian Group was the demolition of the Adelphi, a magnificent range of apartments in terraced houses facing the Thames along the Strand in London. The Adelphi, designed and built by the Adam brothers between 1768 and 1774, was a superb urban composition. Robert Adam had been much taken by the Palace of Diocletian, Spoleto, and worked hard to shape a terrace of houses that looked, from a distance, like a modern Classical palace. The terraces stood over huge vaulted cellars facing the river and, as a composition, had a truly magisterial appearance. London, hungry as ever for property development, went for the kill in 1936 and much of the Adam brothers' inspired scheme was smashed down. Fragments survive such as the truly elegant home of the Royal Society of Arts in John Adam Street. The Adam brothers were themselves property developers and the Adelphi was raised on the cleared ruins of medieval Durham House.

Above A print from 1795, hand-coloured by Joseph Constantine Stadler [active c.1780–1812], showing Somerset House, London – still very much with us – in the foreground and the doomed Adelphi by the Adam Brothers further upstream with the spire of St Martin-in-the-Fields rising above it.

Opposite The Adelphi, as handsome as ever, caught by the German-born photographer Emil Otto Hoppe [1878-1972]. By this time, the Thames had been embanked and so the Adelphi stood back from the water. The background building is the brand new Shell-Mex House [1931], by Ernest Joseph.

Above left Fine ironwork was a much loved feature of London streets before much of it was ripped out, unnecessarily as it happened, for the "war effort" between 1939 and 1945. Here, the railings and lampstands of the Adelphi are shown in 1931. Photograph by E O Hoppe.

Above right Ornate façade of one of the terraced houses in the Adelphi, photographed by E O Hoppe in 1931. One of the reasons why so much London architecture form this period is missing today is the rise of such massive new buildings as Shell-Mex House, seen behind.

Above Oil painting by William Hodges [1744–97] celebrating the spectacular coffered vault of the dome of the Pantheon, Oxford Street, London. Everyone seems to be impressed, although not the exotic turbaned visitors who will have experienced such magnificence on their travels from India through the Near East and Italy.

Left The entrance of the Pantheon, Oxford Street, in 1829 illustrated in an engraving by J Hinchcliff made from an original drawing by Thomas Shepherd [1792–1864]. Shepherd was a prolific artist who captured much of the character, street life and architecture of Regency London.

Below A masquerade party held in the Pantheon in 1809. The artist and caricaturist Thomas Rowlandson [1756–1827], a man who enjoyed contemporary London life to the full, was there to capture this rumbustious scene. Wyatt's architecture and playful decoration was the perfect backdrop for such popular events.

The year 1937 marked not just the formation of the Georgian Group, but also the demolition of what remained of the Pantheon in Oxford Street. One of the most spectacular buildings of Georgian London, this great pleasure dome was replaced with a branch of Marks and Spencer. Designed by James Wyatt [1746–1813], a rival of Robert Adam, the Pantheon opened in 1772. Its name was derived from the Pantheon in Rome, one of the surviving temples of ancient Rome. The London building boasted a vast rotunda set under a huge dome with various reception and "card rooms", as well as a tea and supper room. This amazing Romanesque building served as the setting for public spectacles, masques, carnivals and balls; it was used as a theatre and an opera house at different times. It burned to the ground in 1792 and was rebuilt by Wyatt, with a theatre replacing the original domed rotunda. The Pantheon fell out of fashion and was closed as a place of entertainment in 1814. Rebuilt as a bazaar by Sydney Smirke,

architect of the original British Library, it retained its original Oxford Street façade, but the theatre was replaced by a barrel-vaulted nave.

In 1867 the Pantheon was bought by the wine merchants W and A Gilbey for use as a showroom and offices. Wyatt seemed doomed to create sensational buildings that somehow failed, including the legendary Fonthill Abbey (p.196). He even came to a dramatic end when his stagecoach overturned in Wiltshire. Despite the lasting popularity of Marks and Spencer, it does seem a shame that such a sensational eighteenth-century building has made way for a shop with branches all over the country.

Today's Oxford Street is wholly dull; its last unexpected architectural treasure was the Pavilion restaurant, designed in the 1950s by the Welsh-born surrealist photographer Angus McBean [1904–90] as a Hungarian tearoom above the much-missed Academy cinema.

Left The Corinthian portico at the north front of Carlton House seen in an engraving dated 1819. The exterior appeared chaste and correct, but it hid a richly coloured and exotic interior that the house's first architect, Henry Holland, would have found rather shocking.

Below The south front of Carlton House in 1819 with elegant ladies taking a stroll in gardens adorned with peacocks. The Gothic conservatory, a later addition to the original design, can be seen, like some prickly architectural hedgehog, on the far left-hand side of the main building.

London's most exciting Georgian buildings could be remarkably short-lived. Carlton House, set between Pall Mall and the Mall, was to become one of the most lavish and exotic of all London residences, designed for the Prince Regent before he became George IV. Although the Prince's chosen architect, Henry Holland [1745–1806] began the work in a chaste and much admired French-influenced neoclassical style, the house soon became an ambitious and colourful palace with the addition, after Holland's death, of a theatrical Gothic dining room and conservatory. Holland would barely have recognized what, by 1820, had become a lavish Regency palace. If you are lucky enough to get inside the exclusive Brook's club in nearby St James's Street, you can still get some idea of Holland's original noble design.

As for Carlton House, the Prince Regent lost interest and decided to spend a less than grateful nation's money on transforming Buckingham House on the western fringe of St James's Park into Buckingham Palace, with John Nash as his architect. Nash declared Carlton House unsound and the building was demolished in 1827. Nash replaced it with a superb range of white stucco-faced neoclassical terraces – Carlton House Terrace – that faces St James's Park at the foot of the Duke of York steps. If you walk up to Trafalgar Square, you will find the handsome portico of Holland's Carlton House; William Wilkins incorporated it into the front of the National Gallery.

Above The Gothic dining room, Carlton House by John Nash. The lavish décor was rooted as much in Chinese and Mughal as Gothic precedent.

Right Another illustration from J B Pyne's *Royal Residences*, 1819; this one offers us a sunny glimpse inside the imaginative Gothic conservatory by Thomas Hopper.

One of Henry Holland's students was John Soane [1753–1837], the son of a Berkshire bricklayer who went on to become one of the most imaginative and important of all English architects. Soane was a prolific designer, but his most important commission in terms of location and prestige was the Bank of England building in the City of London. Soane began work on the design of this cavernous building in 1788 and continued to do so over the next 45 years. In later life, he described his role at the Bank as "a situation which has long been the pride and boast of my life."

The Bank had been established in 1694 and had been worked on by other architects, but it was Soane who made the Bank of England one of the most distinguished and fascinating buildings in the world. Behind the windowless neoclassical screen Soane wrapped right around the Bank in 1828, there lay a labyrinth of wonderfully romantic offices and rooms. The Bank's governors gave Soane a remarkably free hand and he experimented to his heart's content with the Classical tradition, reinventing it as he went along much to the disgust of academically correct architects who thought his work over-the-top and even absurd. It was no such thing; Soane was playing what Edwin Lutyens, another of Britain's most ingenious architects, described as "the high game of Architecture".

The offices inside the three-storey high bank had such unromantic names as the Four Per Cent Office, which belied their extraordinary designs. Sadly when the Bank decided it needed more space in the 1920s, Herbert Baker [1862–1946] demolished nearly everything Soane had built, except his fine wall. Pure architectural genius was replaced with a heavy-handed and half-baked Classicism, described by Nikolaus Pevsner, the architectural historian and editor of the well-known *Buildings of England*, as "the greatest architectural crime, in the City of London, of the twentieth century."

In 1988 the Bank reconstructed one of Soane's finest rooms, the Stock Office, on its original site; this serves as the Bank's museum and reveals just how wonderful Soane's superlative building must have been. Fortunately the architect's London home in Lincoln's Inn Fields became Sir John Soane's Museum after his death. All but unchanged, this haunting labyrinth of unexpected rooms and spaces stuffed full with paintings and equally unexpected artworks, remains almost as it was in 1837. Soane designed this conjuring trick of an interior to demonstrate what he liked to call "the poetry of architecture." This Soanian sonnet is truly special, a walk through the mind and spirit of this great, if tortured, soul.

Below left Soane's magnificent wall surrounding the Bank survives. Here it is *c.*1880 on a busy City day. The capitals crowning the columns were adopted from the Temple of Vesta at Tivoli, a Roman building still standing.

Below right The modern reconstruction of Soane's demolished Four Per Cent Office at the Bank of England, recreated by Donald Insall Associates in the 1990s. The lanterns, supported by Soane's characteristic pendentive domes, are peopled by Greek caryatids adopted from the porch of the Erechtheion, Athens.

Opposite A fine 1920s study of the Old Dividend Office in John Soane's Bank of England. The Bank's magical interior was something like a walk through a sequence of intimate Roman basilicas, each ingeniously lit, and all very much missed. The rooms were known to staff as "parlours".

The City of London has long been the financial engine of the English, the British and now the global economy; a machine for making money. It has been endowed with some superb architecture, including Sir Christopher Wren's St Paul's Cathedral, and yet it has also destroyed fine buildings with abandon when these have stood in the way of economic development. In Sydenham, a suburb of south-east London, a walk down a nondescript cul-de-sac lined with 1960s houses leads to a real surprise: here, in the former garden of the printer Robert Harrild, stands the top section of an octagonal seventeenth-century Portland stone spire capped with a weathervane. This was once the top of the spire of St Antholin's, Watling Street, one of Wren's famous City churches built from medieval ruins in the years following the Great Fire of London of 1666. The church was demolished to make way for a major new Victorian thoroughfare in 1874–75. It had already been bashed about, which was why Harrild was able to buy the top of the spire for five pounds in 1829 and cart it back to his home in Sydenham.

The idea of demolishing a Wren church might seem anathema to us today, but as late as 1940, when the Luftwaffe did the job very effectively, even the finest churches were under threat. In his unintentionally hilarious, yet disturbing book *The Face of London* (1932), the commentator Harold Clunn advocated the demolition of Nicholas Hawksmoor's stunning Baroque church, St Mary Woolnoth, sited just around the corner from the Bank of England. Clunn's case hinged on the fact that the church occupied valuable land that would be more profitable it if was a bank, for example, and that it had become out of scale with the new commercial buildings erected in the City after the First World War. Thank goodness, common sense prevailed and this much-loved and brilliantly designed church survived, continuing to thrive today.

Eighteenth-century churches outside London were also fair game for ambitious local authorities. One of the saddest losses of all city churches in England was that of St Paul's in Sheffield. This was a particularly handsome Roman Doric Baroque design by Ralph Tunnicliffe [c1688–1736] and the builder John Platt. It stood in the way of the ambition of Sheffield's mean-minded councillors who had no time for architectural pleasantries; in a bid to build a much bigger town hall, they had the church smashed down in 1938. Before they built their grim new town hall extension, Great Britain had declared war on Germany and such vainglorious projects ground to a halt. After the war, the church grounds were turned into the Peace Gardens, a haven for drunks and feral youths.

St Mary Somerset   Steel Yard   Bow Church   Stairs   Queenhithe   St James Garlick Hill   British Copper Company   St Antholin   St Coll

Opposite above Charming early nineteenth-century watercolour looking along Watling Street towards the lost church of St Antholin's, designed by Christopher Wren. A few of the streets to the east of St Paul's, including Watling Street, retain something of the character shown here even if overshadowed by modern buildings.

Opposite below The octagonal steeple of St Antholin's can be seen, second from right, peering up over the roofscape of the City of London in this early nineteenth-century engraving. After the Great Fire of 1666, Wren shaped a lovely necklace of parish churches, many since destroyed, around St Paul's.

Above Here is the ill-fated, and seemingly rarely photographed, St Paul's, Sheffield, and its graveyard, at what must have been the beginning of the twentieth century. It seems astonishing, today, that local politicians were so keen to rid their steely city of this fine Baroque church.

Left A rare photograph of the wonderfully unspoiled Baroque interior of St Paul's, Sheffield, showing a fine arcade of lofty Corinthian columns rising from neat box pews along its well-lit nave, and plenty of well polished oak. Those who ordered the demolition of this building should have been arrested.

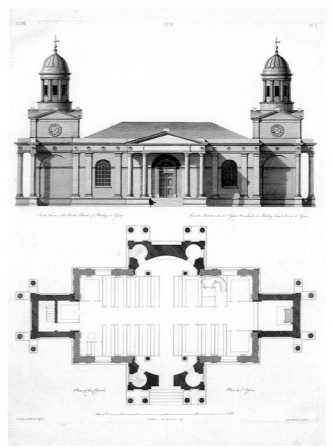

Religious righteousness was a further reason that other wondrous eighteenth-century churches bit the dust in England. Many visitors to the small riverside town of Mistley, Essex, are puzzled by a pair of exquisite neoclassical towers standing alone among flocks of local swans by the River Stour. These are all that remain of what was once the church of St Mary the Virgin designed by Robert Adam in 1776. The main body of the church was set between the towers. The church was rather low-key and hidden by a handsome portico, but the scale and quality of the towers made the overall effect very grand indeed, even if not the great, domed cathedral one imagines might once have stood there.

The church of this small town was given such a powerful presence because a wealthy local politician, Richard Rigby, had plans to transform Mistley into a fashionable spa town; so Mistley needed fashionable architecture and a handsome church for its preachers. It never quite worked out and in 1870 the main body of the church was demolished and services transferred to a rather plain Victorian church that was more in tune with the serious, evangelical spirit of the time than a playful spa-style neoclassical temple.

Conservation of historic buildings in the United States remained limited up until the 1960s. Until then, it had been the case of a young country building itself up, physically as well as politically and economically, and knocking down any building that stood in the way of progress.

The Montgomery Block, San Francisco's first "fireproof" and "earthquake proof" building, was a handsome office building erected in 1853 on behalf of Henry Wager Halleck, later a Union Army general, to designs by local architect, G P Cummings. It lived up to the claims made for it by surviving the cataclysmic earthquake of 1906 that brought San Francisco to its foundations. Over the years, the tenants of this robust and fondly remembered building included Mark Twain, author of *The Adventures of Huckleberry Finn*, and Jack London who gave us *White Fang* and *The Call of the Wild*.

In its day, the biggest building west of the Mississippi, the Montgomery Building was raised around two courtyards. Its public spaces included salons, libraries and billiard rooms. Ingeniously, it floated on a raft of layered redwood logs laid on marshland by an army of Chinese labourers; it was this that made it impervious to earthquakes. None of these claims to greatness saved the Montgomery Building from summary execution in 1959, when it was pulled down and replaced with a car park.

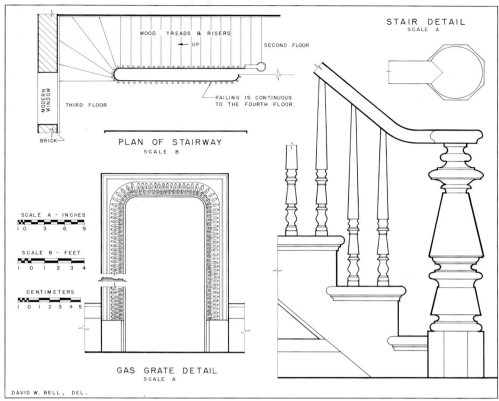

Above For its time, the Montgomery Block was an ambitious design, and one of the largest buildings west of the Rocky Mountains. It was also, as can be seen in this photograph from the late 1930s, a well-mannered building that marched crisply along the streetscape of San Francisco.

Right The interior of the Montgomery Block was as well organized as a contemporary ocean liner. Details were well made (above), if matter of fact, while corridors (below) were wide and well lit. It is fascinating to think of writers such as Jack London and Mark Twain working here.

Above Detroit City Hall c.1930, surrounded and overwhelmed by new skyscrapers. Perhaps local politicians felt demeaned by the fact that their once dominant building was so quickly overshadowed by a new wave of giant buildings. Whatever, City Hall was replaced by a parking lot in 1961.

The grandiose and beautifully built Detroit City Hall designed by James Anderson was opened to rapturous applause on July 4, 1871, but was demolished in 1961 to make way for another car park. Detroit was founded in 1701 by a Frenchman, Antoine de la Mothe Cadillac, who lent his name to one of the world famous car manufacturers who set up in business in the city that became universally known as Motown. Perhaps due to its French foundation, by the 1890s, when Paris itself was the most fashionable city in the world, Detroit was known as the Paris of the West, not least because of its ambitious architecture.

Built in creamy yellow sandstone and in a style that owed something to contemporary developments in France, Italy and the Low Countries, the City Hall rose 180 feet (55 metres) above a

grand public square. No amount of special pleading could save it in 1961 when Mayor Louis C Miriani declared that what central Motown needed most was another car park. Today it is a moving experience to come across some of the building's great stones strewn through what are now overgrown glades in Detroit's historic Fort Wayne; one of these bears the once-proud inscription, "James Anderson, Architect."

Destruction of key historic buildings in American cities has continued apace even though a powerful conservation movement has developed over the past 45 years. One recent and inexplicable loss was that of the handsome St Louis Century Building in the centre of the Missouri capital's historic district. Completed in 1896 to designs by the wonderfully named Raeder, Coffin and Crocker architects, this great example of American Renaissance beaux-arts style was demolished in 2004.

Above Detroit City Hall in its heyday. This is October 6, 1908 and the crowds are gathered outside the building, jubilant that the Detroit Tigers had just clinched the American League baseball championship for the second time. This was civic pride in full-throated action.

Left The handsome US Renaissance-style St Louis Century Building not long before it was demolished in 2004. Buildings like this have long been liked by local conservation movements and local people, but have been seen as standing in the way of progress by politicians and developers.

The centres of even the most historic world cities have not been safe from the wiles of politicians, developers and the suspect idea of modernization at any cost. In Paris the glorious old Les Halles wholesale market was demolished in 1971, only to be replaced with a horrible underground shopping labyrinth dubbed "Forum des Halles". Completed in 1979, this banal eyesore is about to be given a heavy-duty face-lift by the architect David Mangin; the development, although apparently popular with tourists, has never been liked, much less loved, by any true Parisian.

Les Halles was founded around 1,000 years ago and enlarged by Philippe II in 1183. It was rebuilt with 10 glass-covered, cast-iron market buildings, designed by the architect Victor Baltard, between 1852 and 1870. From 1969 the "stomach of Paris", as Les Halles was known, was relocated to an out-of-town location at Rungis, and the iron and glass buildings and the wealth of wonderful food on display inside them had wholly vanished by 1973. Like so many other European cities desperate to appear modern, Paris had begun to sanitize itself. Two of the old buildings survived, shipped to new sites at Nogent-sur-Marne in the eastern suburbs of Paris and to Yokohama in Japan.

Opposite above Les Halles market, Paris, 1950. The idea of such useful markets existing in city centres is anathema to planners today. This is sad as markets like Les Halles were truly the stomachs of great cities as well as being enjoyable buildings to stroll through, all senses fully engaged.

Opposite below A chalk lithograph of 1861, coloured by Jules Arnout after a drawing by Felix Benoist, showing Les Halles before it was even completed. The view is happily optimistic; the streets around the market were never so neat and tidy; but they were very special, and a daily delight.

Above Les Halles on a wet morning in 1950 captured by the distinguished French photo-journalist, Paul Almasy [1906–2003]. The juxtaposition of such earthy, lively, workaday places and buildings with great monuments, grand avenues and densely packed streets is part of what makes city life special.

If the iron and glass pavilions of Les Halles had been a loss for Paris, then the demolition of the Galerie des Machines, one of the greatest engineering-led buildings ever constructed, was a catastrophe. This vast exhibition hall was built for the Paris Exhibition of 1889, where it shared a starring role with the brand new Eiffel Tower. Outwardly it was a little on the conservative side, a giant glass house with some fanciful architectural details, but its interior was simply breathtaking. Inside the architectural carapace designed by the architect Ferdinand Dutert [1845–1906] was a sensational open space – 1,178 feet (420 metres) long, 320 feet (115 metres) wide and 144 feet (44 metres) high – supported by 23 steel trusses. Touching the ground with all the delicacy of a ballet dancer, these revolutionary arches created a vast gallery entirely free of columns. Nothing like it had ever been seen before. It was, as contemporary accounts underline, a magnificent and daunting sight. The engineer who dreamed up this technological *tour de force* was Victor Contamin [1840–93]. Visitors were able to travel through the steel and glass hall on a moving pedestrian walkway set 33 feet (10 metres) above its floor. From here, they could view vast new machines lined up inside the hall, lit up by electric lamps. The Eiffel Tower lived on, but the Galerie des Machines was demolished in 1910.

England had hosted the first of the universal exhibitions or Expos in 1851 inside the Crystal Palace (p.148) in London's

Above left The great glazed entrance to the Galerie des Machines built for the Paris Exhibition of 1889. Although the form of the entrance appeared to be traditional, its filigree and show-off glasswork was a fine demonstration of what French engineers and industry could achieve in modern construction.

Left Inside the wondrous Galerie des Machines. Every sort of engine or mechanical device then available could be found in this vast iron and glass cavern. Not a single column interrupted the giant floor, while visitors rode around the building on a moving pedestrian walkway.

Hyde Park. This was almost the beginning of the era in which manufacturers felt the need to exhibit as well as sell the iron fruits of their great and smoky enterprises. In 1850 what must be the first proper such exhibition hall opened at Bingley Hall, Birmingham. It had been built on the site of Bingley House, a fine eighteenth-century house demolished for the purpose. The exhibition hall was put up in just six weeks under the direction of the architect J A Chatwin [1830–1907] using steel girders surplus to the building of Euston station.

Chatwin's building was conservative in appearance, realized in a Roman Doric style in red and blue bricks, but the scale of the hall was decidedly modern, measuring 224 by 221 feet (68 by 67 metres) and covering one and a quarter acres (5,058 square metres). One of Chatwin's first employers would not have had anything flattering to say about the design of the exterior of Bingley Hall; this was A W Pugin, the great Gothic revivalist, who thought Classical architecture pagan and thus wholly inappropriate for use in a Christian country.

Bingley Hall was home to any number of local shows and events, but it was also the venue where the very first political speech to have been recorded took place in November 1888; the speaker was William Gladstone, the leader of the Liberal opposition at the time, but later to be the British Prime Minister four times between 1868 and 1894.

Bingley Hall was demolished after a fire during the 1984 Midland Caravan, Camping and Leisure Exhibition and was subsequently demolished. The site is now occupied by Birmingham's International Convention Centre and Symphony Hall. Birmingham, once known as the "workshop of the world" has, in recent years, recreated itself as a kind of giant shopping mall. Historic buildings here seem as rare as a contemporary British town without a supermarket, but they still exist in the interstices between brash new designs that shout for attention. Even these surviving buildings may soon vanish as we demand ever more money, faux-luxury and consumer goods.

Above A 1907 exhibition celebrating the many proud achievements of Britain's "Premier Line", the London & North Western Railway, featuring what are clearly some fine photographs, at Bingley Hall, Staffordshire. Today, Britain's first purpose-built exhibition hall would be worthy of a show of its own.

Left An engraving of Bingley Hall [1760], made c.1830, twenty years before it was demolished to make way for a railway tunnel and the new exhibition centre. The landscape of this part of England changed with the speed of an express train at the time of the Industrial Revolution.

3 LOST IN WAR

The German Luftwaffe's raid on Coventry and its cathedral on November 14, 1940, was to many British people both an attack on their very soul and the beginning of a new form of warfare. The British, and the English in particular, might not be the most religiously minded people, instinctively distrusting all forms of religious fundamentalism, bigotry and excess, but they are sentimental. The loss of a medieval cathedral was a raid too far. The British government did nothing to hide the loss of lives, property and heritage, as the raid had clearly been aimed solely at civilian targets in the city, despite the surrounding area being dominated by many of Britain's weapons and armaments factories.

Adolf Hitler had ordered the raid in retaliation for a rather ineffective attack by the RAF on the centre of Munich on November 8; Munich had been the cradle of the Nazi movement and Hitler rightly saw the raid as a personal one. He struck back at Coventry. The Midlands city was ill prepared for such an attack. Much had been done to defend the city as people saw fit at the time, but 56 barrage balloons and some small anti-aircraft guns were unable to hold up the Luftwaffe's bombers. They got through to the centre of Coventry all too easily, dropping a mixture of incendiaries, high explosives and oil and mortar bombs.

The roof of the cathedral was soon ablaze, and with incendiaries trapped in the gap between the lead roofing and the timber vaults below, it was extremely hard for local emergency services to deal effectively with the fire. Ironwork added as supports for the roof by Victorian restorers in the 1880s transmitted intense heat from the roof above to the pillars of the nave below, causing these to crack and fall. By the morning all that was left of the medieval cathedral was its outer walls, its tower and proud 295-foot (76-metre) high spire.

In the scorching rubble, Jock Forbes, the cathedral's stonemason, discovered two charred roof timbers that had fallen in the shape of a cross. These still stand on an altar made of rubble with the words "Father Forgive" inscribed into the Sanctuary wall behind it. King George VI came to visit, as did the Prime Minister, Winston Churchill, and the announcement was made that the cathedral would be rebuilt not as an act of defiance but in a spirit of "faith, trust and hope for the future of the world".

This gracious sentiment was acted out and on May 25, 1962, the new Coventry Cathedral was consecrated. On the same day, the remodelled Kaiser Wilhelm church in Berlin, which had been all but destroyed in an Allied bombing raid, was also opened.

Coventry Cathedral serves as an example of the many religious buildings destroyed in wars around the world and throughout the centuries. The armies of conquerors have often destroyed places of worship in order to try and crush the spirit of a people. Today, not a year seems to go by without news of a church or other place of worship being burned down or attacked, often with worshippers trapped inside, by some vicious mob, maddened by its own sense of right.

Opposite A striking shot of Coventry Cathedral taken the day after the Luftwaffe raid of November 14, 1940. By hitting at the emotional heart of Coventry, and destroying such an architectural, religious and social focal point, Hitler ensured that the British would fight him to the bitter end.

What was lost at Coventry was the physical heart of a dignified medieval parish church, dating from the late fourteenth and early fifteenth centuries. St Michael's was the largest parish church in England and had only been raised to cathedral status in 1918. What Coventry gained was a beautifully crafted, modern cathedral set in and around the medieval walls. The Scottish architect, Basil Spence [1907–76], won the competition to design the new cathedral in 1950; work began six years later and was completed in 1962. Inside the folding and re-folding walls are superb contemporary art and craftworks by John Piper (stained glass), Graham Sutherland (tapestry) and John Hutton (engraved glass). Spence's cathedral, although idly compared to a factory by some, was a *tour de force*; it was also deeply moving, garbing its new form with the stone cloak of the blitzed cathedral's walls.

Although Coventry lost other buildings in the 1940 raid, it has to be said that the city council had not exactly been careful with its built heritage before the Second World War. If you look at old photographs of streets including Little Butcher Row, Cross Cheaping and Palmer Lane, all demolished in the 1930s for a brash new commercial venture, you will see how the medieval core of the city was already in a poor condition, well before the Luftwaffe arrived to do the job in a savage and scientifically modern fashion.

While Coventry decided to build its cathedral afresh, other cities chose to recreate bomb-damaged churches more or less exactly as they had been before the war. The most remarkable, inspiring, although controversial, example of this is the complete reconstruction

Left An illustration from Jarrold's *Warwickshire*, 1905, showing Coventry Cathedral soaring proudly above the busy manufacturing city spread out around it. This drawing was based on a photograph of 1880 showing the church in a far less idealized state. By the Second World War it had been fully restored.

Below Coventry Cathedral in 2005. The ruins of the blitzed cathedral are matched by the new cathedral designed by Basil Spence. Although controversial at the time of its construction, the 1950s design is a beautifully crafted building and a fine foil to its medieval predecessor.

Right Wounded American soldiers attending a Mother's Day service in the nave of Coventry Cathedral on May 13, 1945. The walls with their huge windows survived their encounter with the Luftwaffe as the cathedral was hit by incendiary rather than by high explosive bombs.

of the Frauenkirche in Dresden. A truly magnificent and daring design by the Baroque master, George Behr [1666–1743], this highly original church with its enormous, bell-shaped stone dome, was destroyed by the huge Allied air raid on the city in February 1945. At first it seemed as if the church might survive the fires, caused by the dropping of 650,000 incendiary bombs, which raged through Dresden, but inside the church, the city fires caused the temperature to rise to a hellish 1,000 degrees centigrade, at which point the structure imploded.

Frauenkirche was to remain a pile of rubble until 1993 when the architect and engineer Eberhard Burger was charged with its reconstruction. The plan had been mooted in 1985, but was made viable after the reunification of Germany when international funds began to channel their way into the former Communist republic of East Germany. British and American contributions amounted to half the total cost of £122 million needed for Burger to complete his task. The church reopened with international media coverage in October 2005. It was an extraordinary sight to stand inside a church one had only known either through pre-war photographs, historic architects' drawings or as a massive pile of rubble.

Burger used computer design techniques to recreate Bahr's Baroque masterpiece, but his completed project has been criticized as being a soulless new version of a great building. Computer techniques were used to position 3,800 charred stones into the overall fabric of the church, but it is true that almost everything you see is brand new. Is this right? One might just as well ask was it right for Victorian architects to virtually rebuild so many of Britain's cathedrals and churches; what they did was often brash, hard-edged and altogether too modern to look or feel right; yet without their zealous ministrations, many of these buildings, largely dismissed as barbarous in the eighteenth century, would have fallen into ruin or been completely swept away.

Above This is the Frauenkirche, in the heart of Dresden, seen from the air in 1935. The Allied bomber pilots who torched the city in February 1945 dropped their incendiary bombs from a great height and would never have been fully aware of the exquisite nature of their target.

Opposite Completely rebuilt, this is the Frauenkirche shortly before it was re-consecrated in October 2005. The original stones are easy to pick out; these are the dark ones, blackened by age, charred by fire. Everything else from the pavement to the top of the lantern is new.

Imagine living in Dresden knowing that your city was once one of the most beautiful in Europe and that so much of it had been destroyed. The desire to rebuild what had gone before was latent, but perhaps it only burned all the brighter and deeper as the years went by. Today, whether or not you really feel that this is where Johann Sebastian Bach once gave organ recitals, the rebuilt Frauenkirche, first completed in 1743, has prompted the beautification of Dresden's old city centre, bathing away the architectural wounds of war. Thirty-five thousand people did not die in vain on that terrifying night in February 1945.

The Blitz on British cities continued throughout much of 1940 and 1941. Liverpool, one of the country's greatest seaports, was a target for heavy bombing. Eight nights of continuous bombing in May 1941 led to the destruction of many fine buildings, but the greatest of these was the handsome Custom House facing the docks on the River Mersey. Designed by John Foster Jr [1787–1846], this impressive Ionic Greek building was crowned with a fine rotunda and dome. Although gutted, it could easily have been restored and today we would revel in such a grand design. Sadly this was not the way of doing things in Liverpool at the time and the Custom House was pulled down in 1942.

Foster was one of Liverpool's finest architects. He had travelled extensively, and amorously by all accounts, through Greece and Asia Minor in the company of C R Cockerell [1788–1863], the architect who was to complete the design and decoration of Liverpool's other great neoclassical monument, St George's Hall, which unlike so much of Foster's work, survives.

Opposite The ornate, Baroque interior of the Frauenkirche on the morning of the day it reopened. The debate over whether or not such buildings should be reconstructed or replaced by something altogether new continues, and yet who would deny Dresden its very special place of worship?

Left The Custom House, Liverpool from *Modern Liverpool Illustrated*, engraved by the painter William Gavin Herdman [1805–82] and James Orr Marples, and published in 1864. The masts of the ships are a fine foil for the massive Ionic portico and dome of John Foster Jr's commanding building.

Above Eat your heart out Louis XVI... the Long Hall in Albert Speer's Reich Chancellery, Berlin, was twice the length of the Hall of Mirrors at Versailles. The mirror-like effect of the room's décor was enhanced by its gleaming marble floor and window reveals.

There would be no justification whatsoever in the survival, much less the recreation of some of the key Nazi German buildings destroyed by Allied assaults in the Second World War. No right-minded person would want to see Albert Speer's Reich Chancellery back in place along Berlin's *Vossstrasse*. Nevertheless, this is one of those lost buildings one longs to explore if only through plans, photographs, historical documents and the imagination. There is no doubt that the architecture of dictators and other powerful political leaders is perennially fascinating. What might. What spectacle. What hubris.

The Reich Chancellery was a symbol of Nazi might and aesthetics, and it was also the palatial Berlin office of Adolf Hitler. It is interesting to think he must have spent almost as much time lurking in the *Führerbunker* hidden deep under the courtyard garden of his Chancellery, or in other military bunkers, as inside the completed Speer building itself.

Albert Speer [1905–81] completed work on the new Chancellery in just less than a year and within 48 hours of Hitler's schedule. Commissioned by Hitler in early 1938 and with limitless resources at his beck and call, the ambitious young architect was able to work with quicksilver speed. Manpower, materials and other resources were drawn from throughout Germany and the Reich.

The building, although beautifully realized in stone, granite and marble, and boasting colossal rooms, was in many ways more theatrical than substantial. Its plan, for example, reveals the long facades to *Vossstrasse* to be just one room deep. Some might see such architectural shallows as signs of weakness, but Speer knew what he was doing. The plan of the building required visitors to walk at inordinate length through lobbies, corridors and a hall of mirrors twice as long as the one in the palace of Versailles, before reaching the Reich Chancellor's office. When the double doors to this inner sanctum were opened, visitors were stunned by its size; Hitler's office measured 4,305 square feet (400 square metres).

When newly completed, Hitler invited all 4,000 or so workers who had built the Chancellery to inspect this new seat of power. The next proletarian visit to the Chancellery must have been in April 1945 when, in the ember days of the hugely destructive Battle of Berlin, Red Army troops made their way through Speer's marble and glass halls. Although damaged by bombing, artillery and small arms gunfire, the Chancellery was still reasonably intact when the Soviets demolished it. Apparently, marble from the Chancellery was used to build Berlin's Soviet war memorial in Treptower Park, while other building materials were employed in the reconstruction of the city's *Mohrenstrasse U-bahn* station, with some red marble being shipped to Moscow where it is incorporated in the walls of post-war metro stations.

No one would have condemned the Russians for doing what they did. Hitler remains a strangely alluring figure for all too many people around the world more than 60 years after his death and had the Chancellery survived, it would have become a kind of shrine, by default, to one of the most destructive politicians of all times. For all his professed love of architecture, Hitler was responsible for the destruction of many of Europe's – and, by extension, Asia's – finest buildings, including many in Germany itself.

Hitler's Alpine retreat, the Berghof, on the Obersalzberg near Berchtesgaden, was a house of his own design and furnishing. Perhaps he had help – he had only to click his fingers – but perhaps no one wanted to take credit for this, the most personal of Hitler's homes. Here, Hitler greatly extended and remodelled an earlier Alpine villa, transforming it into an interesting marriage of the cosy and the overbearing. The Great Room on the raised ground floor was a baronial affair, where all those infamous meetings took place between

Right The main entrance to the Reich Chancellery, seen here in 1939, goose-stepped the entire length of Berlin's Vossstrasse. Here was architecture standing to attention and very much on public parade.

Below right Portrait of a Faustian pact, or the Architect sells his soul to the Devil. Here is Albert Speer at Obersalzberg in 1934 showing Adolf Hitler plans for new buildings. Hitler had originally intended to be an architect, and Speer lived out that side of his ambitions for him.

Hitler and European politicians hoping against the odds to appease the German dictator. This is the room famous, too, for its colossal picture window that could be lowered entirely into the fabric of the building to afford unbroken views of the Wagnerian mountain landscape beyond.

I remember sitting in the library of a furniture-maker friend's house in France, thumbing through old bound copies of *Illustration* magazine and coming across a fascinating pre-war interview conducted by one of the magazine's younger members of staff with Hitler at the Berghof. What begins as a polite discussion about fabrics, wallpaper and domestic architecture ends up as a full-on declaration of intent by Hitler to make good the humiliation suffered by Germany because of the 1918 Treaty of Versailles, and thus, by implication, war. The Berghof was never exactly an innocent retreat.

Here, Hitler and his entourage would engage in more or less polite conversation, watch Hollywood movies in the Führer's private cinema, eat in his panelled dining room and drink cocktails – except for the teetotal, vegetarian, dog-loving leader – on a balcony looking out across superb views of the Alps.

The RAF raided Berghof on April 25, 1945 and when the game was up and Hitler was dead, members of the SS set the house on fire on May 4. That very same day, troops of the 3rd US Infantry Division arrived and settled down outside in the fine weather with well-earned bottles of wine and cognac from the Berghof's fire-proof cellars. The substantial remains of the house were blown up by the Bavarian government on April 30, 1952, the anniversary of Hitler's death. There is nothing left to see today.

However, you can take tea in the "Eagle's Nest", or *Kehlsteinhaus*, a mountain chalet built for Hitler as gift from a grateful Reich on the occasion of his 50th birthday in 1939. A beautifully engineered four-mile mountain road, passing through five tunnels and with just with one horse-shoe bend on the way, takes visitors up from Berchtesgaden to the foot of the mountain ridge the house sits on, 6,017 feet (1,833 metres) above sea level. A grand architectural entrance in the rocks leads into a barrel-vaulted corridor 417 feet (127 metres) long, ending in a circular, domed chamber cut into the rocks. From here a double-deck lift – the top compartment for passengers, the bottom for goods – climbs a further 417 feet vertically up through the mountain to reach the guesthouse, one of the world's strangest restaurants.

The fact that the Eagle's Nest survived appears to be down to the fact that Hitler only ever came here around 20 times, although Eva Braun was clearly fond of it. You can find photos easily enough – but, not on display at the Eagle's Nest – of Eva sharing jokes with family and friends at the wedding reception held in honour of her younger sister, Gretl, and her husband, *Obergruppenführer* Hermann Fegelein, a member of Heinrich Himmler's personal staff. What fun they were having!

Possibly the real reason the house survived is that no one was ever going to build a guest house like this again – Nazi or not. That lift and the shaft it climbs up through mountain stone is a magnificent piece of engineering and, unlike Hitler and his regime, the Allies seemed to have agreed that this was a special place worth saving.

Above The newly remodelled Bergholf at Obersalzberg near Berchtesgaden in the Bavarian Alps photographed in 1939. This was Hitler's mountain retreat and a house very much the Fuhrer's own work, and to his taste. It was a mixture of grandiose and *gemütlich*, or sweetly sentimental, design.

Opposite above The enormous picture window in the Great Room of the Berghof overlooking Alpine peaks. The entire window could be opened and lowered into the wall.

Opposite below In June 1945, American GIs stand in the frame of the Great Room window. They had fun partying in the ruins of this ill-fated house.

The buildings the Allies were keen to destroy were those most closely associated with Hitler himself. Today, Berlin's mighty 1936 Olympics Stadium [Werner March, 1894–1976], is still a sports stadium and what was Hermann Goering's Air Ministry headquarters in 1934–36 [Ernst Sagebiel, 1892–1970] is now an office for the Ministry of Finance; these are useful buildings and essentially free of association with the horrors of Nazism. Indeed, it would be hard not to shed a tear at the loss of the superb, yet doomed, art deco-meets-Thirties Classical Tempelhof Airport designed by Ernst Sagebiel in 1935–41. Until recently, it was possible to fly in and out of this city centre airport, which was once one of the proudest architectural and technological achievements of the Third Reich. While many buildings are able to outlive the nastiness of the regimes that created them, few prove to be a match for the commercial guns of property developers.

The fortunes of war and the colours of political regimes do indeed determine the fate of buildings. If you knew nothing about the politics and the sheer horror involved, it might be tempting to say that Albert Speer's Reich Chancellery was a finer and better-looking building than Paul Wallot's Reichstag, the seat of the unified German government from 1894 until 1933. Where the former had a certain neoclassical Prussian restraint about it, the bulbous Reichstag was an overblown essay in the uneasy, overwrought Classicism favoured in much of

Europe towards the end of the nineteenth century. It had the look of an over-egged architectural pudding.

When Otto von Bismarck succeeded in uniting Germany in 1871, a new central parliament house was deemed necessary. After two awkward architectural competitions, the commission was awarded to Paul Wallot [1841–1912] in 1882. Work commenced in 1884 and the building was completed 10 years later. When Hitler was appointed Chancellor in January 1933, he needed an excuse to set in motion his plan to undermine and then to ban parliament, or at least, to turn it into a supine rubber stamp for his Nazi regime. Like all cynical politicians, Hitler knew that the best way of gaining greater power for himself while curbing civil liberties was to play the national security card. If the German *volk* could be persuaded to see itself under threat, then it would be prepared to go along with a Nazi security clampdown in the interests of the state.

Above The Reichstag in full Prussian glory, 1930. This was just three years before the Nazis set fire to the building. It had never been beautiful, yet it deserved a better fate. It would wait the best part of seventy years before it came fully back to life.

Left A famous (posed?) photograph by Yevgeny Khaldei showing a Red Army T-34 tank and Soviet bombers triumphing over the Reichstag. May 1945.

Above The restored and remodelled Reichstag, now known as the Bundestag, in May 2005 by which time it had become not just the seat of a unified German government, but one of Berlin's top tourist attractions. An ugly duckling had, almost, become a swan.

Right The enormous abstract glass lightwell that passes through the new Bundestag dome and shines light on to the political proceedings of the parliamentary chamber far below. This is the spectacular centrepiece of Norman Foster's eight-year redesign of Paul Wallot's once rather lumpen building.

Hitler had been in office for less than a month when a major fire broke out in the Reichstag. A young Dutch communist was blamed and after a summary trial he was executed. Hitler, whose own men (it was suspected) had committed the deed, began his clamp down on civil liberties and human rights.

As for the Reichstag building, it never recovered and was barely used until a decision was made to convert it into government offices in the early 1960s. The work was carried out by the architect Paul Baumgarten between 1961 and 1964, but this was routine stuff and Bismarck's building looked as glum as it had ever done. In 1991 a newly unified German parliament voted to establish the country's capital in Berlin (after the Second World War, Bonn had been the capital of West Germany), and a competition was held to rebuild the Reichstag. Remarkably, the commission went to British architect, Norman Foster, who transformed the old building into a rather magnificent monument to a unified and democratic Germany.

Foster capped the building with a magnificent glass dome, up which visitors could walk to look out across the city and view, through a glass oculus, their political representatives busy at work below. The rooftop was equipped with a café, and the glum old Reichstag – renamed the Bundestag – took on a new life as a place for people to visit, meet and relax as they watched the world turn around a very different Berlin from the one Hitler and his pet architect, Albert Speer, had once hoped to build. Here is a case of a lost building found.

Peace did not descend upon the world with the fall of Hitler and Hirohito's Japanese imperial regime in 1945. Wars continue to be fought around the globe today, as humans try to dominate one another with their various puerile beliefs and pathetic power games. Not a month goes by without one building or another being damaged or destroyed, each of them marking the taking of human lives and the

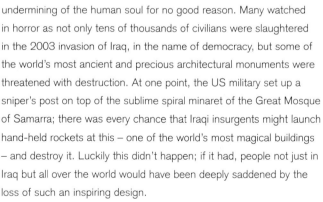

undermining of the human soul for no good reason. Many watched in horror as not only tens of thousands of civilians were slaughtered in the 2003 invasion of Iraq, in the name of democracy, but some of the world's most ancient and precious architectural monuments were threatened with destruction. At one point, the US military set up a sniper's post on top of the sublime spiral minaret of the Great Mosque of Samarra; there was every chance that Iraqi insurgents might launch hand-held rockets at this – one of the world's most magical buildings – and destroy it. Luckily this didn't happen; if it had, people not just in Iraq but all over the world would have been deeply saddened by the loss of such an inspiring design.

There have been some more understandable losses. In April 1999 a NATO air attack on Belgrade targeted and destroyed the 656-foot (200-metre) high transmitting tower on the city's Mt Avala, belonging to Serbian state television. This strike against a brutal regime led by Slobodan Milosevic was aimed at lowering Serbian morale as well as putting an end to its propaganda broadcasts; the 34-year old tower had been the tallest structure in the Balkan republic and a symbol of the controlling might of its crypto-fascist government.

It was also a source of pride and an object of affection, much like the Post Office Tower (now the British Telecom Tower) in London or the CNN Tower in Toronto. In June 2005 the Serbian Prime

Minister, Vojislav Kostunica, stood among the rubble on Mt Avala and announced that the tower would be rebuilt. "This is not just a message of reconstruction", he declared, "but an appeal to faith that every creation is stronger than every act of destruction." On a personal note, the Prime Minister said, "I could not believe Belgrade had lost the Avala Tower; I felt as if I had lost someone close."

The reconstructed tower is to be identical to its predecessor, except for a restaurant on the top; this time around, the Serbs aim to have a little more fun than they used to now that Milosevic's murderous regime has been brought to an end.

The most spectacular attacks on buildings in recent years have not been by conventional armies fighting conventional wars, but by terrorist groups aiming to kill as many civilians as possible in attempts to draw attention to their causes. The most infamous was, of course, the attack by al Qa'ida on New York's World Trade Center on September 11, 2001. This story is so familiar that few details need to be repeated here. Two Boeing airliners were hijacked and flown into the twin towers; each imploded killing thousands and striking a blow that led the United States to launch its "war on terror". The attack has also led to the curtailing of civil liberties in the western world and to the establishment of a culture in which we are all presumed to be guilty as we skulk through airports, ports, border controls and international railway stations.

Above left The Avala Tower, Belgrade, headquarters of Serbian state television, at the moment it was struck by a NATO missile on April 23, 1999. NATO had warned of the attack, but the state television director, Dragoljub Milanovic kept his staff on site. Sixteen people were killed in the attack.

Above right Twisted remains of the Avala Tower photographed a week after the NATO attack. The tower is to be rebuilt since, despite being little more than a tall steel platform supporting huge broadcasting dishes, it was a popular public monument in Belgrade.

There are a number of curious back-stories to be told in the aftermath of the attack. From a strictly architectural viewpoint, it was sad to see the work of the Japanese-American architect Minoru Yamasaki [1912–86] meet such an end. On March 16, 1972, Yamasaki's first major work, the Pruitt-Igoe urban housing project in St Louis, Missouri, was also blown to pieces. This was not an act of terrorism, but because the 33 concrete blocks containing 2,870 apartments had become one of the most notorious modern slums in the United States. Smothered in graffiti, dirty, violent and suffering from damp and any number of technical deficiencies, this "project" was sentenced to death by democratically elected city authorities. Charles Jencks, the eminent architectural critic and historian, declared March 16,1972, as "the day Modern architecture died."

Significantly, Mohammed Atta [1968–2001] the Al Qa'ida terrorist who flew American Airlines Flight No 11 into one of the twin towers of the World Trade Center had trained as an architect at Cairo University, and had written a thesis while studying at the Technical University of Hamburg on the issue of how modern high-rise buildings were destroying the fabric and spirit of traditional Arabic cities. Atta despised the housing blocks that Yamasaki had designed in St Louis, while the twin towers were, for him, a symbol of all that was wrong with western modernism. The attack on the World Trade Center appears to have been tailor-made for this fierce opponent of modern design.

Yamasaki saw things very differently. When asked about the towering design of the 110-storey, 1,350-foot (411-metre) towers of the World Trade Center, he said:

"I feel this way about it. World trade means world peace and consequently the World Trade Center buildings in New York… had a bigger purpose than just to provide room for tenants. The World Trade Center is a living symbol of man's dedication to world peace… beyond the compelling need to make this a monument

Below The north tower of the World Trade Center, Manhattan, under construction in 1972. Unlike most skyscrapers, it was the external walls of the Twin Towers that supported the buildings' weight, rather than a grid of steel columns. Office floors could thus be free of columns to maximize usable floor space, and rents.

to world peace, the World Trade Center should, because of its importance, become a representation of man's belief in humanity, his need for individual dignity, his beliefs in the cooperation of men, and through cooperation, his ability to find greatness."

From a purely architectural and urban planning perspective, it is hard to know exactly what to say about the loss of the twin towers. I remember taking a long while to come to terms with them; they seemed so aggressive, so unexpressive of anything much beyond commercial might. When I visited them, they seemed scary and just a little tinny. You could hear the wind howling demonically down the elevator shafts as you waited for a surprisingly bumpy, clattering – and very fast – ride to the Windows of the World restaurant and to the public viewing platform on top of one of the towers. The views were glorious, while the décor of the bars and restaurant were enjoyable Seventies' kitsch.

And yet, like many visitors to New York, I came to see the twin towers as a kind of giant architectural anchor holding the southern tip of Manhattan at berth. The gaping hole left where the World Trade Center once stood, known as "Ground Zero", is slowly being built over as New York gets back into its commercial stride. "The business of the United States", as President Calvin Coolidge once said, "is business." Plans were quickly drawn up for an equally dramatic architectural project, at first led by the design for a 1,776-foot (541-metre) tower (1776 is, of course, the date of American independence) by the American architect Daniel Libeskind [b.1946], surrounded by a sensational new public space. The plans have been tamed since, but within a couple of years the site will add up to far more than "zero",

although the ghostly presence of the twin towers and the story of "9/11" are unlikely to be forgotten.

Terrorism was also responsible for one of the two largest bomb blasts in London since the Second World War. The first of these bombs was detonated in the City of London on April 10, 1992 from a white van stuffed with fertilizer and a Semtex detonator by the Provisional IRA (Irish Republican Army). The blast rocked the foundations of the old Baltic Exchange at 30 St Mary Axe [Smith and Wimble, 1903] so hard, that after heated debate amongst conservation lobbies, City planners and the government, the go ahead was given for the demolition of the shaky building and it was finally demolished in 1998. This was a sad loss, as the Baltic Exchange was the last of its kind, an original City trading floor wrapped in an opulent stone, marble, stained glass and bronze architecture that appeared to have drawn its inspiration from the design of contemporary ocean liners.

Above Jagged remnants of the World Trade Center after the attack of September 11, 2001. There was much discussion at the time of just how strong and fireproof the Twin Towers were; yet very few buildings could withstand the impact of a 150-ton jet airliner laden with fuel.

Opposite The Twin Towers soaring above Battery Park on the southern tip of Manhattan. These were skyscrapers higher than the Empire State Building, realized on the scale of entire towns, enormous, stand-out machines for making money that drew the wrath of extremists in love with death and destruction.

It was replaced by a stupendous new conical 600-foot (183-metre) skyscraper known to Londoners as "the Gherkin", designed by Foster+Partners. The old building was taken apart and many of its components as well as its décor sold off to salvage dealers. In June 2006 an Estonian businessman, Eerik-Niiles Kross, discovered some of the remains in a warehouse near Canterbury in Kent, while searching the web for old tile flooring. He flew to England with his business partner, Heiti Haal, made a deal and shipped 49 containers of pieces of the Baltic Exchange back to Tallinn where the Exchange is to be rebuilt – a curiously happy ending to a sad tale. As for the IRA, not content with the loss of four lives in the 1992 explosion, it tried again, setting off another huge bomb in the City of London on April 24, 1993. One person was killed and the blast all but destroyed the

charming little medieval church of St Ethelburga; this has since been rebuilt by the Classical Revival architect, Quinlan Terry [b.1937].

The British might have felt justified in calling the Indian Mutiny of 1857 a collective act of terror, but to Indians, it was the first blow struck in the Indian War of Independence. Whatever you wish to call it, the uprising turned out to be a vicious bloodbath with atrocities

Above The luxurious trading floor of the Baltic Exchange in the City of London, all marble columns, parquet floors and elaborately plastered vaults, seen here on May 3, 1920.

Opposite The grand stone and marble exterior of the Baltic Exchange that stood in St Mary Axe before it was very badly damaged by the IRA blast.

committed on both sides. The one major architectural loss was the Residency at Lucknow, the dignified neoclassical home of the British Commissioner of Oudh. The house was a handsome affair, all white stucco walls, porticos and verandahs. Built between 1780 and 1800, it would have looked perfectly happy standing next to the villas and terraces designed by John Nash around Regent's Park. For a total of 148 days and during two sieges, the Residency was the object of a fierce rebel attack that saw some 2,000 British and Indians die here, and the house reduced to a ruin.

The Indian Mutiny had been in the offing for some while, but the spark that set it in action was one that may seem odd to western sensibilities. On May 1, Muslim soldiers of the 7th Oudh Irregular Infantry refused to bite the cartridges for use in their newly issued Enfield rifles, because they believed that the cartridges were greased with an unholy mixture of beef and pork fat. This offended their religious sensibilities and when disarmed by non-Muslim regiments, they were more than ready to rebel. The fighting spread through several parts of India, but the Siege of Lucknow remains one of the most infamous episodes in this inglorious "war".

Today the ruins are like those of an ancient Roman site, peaceful, romantic and rather beautiful. It takes some effort to imagine the terrible fighting that took place here in the searing summer heat of 1857 and of rescue efforts, ultimately successful, made by the British through the monsoon and into the following year. Here in Lucknow, the savagery and hate has been lost; what remains is a testament to India at a very different time in its dramatic history.

Above The Residency, Lucknow, all stucco, Ionic columns and louvred windows shortly before the siege of the city that would see its destruction in 1857 at the time of the Sepoy Mutiny. Here is a house that would have been happy to see out its days in London's Regent's Park.

As the years, centuries and generations pass, it becomes increasingly hard to associate some of the world's most haunting ruins with blood, violence, war and terror. High in the mountains, some 50 miles (80 kms) beyond the beautifully recreated medieval walled city of Carcassone in southern France, stand the ruins of the Castle of Montségur. Although the ruins you see today date from some time between 1400 and 1700, they stand on the lost ruins of an infamous earlier castle. It is hard to believe that this beautiful place marked the culmination of the Vatican's "crusade" against the Cathars, Christians of a very different persuasion from Roman Catholics who thrived in Languedoc before they were seen as a threat to power-crazed Popes. Cathars believed that Christ came to live, and not to die, for us; this belief alone was enough to undermine the foundations of the Roman Catholic Church. So in 1209 the far-from-innocent Pope Innocent III launched his Albigensian Crusade, aimed at destroying the Cathars.

The bloodshed was revolting by any standards and during the Crusade's first 20 years, up to a million people died. Nothing and no one was allowed to stand in the righteous path of the Papal juggernaut. When asked how to deal with citizens captured in the towns besieged by the Crusaders, many of whom were Catholics (the Cathars were tolerant of other creeds), the Papal legate in the field, Arnaud-Armaury, infamously replied, "*Caedite eos! Novit enim Dominus qui sunt eius.*" ("Kill them all! God will recognize his own.") After the siege of Beziers, the bloodthirsty legate wrote to Innocent, "our men spared no one, irrespective of rank, sex or age, and put to the sword about 20,000 people. After this great slaughter, the whole city was despoiled and burnt."

The Nazis were fascinated by the story of the Cathars. Himmler and some of his questionable archaeologists believed they might discover the whereabouts of the Holy Grail; there were stories that the Grail had been held in what was once the mountain fastness of Montségur. Legend has it that when Montségur itself was starved into submission in 1244 and the Cathar survivors were rounded up and burned alive in a wooden cage below the castle, two or three of the defenders escaped with a secret treasure; their traces and the

treasure they valued have yet to be discovered, if it ever existed.

After Montségur, the Cathars all but vanished from history. Their final stronghold, Queribus Castle, fell in 1255 and the last Cathars were burned alive by the Church in 1321. Strangely, the highly imaginative and perhaps greatest of all Modern architects of the twentieth century, Le Corbusier, began to believe that he might be a descendant of the Cathars. Perhaps this was just a romantic notion, but at least they were not entirely lost to the passing centuries. Today the Cathars are the focus of a buoyant tourist industry in Languedoc; their buildings might have been razed to the ground, yet their spirit still haunts these southern French skies. Buildings may last for centuries, but the spirit that shaped them can endure even longer. It is a fascination for such buildings as Montségur that leads some of us in a quest to uncover these forgotten souls.

Top left The daunting setting of Montségur in the Languedoc, south-west France. The last stronghold of the Cathars stood more than 1,200 metres (1,300 yards) above sea level. The name means "safe mountain", although the Cathars were unable to withstand the siege by the armies of the Pope's savage crusade against them.

Above left The triumph of religious bigotry: Dominican monks enjoy burning 220 Cathars in a wooden cage at the foot of Montségur after the siege of 1244.

Above Ruins of Montségur: this is actually a later castle built on the foundations of the Cathar fortress. It fell into a less dramatic decline.

Opposite The view from the uppermost walls of Montségur looks across to a mountainous landscape and, beyond, into the peace of infinite space.

4 LOST TOO SOON

T he *New York Times* reported on October 30, 1963: "Until the first blow fell, no one was convinced that Penn Station really would be demolished, or that New York would permit this monumental act of vandalism against one of the largest and finest landmarks of its age of Roman elegance."

The shocking demolition of Pennsylvania Station, one of the greatest buildings of all time, was an act of wanton stupidity and naivety that kick-started a latent American conservation lobby into action. Designed by the inventive and highly accomplished American architects, McKim, Meade and White, and opened in 1910, Penn Station was a truly magnificent reinterpretation of an ancient Roman building recreated at the beginning of the twentieth century to serve what was, at the time, one of the nation's most dynamic railroads, the Pennsylvania. McKim Meade and White adopted much of the plan, scale, design and décor of the once mighty Baths of Caracalla to shape their Manhattan masterpiece, adding a dramatic steel and glass train shed from which, in the heyday of the Pennsylvania Railroad in the 1940s, luxurious express trains ran to and from Chicago and other industrial cities.

The ruins of the Baths of Caracalla still stood in McKim Meade and White's day, as they continue to do today. Here was an antique building constructed on a scale appropriate not just for third-century Rome, but for twentieth-century Manhattan. Commissioned by Septimus Severus in 206 AD and inaugurated in 217 AD by Caracalla, the vast marble-clad Baths were designed for up to 1,600 people at a time. The main, centrally heated building was 750 feet (228 metres) long, 380 feet (116 metres) wide and 125 feet (38 metres) high, set in 33 acres (133 square metres) of public gardens. Aside from thermal baths, this huge civic meeting place and pleasure palace included a swimming pool, gym, libraries – one Greek, one Latin – shops and dining rooms, all housed under magnificent and highly decorated vaulted roofs.

The Baths fell into disuse after the fall of the Roman Empire and the building was allowed to go to rack and ruin. Some of its beautifully carved columns were re-used in Christian churches – there are no fewer than 22 of these in the church of Santa Maria in Trastevere, one of the very oldest in Rome. The walls of the Baths, long stripped of their marble cladding, serve as a backdrop each summer for open-air performances by the Teatro dell'Opera di Roma. This is where the "Three Tenors" – Placido Domingo, Jose Carerras and Luciano Pavarotti – sang their hearts out at a gala performance to mark the end of the 1990 FIFA World Cup.

Right Surely no one could ever have wanted to demolish this truly magnificent New York building. Pennsylvania Station, seen here in 1911, a masterpiece of American design, was destroyed neither by war nor by "Act of God", but by political stupidity and rank commercial greed. Look at it, and weep.

Left Mosaic floor from the Baths of Caracalla. These were made of stones drawn from across the Roman Empire. Floors were heated. Even the latrines were magnificent. One of Rome's most popular public buildings, it lost its purpose when the water supply was cut off by Ostrogoths in 537.

Above Penn Station was based, in large part, on the monumental Baths of Caracalla, built in Rome between 212 and 217 AD. The gentleman sitting here admiring its ruins could easily be mistaken for a commuter waiting for a train home from Penn Station.

At least something remains of the Baths of Caracalla, but its twentieth-century offspring, Penn Station, was wiped off the map and replaced by a truly dismal station. Largely subterranean, it seemed deliberately designed to put people off travelling by train at the very time that New Yorkers were beginning to fly more frequently to cities like Chicago, or to drive on the new interstate highways, once served by some of the finest trains in the world.

Penn Station had arrived late in Manhattan itself; until an electrified line was built under the Hudson River into the city, Pennsylvania Railroad trains had to terminate on the western side of the river at Exchange Place, New Jersey, and passengers completed their journey by ferry. Once electric trains arrived, a tunnel was dug and Penn Station built. At least we can look at the many superb photographs that were taken of this railroad temple; it is hard to believe just how awe-inspiring this building was. When it was demolished and its site covered over with the lacklustre Madison Square Gardens complex,

the architectural historian, Vincent Scully, was moved to compare the old and the new Penn stations, noting that where once "one entered the city like a god, one scuttles in now like a rat." If Penn's demolition in 1964 marked the death of great historic architecture in New York, the horrid new station was spookily to claim the life of one of the greatest of all Modern American architects, Louis Kahn [1901–74] when he suffered a heart attack and died in the station's restroom.

A new and better Penn Station was first announced in 2005, but plans have come and gone, and commuters continue to suffer the indignity of creeping underground to leave the city by train. One of the most intriguing plans was one that would have incorporated the fine Roman-style General Post Office Building, also designed by McKim Meade and White, and first opened in 1912. The building is listed and cannot be demolished, and today only the most shark-like developer and least scrupulous local politician would want to see it destroyed.

Above Penn Station at its zenith in July 1954, and yet just nine short years from destruction. The station was impressive, easy to use, well kept and made everyone who entered its mighty Roman-meets-Beaux Arts portals somehow special. All this must have counted against it.

Left Passengers at the booking office of Penn Station. Note the consistency of the design, the quality of the fittings and the general pristine nature of this great building. It looks as if it had been designed to last five hundred years rather than fifty.

Below With the Empire State Building watching over the tragedy unfolding on New York's Eighth Avenue, Penn Station is demolished to make way for the glum Madison Square Gardens and a replacement station underground that continues to belittle passengers, although a new station is due soon.

Right Savannah's Union Station in the 1940s. US railroads were at their peak at this time in terms of handling passenger traffic. This declined rapidly with the arrival of inter-city aircraft and Interstate freeways in the following decade. A freeway pushed the Union station out of existence in 1962.

Below right Union Station when brand new in 1902, looking just right for a railroad generation *Gone with the Wind*-style clientèle. Because of "Jim Crow" laws, there was one waiting room for white folk and one for coloured. Perhaps the Civil War had never happened.

The early 1960s were a bad time for railroad stations in the United States; this was a time of "modernization" when planes and automobiles, rather than trains, were seen as the way to go. A year before the destruction of Penn Station, the exotic Union Station in Savannah had fallen. Designed by Frank Pierce Milburn [1868–1926] in a style, or styles, that the architect liked to call Spanish Renaissance and Elizabethan – a case of having your stylistic cake and eating it – Union Station was a delightful building, best known by the many passengers who passed through it for its ample octagonal waiting room. Actually, there were two waiting rooms; right up until the station's demolition, "Jim Crow" laws enforced segregation between black and white passengers. The street in which the station once stood is now named Martin Luther King Jr Boulevard in memory of the inspired black American preacher and human rights campaigner. Sadly, though, the station made way for the path of what at the time was known simply as Interstate 16 and today it is marked by nothing more than an Enmark service station. As for Milburn, this eclectic architect designed grand buildings – churches, town halls, office blocks – in many styles across the Southern states and much of his best work survives.

The losses of Savannah's Union Station and New York's Penn Station marked more than a careless, destructive attitude towards historic architecture, they also underlined the fact that America's once-magnificent railroads would never be the same again. Although the railroads are busy today, they carry mostly freight and very little in the way of passenger traffic. Given the revival of railways in Europe and their continued development in such giant countries as China, Russia and Australia, this seems a sorry state of affairs.

In the 1960s the United States went on a demolition spree as the notion of Space Age modernization went hand-in-developer's-hand with the notion that anything old that stood in the way of "progress" had to go. The idea that it was perfectly possible to send rockets into space and still travel by train from Roman-style railway stations

Above The Singer Building's tower rising into the Manhattan skyline in 1908. This picture well conveys the spirit of commercial, architectural and engineering adventure that guided the first skyscrapers so optimistically upwards.

Opposite The brand new Singer Building, thrusting priapically above nineteenth-century rooflines. The manner in which the floors were divided into bands of six to give definition to the building was particularly skilful.

doesn't seem to have occurred to many people in positions of power and influence. The destruction of so many twentieth-century buildings in the same century is not just sad, but irresponsible. The sheer waste of energy involved can no longer be readily sanctioned in an age that, superficially at least, expresses ever-greater concern about the use of fossil fuels, carbon emissions and the environment in general.

Several famous New York towers came tumbling down to make way for shinier, energy-gobbling replacements. If you look at certain photographs of the Singer Building, for example, it's hard to tell if these are construction or demolition shots. When it was completed in 1908, the Singer Building, resembling some outsized Italian campanile, was the world's tallest building, a record it held – this being New York – for less than a year. It survived just 60 years. Developers claimed that its small floor plates – the floors of its towers measured just 65 square feet (6 square metres) – were too small for modern business needs, so it was pulled down and replaced with One Liberty Plaza, an admittedly impressive 783-foot (239-metre) tower, damaged in the infamous al Qa'ida attack of September 11, 2001.

Today new forms of communications technology mean that city offices need not necessarily be as big as One Liberty Plaza and if the Singer Building had survived, it would have a made a fine suite of offices and studios for young businesses much lighter on their feet than the titanic corporations of the 1960s. The 612-foot (186-metre), 45-storey Singer Building, designed by Ernest Flagg [1857–1957] has a rather peculiar claim to fame; it is the tallest building ever legally demolished.

The Chicago Federal Building's claim to fame is that its mighty domed rotunda was bigger than that of the Capitol in Washington DC. Chicago always liked to go one bigger and better than any other American city and its Federal Building, designed by Henry Ives Cobb [1859–1931], was certainly big. A bruiser of a *beaux-arts* building, the mighty Federal Building replaced an earlier design of 1879. Cobb shaped an enormous, 16-storey office block arranged in the form of a Greek cross, resting on top of a grandiloquent, Roman-style square base and topped the whole thing with that mighty rotunda and a dome that rose almost 300 feet (91 metres) above the city's sidewalks. The building opened in 1905.

The Federal Building housed courts, a post office and civic offices. By the 1960s it was regarded as not only too small, despite its bulk, but far too old-fashioned for a new-look Chicago. The fashionable and brilliant German-American architect, Ludwig Mies van der Rohe [1886–1969] designed a sleek steel-and-glass 45-storey replacement, and in 1965 Cobb's Federal Building came down. Mies's building is very fine; demolition of historic buildings does not always mean they are replaced by something worse, and yet it is intriguing to see buildings barely in their prime being destroyed. While it is possible to see why, for example, the city bosses of Chicago would have thought Cobb's Federal Building frumpy and outmoded, in recent years even some of the most lumpen civic buildings, such as the Reichstag in Berlin, have been renovated in ways – in this case by Norman Foster in the 1990s – that make them freshly compelling. In the 1960s it was all too often a case of out with the old, in with the new, but since then a developing concern for conservation combined with a desire not to lose traces of our past has encouraged many cities to remodel time-worn buildings, bringing them up to date without destroying them.

Opposite Hand-coloured photograph of the Singer Building, *c.*1908. Skyscrapers were the defining building type of Manhattan as the city found ever-increasing fame and fortune on the international stage in the early twentieth century; they were clearly something to celebrate rather than to be feared.

Right Although an imposing building and with a dome bigger than that of the Capitol in Washington, the Chicago Federal Building seems to have been rather unloved and perhaps even unmourned; there are surprisingly few photographs of this muscular, if rather pompous, public building.

Below The Chicago Federal Building was replaced by the sleek steel and glass towers of the new Federal Centre designed by Ludwig Mies van der Rohe, while the plaza it stood in was adorned by this energetic and colourful abstract modern sculpture, "Flamingo", by Alexander Calder [1898–1976].

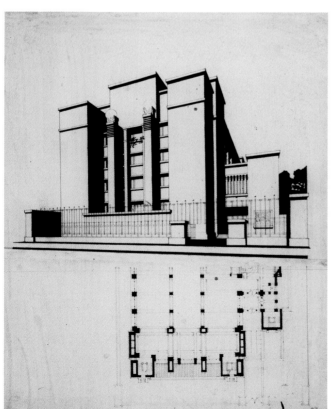

Sometimes the demolition of an office building – not always a much-loved building type – can be shocking. Why, for example, did anyone ever think of demolishing Frank Lloyd Wright's Larkin Building? Wright [1867–1959] is the most celebrated of all American architects, and perhaps best known for his "Prairie" houses – open-plan living for the modern Chicago middle classes in the early years of the twentieth century – and for the utterly unexpected form of the Solomon R Guggenheim Museum on New York's Fifth Avenue. A charismatic, quixotic and even eccentric figure, Wright did much to revolutionize American architecture from the 1890s and virtually every building he designed had something special about it. It is a shame to lose any of them, but the loss of the Larkin Building in 1950 when it was just 46 years old was a tragedy.

What was so special about the Larkin Building? It was the world's first truly modern office building. The core of the building, designed for a mail-order business operating from Buffalo in upstate New York, was an atrium. Judging from photographs of the building, the whole place looks rather gloomy, but in fact it was beautifully lit inside. Not only

Above left The Larkin Building was designed to handle the mail-order side of the company's business. This included not just soap, but groceries, dry goods, china and furniture. Here the sales clerks are busy at work surrounded by edifying slogans encouraging such virtues as "co-operation", "economy" and "industry".

this, but the interior boasted elevators as well as stairs, air-conditioning (a first), glass doors and steel furniture. Wright made maximum use of the site in Buffalo by pushing the stairwells and elevator shafts to the sides of the building; this was a way of designing major office blocks, which was only really taken up again three-quarters of a century later. The design of the determinedly futuristic Lloyd's Building [1978–86] in the City of London by Richard Rogers, for example, draws much from the plan of Wright's historic design.

The exterior of the building has always been a little baffling; it is not exactly what we expect of an office building, either then or now. I think what Wright was doing here was to shape a building that called to mind the great modern farm buildings of contemporary America. The Larkin Building's somewhat formidable appearance is surely based, at least in part, on the great storage silos and other industrial-era agricultural buildings rising on the endless mid-western wheat plains he knew so well. The loss of this fascinating building and its replacement with a parking lot remains as inexplicable as it is haunting and sad.

Above right The interior court, or atrium, of the Larkin Building in 1905 with clerks and typists dealing with orders. Wright designed pretty much every last fixture and fitting in the building. It seems sad that such a thoroughly crafted building was replaced with nothing more than a parking lot.

Above The lily pond and entrance front of the Imperial Hotel, Tokyo, in the late 1950s. This extraordinary design owed as much to Mayan as it did to Japanese precedent. An intriguing building in every way, the short-lived Imperial would be a cult destination hotel today.

Equally inexplicable, by the standards of anyone who cares for great architecture, is the loss of Wright's Imperial Hotel in Tokyo. Wright was hugely influenced by traditional Japanese design; the free-flowing, largely open-plan interiors of the many houses he designed over his long career owed more to Japanese precedent than it did to design ideas emanating from the Bauhaus, the German powerhouse of Modern Movement design that was to so affect the look of many American city centres from the 1950s.

The commission of a building in Tokyo must have meant a great deal to Wright, yet the extraordinary hotel he created between 1916 and 1923 owed as much to Mayan design – another of Wright's favourites – and to art deco as it did to anything recognizably Japanese. From some angles the hotel looked as if might have been flown in from the ancient Mayan site of Chichen Itza in the Yucatan and from others it looked liked an obscure Japanese temple. Arranged around pools and courtyards, the low-lying hotel was a truly exotic creation. Low corridors led into a lofty banqueting hall and gold-leafed reception rooms. Architectural details – built into the internal structure – included large-scale abstract representations of turtles, peacocks and scarab beetles. Carpets in public areas boasted Native American patterns, while guest rooms featured

Japanese screens and antiques neatly mixed with the very latest American furniture.

The hotel won the hearts of the Japanese when it survived a major earthquake in 1923, one that damaged much of Tokyo. Wright believed that the low-lying, concrete structure sitting on swampy soil had saved the day. Perhaps it was just good luck that the hotel escaped so lightly during an earthquake that measured no less than 7.9 on the Richter scale. However, it proved not to have been such a good idea to build the hotel on soft ground after all; as the years passed, the structure slowly began to sink, causing increasing damage. In 1968 the Japanese hoteliers reluctantly demolished this intriguing building. Nowadays it could be possible to underpin such a building, but this wasn't the case 40 years ago. The Imperial Hotel's successor, no matter how comfortable and well run, resembles a rather dull office block. Tokyo is a city famous for knocking down new buildings even before their completion; this happened during the economic boom of the mid to late 1980s when land values in central Tokyo were so inflated that developers tore down new buildings to erect even bigger ones and make ever more money. Architecture was a pure commodity, something to be raised and torn down whenever a fast buck, or yen, beckoned.

Left A luggage label, of 1932, from the Imperial Hotel. Every last detail of this unexpected hotel was designed with care. Wright had long been captivated by Japanese art and architecture before he began work on the building; it is rather sad that his enthusiasm was so shabbily repaid.

Above US naval officers lounging in the exotic lobby of the Imperial Hotel in the late 1940s. Note the complex changes of level, the half or even quarter floors projecting overhead, the use of exposed brick and the lovely play of diffused sunlight across ceiling, walls and floor.

In Britain, once thought of by the Americans and the Japanese as an old-fashioned country imbued with courteous manners, such unseemly demolition began to gather pace in recent years. Only recently, Drapers Gardens, a svelte 328-foot (100-metre) 1960s office block in the City of London, was demolished and replaced by a lower, but altogether more complex office commissioned by the Royal Bank of Scotland. For me, it was a shock to see one of the tallest buildings erected in the City of London during my own childhood come tumbling down. Completed in 1967 to designs by the prolific Seifert and Partners, the lifespan of Drapers Gardens was briefer than the "prefab" houses bolted together after the Second World War as temporary replacements for homes lost during the Blitz. Where architecture was once a rock of ages, now it seems to be as temporary as anything else in our lives.

Drapers Gardens was not a great building, but it had a certain slick élan – all cantilevers and curves – and it was a personal favourite of Richard Seifert [1910–2001], or the "Colonel" as this former wartime army engineer liked to be known. Seifert's practice designed something like 500 office blocks in Great Britain and Europe; these include Centre Point tower in London's West End and Tower 42 in the City of London, two distinguished buildings that have gained increasing enchantment, or bravura, over time. Seifert's were some of the most stylish of Sixties office blocks and many have a good chance of surviving for a long while, if they don't happen to stand, as Drapers Gardens did, on some of the most costly land in the world.

Skyscrapers had never been immune from demolition in any part of the world. The first skyscraper – usually taken as a building of 12 storeys or more – to be built in the southern hemisphere was, I think, the Australia Building, for the Australian Property and Investment Company in Melbourne. Opened in 1889, on a corner of Elizabeth Street, this was a fascinating design. It was an early attempt to stretch a historic style of architecture or nineteenth-century version of a historic style, into a high-rise office block. The style chosen by its architect, Henry Kemp [1859–1946] was "Queen Anne Revival" favoured by the British architects Richard Norman Shaw and E W Nesfield who were Kemp's especial contemporary heroes.

Kemp had been born in Lancashire and educated in London before he emigrated to Australia in 1886. He sailed to Melbourne and the following year was made a partner of a new firm, Oakden Addison and Kemp. This was short lived as a sharp economic downturn in 1892 put

Above Drapers Gardens was a very short-lived London office block, completed in 1967, demolished in 2006. It was the tallest building yet to be demolished in Britain, although given that the City of London wanted larger trading floors than Sixties towers could offer, others are likely to go, too.

Right Detail of Drapers Gardens rising above and between Victorian City of London offices. This was Colonel Seifert's favourite office block, of his own design, of which very many remain in central London. They are some of the best commercial buildings of the era, but prey to economic forces.

Right Flared trousers and Coke-bottle styling for cars are clearly in, so this is obviously the 1970s – 1979 to be exact – and this is the Australia Building on Elizabeth Street, Melbourne, soon to be demolished despite its fascinating high-rise "Queen Anne Revival" design.

a sudden halt to ambitious commercial design. Kemp, a hard-working, devout Presbyterian, still prospered in his own right and went on to become one of Australia's leading architects in the period leading up to the Second World War.

The Australia Building towered over Melbourne in tiers of brick, terracotta, pediments and gables. It was a handsome building, full of character, and a true landmark in the history of Australian architecture, yet who really cared about its claims to fame? It was demolished in the early 1980s in the name of lucrative downtown redevelopment.

Just as the worlds of real estate, office management and technology and corporate culture change, so does the world of entertainment. In the same way that a creaking, black-and-white Laurel and Hardy "short", no matter how funny, seems as ancient as a Mayan temple today, the picture palaces of the early twentieth century appear obsolete to those running the entertainment business in the era of digital movies, interactive DVDs and home computers connected to the Internet. Many cinemas have vanished worldwide in recent years, even though they might have been given new uses or even revamped as modern cinemas.

The Alhambra Theatre, Sacramento, California, first opened in 1927 and demolished in 1973, serves as an example here for all the many fine and imaginative picture houses that have disappeared in recent decades, buildings that had once seemed so glamorous – architectural counterpoints to Busby Berkeley musicals and to Fred Astaire and Ginger Rogers singing and dancing their way across glittering art deco film sets.

Dressed up in the guise of some ineffably romantic Moorish palace, the 1,990-seat Alhambra was entered through a courtyard fountain garden. Inside, it was an artful creation of Moorish lamps and screens, plush red carpets, gold leaf, intricate decorative mouldings and an ambitious pipe organ. Its architects were Nacht and Lewis. When this much-loved building came down, it was replaced by nothing more exciting than a Safeway supermarket. One fountain from the cinema's courtyard remains standing on a corner of Safeway's parking lot.

If anything good came out of the destruction of this theatre, it was the rise of a strong conservation movement in Sacramento, and just as patriotic Texans like to cry, "Remember the Alamo!" so many conservationists in Sacramento still rally to the call "Remember the Alhambra!"

Hollywood stars themselves were for 20 years or so enamoured with another glamorous art deco setting; the Garden of Allah Hotel on Hollywood's Sunset Strip. Opened in 1927, this was the centre of the raunchy side of Hollywood life. Charlie Chaplin, Errol Flynn, Greta

Above top The Alhambra Theatre, Sacramento, in 1935 when this glistering Art Deco cinema was in its prime. It didn't really look much like the famous Andalusian fortress-palace from the outside, but it did have the look of some exotic Arabian Nights stronghold. It was much mourned when demolished.

Above Detail from the Alhambra Theatre of an electrolier hanging over the entrance lobby. The Californian cinema opened when the first movie with synchronized sound – *The Jazz Singer*, starring Al Jolson – was released, and closed with *The Exorcist* which was scaring audiences witless at the time.

Garbo, Ginger Rogers, Marilyn Monroe and the Marx Brothers came to play here. This is where Humphrey Bogart and Lauren Bacall began courting while working on the set of *To Have and To Have Not* (1944), and this is where the American literati – Dorothy Parker, F Scott Fitzgerald and Ernest Hemingway came to join the fun.

The hotel came about after Alla Nazimova [1879–1945] the Russian-born star of Hollywood's silent screen began to worry about her bank balance. Her most recent films, such as *Salome* (1923) based on Oscar Wilde's risqué stage play, had not been a commercial success and so she extended the Spanish hacienda-style Hollywood mansion she had leased in 1918 and converted it into what became the Garden of Allah Hotel.

Apparently the construction was fairly flimsy, the food lousy and the whole place run in an amateurish manner, but it was somewhere for the rich and famous to hide away in and make whoopee, not a perfect example of Californian architecture. After the Second World War the hotel fell into a slow decline and was demolished in summer 1959. It might well have become a cult place to stay today; before its closure the hotel hosted one last, riotous party, said to be attended by 1,000 guests including some, like Chaplin, who had attended the opening party more than 30 years before. An auction of furniture, fixtures and fittings was held during this boisterous swansong and the story goes that there was an unseemly jostle when it came to the bidding for a bed much favoured by Errol Flynn. The Garden of Allah was a joint that existed in haze of alcohol and hedonism; the wonder is that it lasted so long.

As for Alla Nazimova, she never made any money from the venture; soon after the opening of the hotel she was living in a small apartment in one corner of the complex. First replaced by a parking lot, the site is now occupied by a West Coast strip comprising undistinguished shops and fast-food chain restaurants like McDonalds. Joni Mitchell remembered the loss of this one-time Hollywood favourite in her 1970 song "Big Yellow Taxi", when she sang:

"Don't it always seem to go
That you don't know what you've got
Till it's gone
They paved paradise
Put up a parking lot"

Above top The Garden of Allah, Hollywood, in 1940, and still very much the place for movie stars to while away time "resting" between engagements. In strict architectural terms, the building was nothing special, but the Garden of Allah was a racy joint and much missed when it was gone.

Right The garden front of the Garden of Allah, with bedrooms overlooking the pool, some protected by faux-Spanish ironwork. The Andalusian-style detailing was pure tokenism, but no one really cared. This was a place to come and be bad in, not to ponder the finer points of art history.

Paradise Street in Las Vegas was the home for over 30 years of a space-age hotel that promised so much, yet ultimately did not deliver enough to make it a going concern in the twenty-first century. This was the Landmark Tower hotel, a superficially exciting design that took eight years to build, from 1961 to 1969, and closed its doors in 1990. After a long wait, the hotel was blown to smithereens in a controlled explosion that brought it down to earth with a bump in just 17 seconds. Caught on film, the footage was used to spectacular and comic effect by Tim Burton in his sci-fi spoof, *Mars Attacks!* (1996).

The Landmark Tower was the brainchild of Frank Carroll, a Kansas City building contractor, aiming to cash in on the booming casino hotel trade in Las Vegas. Carroll employed the Californian architect John W Jamieson [d 1989] and they soared off into structural space. Carroll's finances, however, were not enough to complete this starry building. He sold out to Howard Hughes, the legendary film-maker, pilot, industrialist and reclusive Californian billionaire, and the hotel was finally completed. Hughes opened the Landmark Tower on July 1, 1969, just 10 days before Neil Armstrong and Buzz Aldrin became the first men to walk on the moon.

This was the zenith of the first space age and the hotel looked set to cash in on its glamour, but with just 525 rooms, the Landmark Tower was small compared to the giant casino hotels that began to open elsewhere in Las Vegas at the same time. Guests found the rooms, stacked up around the shaft of the tower, too small, and sited slightly off the map, there was little passing trade for the hotel's casinos. By the mid-Eighties the hotel appeared to be a lost cause. If it had survived a little longer, it might just have made the grade as a cult hotel. It didn't and today it has been replaced by – you guessed – an all-American parking lot, serving the Las Vegas Convention Center.

Was the hotel ever any good? I did visit, although I never stayed there, and was disappointed because it wasn't the truly NASA-style experience it could have been. It was topped with a spectacular three-storey steel and glass flying saucer-shaped "flight-deck" reached by glass elevators climbing up and down the external walls of the concrete tower (these made an appearance in the Bond film, *Diamonds are Forever* (1971), but the interiors were far too conventional to make the experience as special as it might have been. On the top, there was a Chinese restaurant, a steak house, casino, coffee shop and nightclub. The views across Las Vegas and the desert beyond were wonderful, but it was a little too earthy for its commercial good.

Top Big Yankee cars roll on by the Landmark Tower before anyone worried about the draining away of natural resources and their personal carbon footprints. The rocket-like hotel was very much the child of the early, optimistic Space Age, and it looked great from the road.

Below When the Landmark Tower was demolished on November 7, 1995, the crowds whooped and cheered, thrilled to see a modern tower being destroyed by high explosives. I wonder why they were so gleeful? The Landmark could easily have been transformed into a unique place to stay.

Above The living room, complete with Andy Warhol on one wall, of the Maslon House, Rancho Mirage, California. This was one of those dream Californian homes designed by a distinguished architect that many of us would love to stay in, or even own.

If the loss of the Landmark Tower was sad, the sudden demolition in 2002 of the superb Maslon House at Rancho Mirage, California, came as a real shock. This beautiful modern villa, built in 1962 for the art-collecting husband and wife team, Samuel and Luella Maslon, was designed by Richard Neutra [1892–1970], the inspired Austrian-American architect who did much to create the dreamlike type of Californian home that many of us think of as perfect. Shortly after the death of Luella Maslon, the house was bought by Richard Rotenberg. Within 30 days of purchasing it, the new owner had won a local demolition order on the grounds that asbestos had been used in its construction – and down it came.

It's clear from the photographs that the house was very beautiful and had been lovingly and intelligently furnished. The way in which this resolutely Modern house charms its way into the local landscape is all but magical. Look how well the house works with the Hockney-esque pool, the surrounding gardens and the big Californian sky. I only really knew the house from pictures in Adele Cygelman's fine book, *Palm Springs Modern* (1999). At the time of its demolition, Cygelman had this to say:

"Luella Maslon took great pride in her house. It was a radically modern commission at the time, and she felt that she and her husband had laid the groundwork for others… to follow suit. Neutra responded to their needs for a family house that could also showcase a growing art collection – the long entrance gallery and spacious living room absorbed their paintings and sculptures and first edition books, but the dining room had a wet bar and indoor grill and the pool was directly outside for easy access. The house was as soulful as the Maslons. It's obviously a trait lacking in the new owners."

Barbara Lamprecht, author of *Neutra: Complete Works*, said:

"It is a kind of raw pain to ponder the gratuitous death of one of his best villas, a residential palazzo of art that embodied sophisticated abstractions about positive and negative space in a structure that was equally sophisticated in construction. I'm sure it wasn't easy to demolish, at least I hope so. All that care, all those beautiful materials used to accomplish richer human relationships with the outdoors and with other humans, placed in ways that spoke to the beauty of asymmetry, gone, and for what? Wasn't another site even considered?"

Neutra was one of the most acclaimed Modern architects of the twentieth century. Born and educated in Vienna, his first major commission in the USA was the hugely influential Lovell House [1929], a vision of white, geometrical perfection set in a superb Los Angeles landscape. The house starred in the famous 1932 International Style exhibition, curated by the architect Philip Johnson and architectural historian, Henry-Russell Hitchcock, and was a major influence on the development of the ideal Modern house – all deeply cantilevered low roofs, cocktails, car ports and swimming pools – dreamed of by art-loving or fun-loving Americans. The Lovell House also co-starred in *LA Confidential* (1997) where it looked several million dollars.

Neutra's houses were brilliantly photographed by Julius Schulman [b.1910], who has shaped the way we look, with delight, on these Californian houses ever since. The Maslon House was a disturbing loss for the American conservation lobby and for anyone with a love of inspirational architecture and good design.

Opposite Swimming pool and garden of the Maslon House. The house was demolished within just thirty days of its new owners moving in. This was in 2002. The fact that the local authority allowed such vandalism without blinking a corporate eyebrow raised great concern throughout the United States.

Below Looking through the Maslon House to the pool and garden. Richard Neutra was a master of blurring the defining line between the exterior and interiors of the houses he built in California. Living in a house like this must have made pretty much every day seem like a holiday.

Above All this fairy-tale wonder is a shopping mall today. This is the White City, the architectural hub of the 1908 Franco-British exhibition which was held at Shepherd's Bush, west London. The principal plaza, with its bandstand, and main buildings, are seen from the top of the Flip-Flap ride.

Major exhibitions, and especially the world Expos that began with the Great Exhibition of 1851 at the Crystal Palace (p.148), London, have been an entertaining and provocative source of inspirational, if sometimes madcap, architecture, design and engineering. Their fate, by and large, is to have been ephemeral things, ambitious shows that come and go in a puff of smoke, mirrors, hype and showmanship. Yet images of these great exhibitions often linger on in the collective imagination. What were they like to visit and were the exciting buildings ever as good as they look in veteran photographs and venerable newsreels? We know for certain that the Eiffel Tower, star of the 1889 Paris Expo, was and is a magnificent engineering achievement, and remains a hugely popular tourist attraction to this day.

One of the great exhibitions that looks magnificent in old photos, but was, I suspect, very much a "smoke and mirrors" affair, was the

London "Expo" of 1908 held in what is still known today as "White City". The exhibition was a celebration, among many other things, of the *entente cordiale*, a political understanding between Great Britain and France. The site was in west London between what is currently the link road between Shepherd's Bush roundabout and the A40 (M) road from London to Birmingham and the BBC television studios, which are themselves under threat of demolition.

The centrepiece of the 1908 exhibition was The Court of Honour, an architectural fantasia in the guise of a truly white city, set around lakes and canals crossed by pretty bridges, adorned with timber and canvas stage-set buildings – some clad in white marble, most in white plaster – drawn from fairy-tale interpretations of Spanish, Arabic and Oriental architecture. Some of the buildings were huge and their fanciful façades drawn up by contemporary architects hid functional steel frames. The whole architectural programme was drawn up by Imre Karalfy [1845–1919], a Hungarian Jewish folk dancer who had gone on to produce spectacular musical shows in Europe and then across the USA before settling in London and re-inventing himself as the great "exhibitionist" of his age. Certainly, the White City must have been an impressive sight; even the illustrious *Architectural Review* was prompted to comment, "By day it is a vision of dazzling whiteness, with its tiled court and plashing cool waters, its pointed arcades and lattice windows. At night it is equally effective with its thousands of lights and the rainbow colours of the cascade." The *Manchester Guardian* took a less lenient and more purist view; Sir Walter Armstrong wrote that the Court of Honour "is neither French nor English, but Mohamedan-Hindoo, and the other buildings have more in common with the architecture of Spanish-America or the Baroque of a united Germany than with anything in the two countries involved." However, it was meant to be fun, a thing of fantasy and not an example of how London or any other British city ought to look.

The exhibition was also a popular success, attracting no fewer than 8.4 million visitors between May and October 1908. Close by was a new athletics stadium built for the 1908 London Olympics; this was demolished in 1985 to make way for a nasty, tin box of a building for the BBC, much disliked by anyone who had to work there.

Several spectacular exhibitions followed in the wake of the 1908 Anglo-French affair; perhaps the most enjoyable was "Merryland", a part of the "Great International Exhibition of the Latin and British Nations". This "wonderful street of adventure" featured such thrilling attractions as the Roly-Poly, the Dingle-Dongle racing swings, the Boomerang, and the 1908 Flip-Flap, a 200-foot (61-metre) high contraption that sent visitors soaring up and down into the London cloudscape for hopeful views for miles around; the new, improved 1912 version revolved on its axis, too. All these machines were designed to hurl people around in space. Two years later, the nation's young men were being blown to pieces as the altogether less innocent machinery of war got into its terrible stride, and the White City must have been little more than a long-lost and happy dream.

White City survived intact until the outbreak of the First World War and then fell into a long decline. When I made a TV documentary on Britain's "Great Exhibitions" for Channel 4 in 1999, I was astonished to find myself walking through remains of the White City exhibition halls and galleries. Very much a secret haunt of London, these were being used partly for ball games, partly for storage, but mostly as a vast and smelly aviary for thousands of feral pigeons. Although every trace – short of old postcards, souvenirs, photographs and snatches of film – of "White City" has gone, it was just possible to imagine what it had been like. The last section of Karalfy's fantasia, which I was able to walk through, is now the site of the enormous and architecturally blank "Westfield London" shopping mall, a giant selling the "brands" Londoners are so desperate for today.

Above top Here is the Court of Honour at the White City. Ladies in bustles and chaps in boaters could take a ride around the 140-acre site in boats around Venetian-style canals. The Flip-Flap can be seen doing its thing behind the domed buildings on the left.

Above This is the Flip-Flap. An outlay of sixpence would take visitors on an exciting 3 minute and 20 second ride up and down, and round and round, the White City with views as far as Windsor Castle and the Crystal Palace on the way.

The next truly ambitious public exhibition in London was the British Empire Exhibition of 1924–25 held at Wembley Park. It was designed to celebrate the Empire and "to stimulate trade, strengthen bonds that bind Mother Country to her Sister States and Daughters, to bring into closer contact the one with each other, to enable all who owe allegiance to the British flag to meet on common ground and learn to know each other". This enormous show, designed under the direction of the architect Maxwell Ayrton [1874–1960] of Simpson & Ayrton, was so successful that it was re-opened for a second year, at the end of which 27 million visitors had come to see it.

While Ayrton took charge of the ferro-concrete, neoclassical pavilions dedicated to Industry, Engineering and the Arts, the mighty Wembley Stadium was largely the work of the brilliant young engineer Owen Williams [1890–1969], among whose last major works are the concrete bridges across the carriageways of the first section of the M1 motorway.

Ayrton's pavilions gradually fell into disuse, although they were used for decades as warehouses, but Wembley Stadium remained the nation's premier football ground until it closed in 2002. This was the scene of England's greatest football triumph when the England team, captained by Bobby Moore, beat West Germany 4–2 to win the coveted World Cup in 1966.

With its Dalek-like twin towers, the stadium appeared to be a highly distinctive and permanent fixture on London's sporting and architectural scene. It has been replaced by an even more impressive 90,000-seat stadium designed by Foster and Partners, which opened, after much delay and a total expenditure of £757 million, to critical acclaim in 2007. The stadium is crowned with a 436-foot (133-metre) lattice-framed arch; this is so enormous that the London Eye ferris wheel could be bowled through it and a London underground train could, if it was fitted with rails, run up and around its vaulting structure.

Above Cowgirls taking part in the British Empire Exhibition line up for the start of the rodeo in May 1924, inside the newly completed Wembley Stadium, Middlesex. The exhibition was repeated the following year. It was a joyous, if occasionally pompous and patronizing, celebration of Empire.

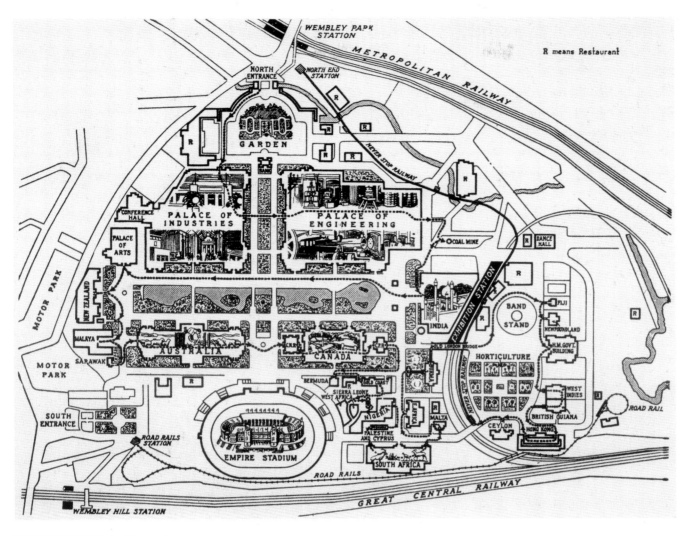

R means Restaurant

Left The plan of the British Empire Exhibition showing Wembley Stadium – bottom centre – and the route of the Never Stop Railway that took visitors around the enormous site, and in doing so, gave them a highly edited whistle stop tour of the world's most expansive Empire.

Below Demolition work under way at Wembley Stadium, December 2002. By this time, the stadium was very much past its sell-by date as far as the millions of people who used it were concerned. Ahead of the game in the mid-1920s, it was doomed by the end of the century.

With the demolition of the original Wembley stadium, the ghosts of the British Empire Exhibition were finally laid to rest. Even so, some of its fixtures and fittings survive. I have sat on the throne King George V sat on when he declared the exhibition open in 1924. It rests, looking slightly out of place, alongside a matching throne made for Queen Mary, in the easily overlooked parish church of St John, Wembley. Meanwhile, two of the six proud carved lions that guarded the British Government Pavilion, demolished in 1973, can be found at the gates of Animal Kingdom at Woburn Abbey, Bedfordshire.

By their nature, exhibitions are ephemeral things, very much of their time and never intended to last for long, but I would still have relished the opportunity to see such extraordinary places and events as "White City" and the British Empire Exhibition. I also wish that Tait Tower in Glasgow had been saved for posterity. This truly thrilling steel structure, designed for the Empire Exhibition, Scotland of 1938, by the architect Thomas Tait [1882–1954] was completely different from Ayrton's imperious work at Wembley. Here was a glimpse into the future, the centrepiece of an exhibition that was decidedly forward-looking.

Despite appalling weather that summer, 12.5 million visited the show held in the extensive grounds of Bellahouston Park. The 300-foot (91-metre) silvery steel tower was set on top of the highest point of the park – 170 feet (52 metres) – and so views from its three public galleries reached by lift and each holding 200 people were, to say the least, dramatic. The tower was demolished in July 1939 a few weeks before the British Prime Minister, Neville Chamberlain, announced that Great Britain was at war

Opposite Looking like a cross between a Russian Constructivist fantasy and a set design from a Fritz Lang movie, the Tait Tower, Glasgow, was quite real.

Above left Glaswegians, taking the sun here, were famed for building mighty ships and locomotives, yet had never seen anything quite like this.

Above right An aerial view of the Tait Tower rising, in flag-waving form, above Glasgow's Bellahouston Park. It was demolished immediately before the Second World War.

with Germany. The story is that it had to go because it would be used as an aiming point for German bombers; this seems unlikely, as their principal target, Clydeside and all the ships being built there, was as clear to the pilot of a Heinkel or Dornier as the full moon in a clear summer sky.

All that remains of this magnificent Modern tower are the 3,000 tons of concrete used to hold it in place, which are concealed in the depths of Bellahouston Park; so for practical purposes the Tait Tower is very much lost to us. The good news is that you can visit some of Tait's superb buildings, including St Andrew's House, Edinburgh, the Kodak Building in Kingsway, London, and the great pylons of Sydney Harbour Bridge.

Tait's tower was really nothing more than a glorified lift-shaft offering spectacular views across Glasgow and the Clyde Valley, so its life could never be guaranteed, although the Eiffel Tower is much the same thing and it has endured since 1889 and remains one of the world's most powerful tourist magnets.

Some structures, no matter how futuristic, are doomed from early on because rapid technological changes make them prematurely redundant. As a child, I loved looking at photographs of the early warning radar station at Fylingdales on the North Yorkshire Moors. These famous "golf balls" seemed so wonderfully mysterious and although they resembled objects that had been sent to Earth by beings from another galaxy, they enhanced the wild landscape they gently

dominated and made everyday life a little more exciting. The fact that they were "top secret" only added to their allure.

The "golf balls" were actually three lightweight geodesic domes, designed according to the structural researches of the American inventor Buckminster Fuller [1895–1983] and connected to one another by a James Bond-style underground corridor. Each housed a radar dish that could be turned to face the most likely source of incoming ballistic missiles. When these "Radomes" were built by the American corporation RCA at the height of the Cold War in 1962, that threat was thought to be the former Soviet Union. Early warning information from RAF Fylingdales would be passed on to similar USAF outfits at Thule in Greenland and Clear, Alaska.

With the collapse of the USSR from the late 1980s, the "Radomes" were effectively redundant. A new "Star Wars" early warning pyramid housing 2,560 aerials was built alongside the "golf balls"; this opened in 1992 and the "golf balls" were demolished three years later. I went to visit them for a TV documentary, "Secret Britain", shortly before they came down. They still looked intriguing, although the machinery inside them already looked as if it belonged in the Science Museum. There was no essential reason why the "golf balls" themselves should have been demolished and some attempts by conservation lobbies were made to save them. However, RAF Fylingdales is very much a part of American foreign policy and we British, living on an island known as "America's aircraft carrier", have little say over such matters.

Above One of the Radomes under construction at RAF Fylingdales, North Yorkshire, 1962. These were the most prominent feature of Britain's ballistic missile early warning station. Top secret for many years, the giant "golf balls" were demolished when new technology outstripped them at the beginning of the 1990s.

Above An RAF officer poses in front of one of the Radomes on Fylingdales Moor. Sitting on top of a ridge in this wild and remote landscape, snow-capped in winter, the Radomes could seem other-worldly. They were a favourite sight for tourists, but strictly off limits to visitors.

Left The three sister Radomes seen together in winter as a bright red Mark IV Ford Cortina battles along the snowy road below; the driver might well be fiddling with his radio to counteract interference from the ineffable workings of these silent, yet powerful and much-missed devices.

Pacifist groups aside, Fylingdales has never been altogether popular. There are those who say that the electronic systems here are a health hazard; perhaps this is true, but the "golf balls" themselves were a special addition to the North Yorkshire landscape and it was sad to see them go.

Few people were saddened by the demolition in 2004 of the Tricorn Centre in Portsmouth. Like early warning radar stations, shopping centres tend to be short-lived affairs, victims of our insatiable desire for the latest in consumer goods and appropriately shiny shops to display them in. Designed by Owen Luder [b.1928], and originally known as The Casbah, the Brutalist concrete Tricorn

Centre opened in 1966 and was a dramatic, sculptural structure designed to house 35 shops, 490 cars, eight flats and a nightclub. In theory, it should have been a groovy Sixties architectural and social adventure. In practice, and despite its radical form, it was always dank and gloomy. Few major shops made their way here and the flats, suffering from excess damp, were boarded up in 1979. All too many people committed suicide by jumping off the decks of the multi-storey car park. This was clearly an unhappy design; it would have taken imagination, determination and a lot of money to make it work as it should have done and to encourage local people to care for it.

Above A corner of the car park of the Tricorn Centre, Portsmouth in March 2004, shortly before this Brutalist shopping centre was knocked down. While largely unpopular with the public at large, it was, like other sculpted concrete buildings of its era, a favourite with photographers.

The Brutalist style adopted by Luder was only ever popular amongst fellow architects and aesthetes doing their best to see the good things in what, for the most part, were tough and unlikeable buildings. Time has been kinder to some Brutalist buildings, such as the Hayward Gallery on London's South Bank, than to others, including the Tricorn Centre. Shopping centres, however, tend to be doomed as soon as their commercial luck runs out; they are big, specialist buildings and difficult to convert to other purposes. Luder was also the architect of the demolished Catford shopping centre in south-east London, as well as the threatened Trinity Court multi-storey car park in Gateshead. Famous for its role as the setting for an exciting car chase in *Get Carter* (Mike

Hodges, 1971) starring Michael Caine, this Sixties building, which once boasted a nightclub on its roof, could be re-used, but like its northern contemporary, Preston Bus Station, it looks doomed by the joint curse of unimaginative local councils and greedy developers. Like those of gun-toting gangsters, the lives of Brutalist buildings, especially those in the retail sector, have usually been short.

One shop that really shouldn't have met the same fate as Catford or Portsmouth, was the superb Schocken department store in Stuttgart. Designed by Erich Mendelsohn [1887–1953] it opened in 1928 and was demolished in 1960. Not only was Mendelsohn one of the finest and most inventive of twentieth-century architects, but

Above The spiralling ramp of the car park of the Tricorn Centre dominates this view of the bold 1960s retail development. With a little bit of imagination this could have been transformed into a fascinating arts centre, with studios and accommodation, but this was not to be.

the Schocken store was also a Modern princess among shops. Its composition was ultra Modern and assured. From the street, a glass stair tower giving access to the various floors was paired with a striking four-storey concrete and brick block dominated by the name of the store in massive, stand-alone lettering. It looked terrific – its interiors were exemplary, too – and it survived the Second World War.

In an act of unforgivable stupidity the city agreed to its demolition, despite international protest. Nothing could stop the juggernaut of modern retailing from stamping its way through Stuttgart. Mendelsohn's magnificent shop gave way to the second-rate Galeria Horten (now, the Galeria Kaufhof) designed by Egon Eierman [1904–70] who could have produced better than this.

However, at least it's possible to sit by the sea and dream of all these lost twentieth-century buildings on deckchairs set along the rooftop of one of Britain's finest 1930s Modern Movement buildings, the De la Warr Pavilion at Bexhill-on-Sea, designed by Serge Chermayeff [1900–96] and… Erich Mendelsohn. This building was also nearly lost, but thanks to the energies and intelligence of local activists it survives, beautifully renovated (by John McAslan and Partners) to show us just how special Modern architecture is and as a reminder of how careful we must be with our modern heritage before we offer it up to the developer's axe.

Above left The destruction of the Shocken department store, Stuttgart, came as something of a shock outside and inside West Germany. What on earth was anyone thinking of when they gave the go-ahead for the demolition of one of the finest buildings of its type in Europe?

Above right The powerful frontage of the Schocken store seen here at the time it opened in 1928. Note how the eight letters of the shop's name line up with the eight bays of windows above them. Mendelsohn's elegantly functional and streamlined design was all of a piece.

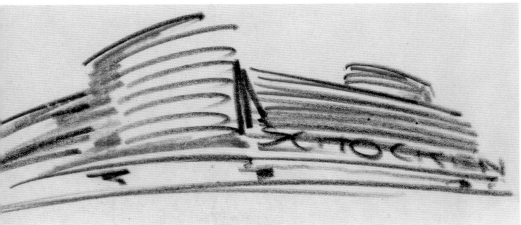

Left This typically dynamic coloured sketch of the Shocken department store, Stuttgart, by Erich Mendelsohn, 1926, captures his energetic "Expressionist" style. The shop was destroyed despite widespread international protest. Mendelsohn himself had long since left Germany for England, Palestine and the United States.

Above A shop floor inside the Shocken store, 1928, displaying rugs, runners and carpets – some with modern abstract designs – lit by the sun and by Bauhaus globe ceiling lamps. The décor is almost non-existent: the goods on display were the only bright colours that this interior needed.

5 ACTS OF GOD

God moves in mysterious ways, His wonders to perform, runs the old hymn. He certainly does. What we choose to call "acts of God" usually means destruction by natural means: fire, flood, storms, plagues and earthquakes. I felt very lucky to have escaped one act of God; not long after I had made a trip to Bam in south-eastern Iran, this extraordinary survivor, an inhabited, 2,000 year-old walled city made of mud, straw and the trunks of palm trees, was obliterated by an earthquake. This act of God took place on December 26, 2003. One moment the ancient city was bustling with activity; the next, it was almost entirely levelled.

No one knows exactly how many people died in Bam, although it seems that at least 25,000 of its 90,000 population perished. Many of these lived beyond the mud walls of what was known as the "citadel" itself, but the great tragedy, aside from the loss of human life, was that the old city really had been so very alive. Although a growing number of tourists had been making their way to Bam, there were never more than a couple of coach loads at a time; it was a city you could wander around believing that you really might have travelled back in a time machine to some distant past. Inside those walls, you could find age-old bathhouses, tea-rooms and laundries. There were some 400 houses. The narrow streets smelled of delicious cooking. Domes rose above roofs. Every last architectural element appeared to blend into a whole as if the citadel was a living organism rather than a man-made structure.

The exact date Bam was founded is not known, although it probably dates back to the third century and reached its zenith during the Safavidi dynasty [1502–1722]. A trading city, it was famous for its cloth and in recent years, for its fine citrus fruits and wonderful dates. The walled city measured two and a half square miles (six square kilometres), was protected by 38 lookout towers and had a population of about 12,000.

In 1722 Afghans seized Bam and it began to decline. A second raid by warriors from the Shiraz region in 1810 only accelerated its downfall and by 1900 the civilian population had moved out of its enfolding walls, leaving the citadel to the military, garrisoned here until the early 1950s when archaeological excavations and some degree of restoration were initiated. The population returned and Bam picked up where it had been several centuries earlier. Its new-found life was brief and although the citadel is being slowly restored, and a new town being constructed nearby, it will be hard to recreate the old ways of life and the age-old atmosphere of this unexpected mud city.

Right Weathered, eroded and battered, this is the Iranian citadel of Bam in September 2003, three months before the mud city was all but obliterated by an enormous earthquake that killed many thousands of people. Until its destruction, Bam was largely unknown to the world of international tourism.

Left Satellite image of Bam on September 30, 2003, showing the ancient street plan and ancient building types of this extraordinarily well-preserved city. This was never a theme park tourist destination but a truly authentic medieval walled city still going about its historic business before the earthquake of December 2006.

Below left Satellite image of Bam on December 29, 2003, three days after the citadel was rocked to its foundations. For many years, Bam was a military town, but in recent decades it had returned to civilian life and was a fascinating snapshot of a long lost world.

Opposite Bam, July 1997. Even before the earthquake, the city was in a state of either disrepair or slow restoration; it was often hard to tell. Imagine, though, these streets full of life, the smell of cooking, the sight of market stalls and the sound of the muezzins' call to prayer.

Earthquakes have of course destroyed many famous buildings in history, beginning with a number of the Seven Wonders of the ancient World. One of these was the Mausoleum of Halicarnassus (Bodrum, Turkey) built by the Greek architects Satyrus and Pythius for Artemisia, wife of Mausolus, governor of the province (or satrap) of Caria, immediately after her husband's death in 353 BC. The 135-foot (41-metre) high marble tomb took three years to complete, which is hardly surprising given the quality of the sculptural reliefs that are said to have adorned each of its four sides, carved by the Greek artists Bryaxis, Leochares, Scopas and Timotheus.

In his lifetime, Mausolus had greatly admired the Greeks and had set about, with Artemisia, turning Halicarnassus into a splendid semblance of an ideal Greek city. Above this city, Artemisia built the legendary tomb that would lend its name – mausoleum – to all grand tombs in the western world ever since. The mausoleum stood in an enclosed courtyard and was reached by a grand marble stair guarded by stone lions, while the platform at the top of the stair was policed by sculpted warriors, some on horseback. A Greek temple sat high above the ground here, capped with a pyramidical roof on top of which representations of Mausolus and his devoted wife rode high above the city in a *quadriga*, a chariot pulled by four horses.

Even when the city collapsed around it, the wondrous mausoleum survived intact. A number of earthquakes in the medieval era gradually destroyed the monument and by the early fifteenth century, only the base remained. The Knights of St John of Malta broke this up when they built Bodrum Castle and in 1522, they strengthened their Crusaders' fortress by taking away the final stones of the antique mausoleum.

Although gone, the Mausoleum of Halicarnassus was never forgotten. It was the subject of many fantasy paintings and illustrations over the centuries, while in 1852 the British archaeologist, Charles Thomas Newton, funded by the British Museum, set out to discover

Above A more or less accurate reconstruction of the Mausoleum of Halicarnassus depicted in a woodcut made in 1890 by Oskar Mothes [1828–1903]. The illustration shows how, far from existing in splendid isolation, the mausoleum was very much a part of the surrounding cityscape.

MAVSOLÆVM.

Martinus Heemskerck Inu.

if anything remained of the mausoleum. Not only did he uncover the site of the monument, he eventually found the statue of Mausolus and Artemisia although only one broken wheel remained from the chariot they once rode together. You can visit the site today, but there is not much to interest anyone except an archaeologist or specialist historian. Some of the finest surviving parts of the mausoleum are to be found in the British Museum, including a broken frieze depicting the battle between the Greeks and the Amazons.

In its own special way, though, the mausoleum did survive; from the time of the Greek Revival, it began to inspire a number of tombs and memorials across the English-speaking world. The tomb of General Ulysses S Grant overlooking the Hudson River at Morningside Heights, New York [John Duncan, 1895] is one example. This is not an exact reproduction of the original mausoleum by any means, yet it does capture something of its grandeur. Mausolus and Artemisia would doubtless have been impressed by Grant's funeral in 1885: a

million people turned out to pay homage to the hero of the American Civil War, forming a procession seven miles long.

In Melbourne, the Shrine of Remembrance [Philip Hudson and James Wardrop, 1927–34] is a chaste, if more archaeologically correct reconstruction dedicated to the fallen of the First World War and to Australians who have died on active service since. The mausoleum was also reproduced in the twenty-first century at the top of the tower of the new Said Business School in Oxford [Dixon Jones, 2003]. My favourite reproduction of the Mausoleum of Halicarnassus is the tower of the church of St George's in London's Bloomsbury, designed by Nicholas Hawksmoor [1661–1736], and featuring the lion and the unicorn fighting for the crown around its stepped base. So although the original building is all but lost to us, we can see what it must have looked like in its glory days.

Earthquakes have destroyed modern monuments and cities, too. It seems remarkable and even downright fatalistic for succeeding

Above One of very many fanciful interpretations of the Mausoleum of Halicarnassus made over the centuries. Although not without foundation, this Baroque illustrator has adorned the Grecian monument with barley sugar columns, niches, arches and other frills and devices belonging to a much later age.

Left A famous photograph by German-born Arnold Genthe [1869–1942], looking down Sacramento Street, San Francisco on April 18, 1906 as the earthquake rocks the Californian city. Some of the people standing here appear to be remarkably unphased. Genthe's studio vanished, but his photographs of the event survived.

generations to rebuild great cities such as Tokyo and San Francisco that have been shattered by earthquakes, yet it would be very hard to abandon cities in which so much energy, spirit and love has been invested.

Much of San Francisco came tumbling down on April 18, 1906, and in the following days when a furious fire raged through the city. Famous photographs taken by Arnold Genthe show San Franciscans sitting above their beautiful ocean front homes as the city collapsed around them. These suggest scenes of orderly retreat from encroaching chaos, but in reality, there was a great deal of panic and looting. Soldiers were ordered to open fire on looters and some 500 were killed. The total number of deaths caused by the earthquake, measuring between 7.7 and 8.3 on the Richter scale, and in the

subsequent fire, was probably around 2,000. The number of buildings destroyed was enormous and the city centre had to be entirely rebuilt, with major works completed by 1915.

San Francisco was rocked by the shifting tectonic plates of the San Andreas fault; on the day these shifted in April 1906, the fault cracked open along 296 miles (476 kilometres) of its immense length, and the after effects were felt along the seaboard from Oregon in the north to Los Angeles in the south; inland, the shock waves rippled out into Nevada. Another such earthquake could hit San Francisco; although many buildings today are nominally "earthquake proof", there is no guarantee that they will be able to withstand the worst that nature can throw at the city.

Above Another Genthe photograph showing a grand Ionic building looking like some newly vandalised Ancient Roman ruin. This image is a powerful reminder that those living in the twentieth century still did so at the mercy of the elements, just as their predecessors did thousands of years before them.

Left Timber framed houses on Howard Street, San Francisco, soon after the 1906 earthquake. Given the severity of the earthquake that hit the city, many of its houses stood up well to the forces of Nature. Today, the city boasts skyscrapers that, up to a point, are earthquake proof.

Left This is the Corinthian courtyard of the House of the Silver Wedding, Pompeii, a first century BC villa designed in a sober, classical style and renovated at some time in the first century AD. Many of its noble rooms seem almost, if not quite, ready for use today.

Below A colour lithograph of Pompeii in the style of Antonio Niccolini [1772–1850] showing the eruption of Vesuvius, with people fleeing the terrifying cloud of volcanic dust descending on the town. You can find all these buildings on a walk through the petrified town today.

Above Pompeii today with Mt Vesuvius in the background. The Volcano is still active. It is a fascinating experience to climb up to its rim and look over into the seething natural cauldron below, but a relief to come back down to Pompeii, and especially to living towns beyond.

The story of Pompeii is quite different. It is one that haunts our imaginations and the fate of the legendary ancient Roman town has made it one of the world's most popular tourist attractions. Pompeii was not destroyed by an earthquake, but by raging currents of molten lava pouring down the flanks of Mt Vesuvius in 79 AD. This volcanic eruption destroyed virtually all life in the town, but it also preserved it under thick layers of ash and pumice. Although we know quite a lot about what happened from the vivid contemporary writings of Pliny the Younger, eighteen years old when he visited his uncle at nearby Misenum, Pompeii itself vanished and remained hidden for almost 1,700 years. It was rediscovered by accident in 1748 and the town was slowly uncovered.

What has been exposed over the past two centuries is breathtaking. Here is a kind of three-dimensional snapshot of life in a first-century BC Roman town. We can not only walk along the town's gridded streets and look at the courtyard houses leading off them, but we can gaze at their frescoes, frown or laugh at graffiti (clearly, this is nothing new), see the baths and theatres where people were entertained and, most remarkably, we can see the people themselves. Striking tragic attitudes in the throes of death, plaster casts reveal the hollow images of bodies set within solidified ash. These are deeply moving, but because so much of Pompeii's day-to-day life and its lively spirit have survived, we can still enjoy visiting the town and its people.

Pompeii was a holiday home for many Romans. It was a place to relax and to have fun. The town was famous for its cheap brothels and the wealth of erotic art found among the ancient ruins led, in 1819, to their being locked away from sight (except for Popes, bishops, priests, nuns, scholars and politicians) in the National Archaeological Museum in Naples for many decades, in case they encouraged Catholic Italians to think unseemly thoughts. I like the fact that until 2005, minors were only allowed to see these not very arousing frescoes if a responsible adult wrote a note on their behalf. Can you imagine it? "Dear Curator, please let little Giovanni see the erotic frescoes. He is a good boy and they will do him no lasting harm. Yours, his Mama." Since 2005, the erotic art of Pompeii has been on public display in the National Museum, although a sign does warn that their unabashed content may cause offence. As for Pompeii itself, each year, more and more of this strangely lost town continue to be uncovered.

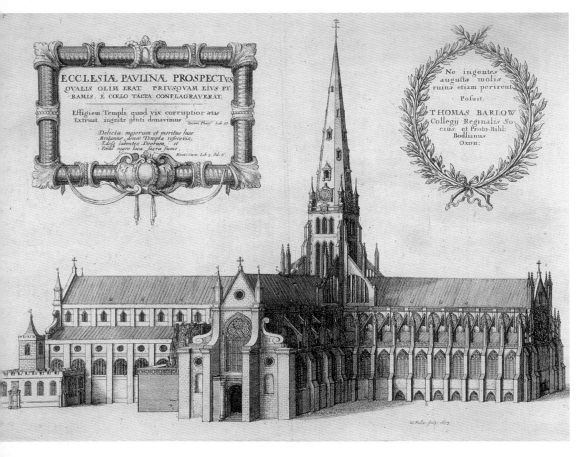

The greatest and most common enemy of buildings is neither volcanic eruption nor earthquake, but fire. As a child, the most famous fire I knew of was the Great Fire of London of 1666. Although it destroyed much of the medieval fabric of the City of London, it also cleansed the city, ridding it of the last vestiges of the Great Plague that had so ravaged London the previous year. Naturally, there was a belief among the more superstitious or conventionally religious that God had been displeased by the city's wayward life, and had, in one of his infamous "smiting" moments, summoned a pestilence followed by fire.

What we know for certain is that the fire broke out in a bakery in Pudding Lane on the night of September 2, 1666, and flamed furiously over the following three days, until a change of wind and the use of gunpowder to blow up buildings in the line of fire, extinguished it. Very few died because they fled in time. After the fire, however, a London mob ran riot in an effort to lynch the French, Dutch and other foreign residents who they believed must be responsible for the conflagration that destroyed 13,200 homes: in other words, 70,000 city dwellers out of a total of 80,000 were made homeless.

Also destroyed were 87 parish churches, 44 company halls, the Royal Exchange, the Customs House, Bridewell Palace, the Grand Letter Office, the city's prisons and three of its gates, Ludgate, Newgate and Aldersgate. The fire had been so hot that it melted the iron locks and chains of the fortified gates, implying a temperature of between 1,100 and 1,650 degrees Centigrade (2,012 and 3,002 Fahrenheit). There were no tabloid newspapers then to record the event with "Phew! What a scorcher!" headlines, but we do have some accurate records of the damage, along with the famous diaries of Samuel Pepys who witnessed the Great Fire at first hand.

Above A beautiful engraved drawing by Wenceslaus Hollar [1607–77] of old St Paul's Cathedral in all its sky-piercing Gothic majesty. This was an enormous church, although it was to suffer from neglect and abuse, during the English Civil War, well before the Great Fire that destroyed it.

Left An engraved drawing of 1814 by John Chapman [1792–1823] showing St Paul's Cathedral as it was immediately before the Great Fire of 1666. The west front of the spireless cathedral had been remodelled by Inigo Jones who also re-clad the building in regular stonework.

The GREAT FIRE of LONDON in the Year 1666.

From the Original Picture in the Possession of

Robert Wilton Esq.r Painted by Old Griffier at the time of the Fire. The Scene is the Original Ludgate taken at the instant of time when the Walls of the Goal adjoining it fell, and exhibited to the View Old S.t Pauls Church just taking fire, and Old Bow Church in the back ground.

The greatest architectural loss was old St Paul's, a cathedral which was built between 1087 and 1314. Its spire had originally reached 489 feet (149 metres) above the narrow city streets; the cathedral was 585 feet (178 metres) long and 290 feet (88 metres) wide across its transepts. By the time of the Great Fire, though, St Paul's, the fourth cathedral dedicated to the disciple on Ludgate Hill, was a shadow of its former self. True, its west front had been rebuilt in an Italian Renaissance style by Inigo Jones [1573–1652], Britain's first Classical architect, who had also re-clad a part of the cathedral walls, but the spire had been lost to lightning in 1561. A London mob, stirred up by angry young Protestant preachers, had run amok through the great church in 1549, destroying many of its finest tombs, statuary, ornaments and decoration. And during the Engllish Civil War, Cromwell's cavalry had, famously, kept their horses in the nave.

The ruins of the cathedral were finally blown up or battered down, under the direction of Sir Christopher Wren [1632–1723], architect of the magnificent English Baroque St Paul's [1675–1710] we know today. One of the losses that followed the fire was Wren's plan to rebuild the City of London along rational, Classical principles. London,

however, was raring to get back to work and to serve its one true god, Mammon. Wren's plan, along with those of several others, was politely dismissed. Together with the scientist Robert Hooke [1635–1703], Wren did get to build not only a new cathedral, but also a towering memorial to the Great Fire. This is the 202-foot (61-metre) high Monument in the City of London, an enormous, fluted Portland stone Doric column crowned with stylized flames completed in 1677. At its base, a description used to read:

"Here by permission of heaven, hell broke loose upon this
Protestant city… the most dreadful Burning of this City; begun
and carried on by the treachery and malice of the Popish faction…
Popish frenzy which wrought such horrors, is not yet quenched…"

Religious bigotry, the cause of so much death and destruction, was encouraged even as the city was rebuilt. Alexander Pope, the eighteenth-century poet, described this corner of London as a place:

"Where London's column, pointing at the skies,
Like a tall bully, lifts the head and lies."

Above A print of 1807 imagining how St Paul's might have appeared looming out of the flames and smoke engulfing the City of London during the Great Fire. The conflagration is said to have destroyed 13,200 homes together, of course, with the grand old cathedral itself.

The inscription was removed in 1831 by which time, London, with a population of over a million, and buoyed up by great trading ventures from her docks, had become the greatest city in the world.

Coleshill House [1649–62] in Berkshire was gutted by fire in 1952 and demolished. Of all the English country houses that have disappeared over the years, this is the one that I would have most wanted to see. It was designed in a style that Sir Christopher Wren was to make very much his own, and as a teenager discovering the works of Wren on my own, I could think of no superior form of architecture than Sir Christopher's or that of his brilliant assistants, Nicholas Hawksmoor and John Vanbrugh. Coleshill was so special because it pre-dated Wren, designed as it was by the well-travelled lawyer and gentleman architect, John Pratt [1620–85].

Educated at Magdalen College, Oxford, Pratt went on to practise law at the Inner Temple in London, but found time to study architecture in Padua and Rome. It is often said that Inigo Jones helped in the design of Coleshill, but Pratt himself said that the great architect had helped only with the design of the ceilings, and judging by the look of them in photographs, that seems to be the case.

What is so sad about the fate of Coleshill is that this grandly modest house had survived intact and almost unchanged for 300 years before it caught fire. Its design set a precedent for that of houses in England and Colonial America, and many of these exist today to remind us of a fine house that was much more than the sum of its elegant parts. Just look at it – with its top-hat chimneys and grand dormered front – and imagine looking out of that cupola on top of the roof across the fields of bucolic Berkshire.

Opposite Coleshill House, Berkshire, was one of the most handsome early Classical houses in England. At the time it caught fire it was still in a remarkably original condition. Gardens and grounds survive.

Above left Grand salon ceiling, Coleshill House, very possibly the work of Inigo Jones, England's first Classical architect, or at least inspired directly by him. This interior was very much as it might have been in the 1660s.

Above right The lantern crowning Coleshill House and lighting the reception hall. This happy structure was very much like the hat of a gentleman perched on the roof of a house that inspired many like it in Colonial America.

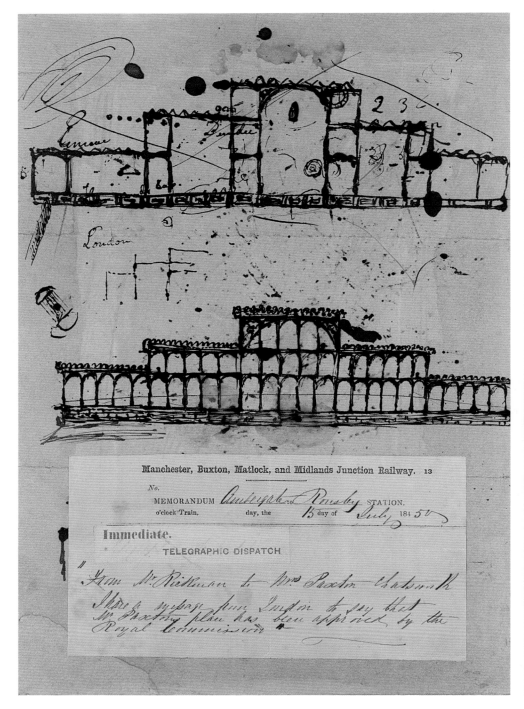

In living memory, the most influential building lost to flames must surely be, whatever the qualities of other candidates from around the world, the Crystal Palace in London. When we watch old newsreels of this magnificent and daring building going up in flames on November 30, 1936, we are witnesses to the destruction of an architectural and engineering revolution as well as the demise of a much-loved public building.

The Crystal Palace was the great invention of Joseph Paxton [1803–65], who had begun his career as a garden boy at Battlesden Park, Bedfordshire. At 23, he became the head gardener at Chatsworth, one of the finest of England's great country estates. Here, he built an ambitious, yet lightweight conservatory, and he experimented with new forms of engineering structure. Paxton was extremely impressed by the giant leaves of a particular species of Guyanan water lily. Measuring up to 12 feet (3.65 metres) wide, these proved to be immensely strong, so much so, that Paxton floated his daughter Annie

across a pond on one of these leaves. The structure of the leaves gave Paxton the clue he needed when he was commissioned at the last moment to design an enormous temporary hall to house the Great Exhibition of 1851 in London's Hyde Park.

Architects had produced plans for heavyweight and highly ornamented structures that were lavish, expensive and ungainly. Paxton came up with his proposal for what the satirical journal, *Punch*, dubbed the "Crystal Palace", on a piece of blotting paper while doodling during a meeting. It is a wonderful thing, that little, blobby sketch and for me at any rate, it was as exciting as holding one of the Dead Sea Scrolls in my hands, when the late Clive Wainwright, a senior curator at the Victoria & Albert Museum, allowed me a close-up look at this historic squib.

The Crystal Palace was a truly revolutionary building. Entirely pre-fabricated, it was made of lightweight timber, wrought iron ribs

and other structural elements together with 293,000 panes of rolled glass. The ironwork was delivered to London by train from foundries in Birmingham and arrived in Hyde Park still warm from the foundry. As soon as the iron had cooled down, it was lifted into place. Once that was done, glaziers working from rail-mounted trolleys would move down the length of the structure installing glass panes at the rate of 108 per man a day. The rate of progress for such a voluminous building was breathtaking; the Crystal Palace measured 1,848 feet (563 metres) long (some accounts believe this to be 1,851 feet (564 metres); a nice conceit, if true), 408 feet (124 metres) wide and 108 feet (33 metres) high.

It was a huge success as the venue for the Great Exhibition, stuffed full of manufactured artefacts for sale in London yet drawn from around the world, and it was much admired by Queen Victoria and Prince Albert who took a great interest in the latest

Opposite You will have heard of designs made on the back of envelopes, but here is a famous design on blotting paper by Joseph Paxton for the Crystal Palace. With little time to spare before the opening of the Great Exhibition, Paxton was forced to think quickly.

Above An idealized contemporary view of the Crystal Palace at the time of the Great Exhibition, 1851. The iron and glass building was a revelation to the six million visitors who came from far and wide to London's Hyde Park to see inside it.

developments in architecture. When the exhibition closed, the prefab palace was taken apart and shipped to Sydenham Hill in south-east London, where, much enlarged, it re-opened as a venue for public entertainment and spectaculars.

Although its popularity slowly waned and the building had begun to look a little shabby by the mid-1930s, the Crystal Palace could easily have been given a face-lift and would have been hugely popular again today. Sadly, like one of the great airships of the time, Crystal Palace went up in flames and despite talk of rebuilding Paxton's masterpiece, this great glass building remains little more than a folk memory for most Londoners. It did, though, lend its name to the part of London it once airily dominated, as well as to the local FA football club. The Crystal Palace has also lived on in the designs of any number of shopping malls built in the wake of the Eaton Centre mall [Eberhard Zeidler, b.1926; 1977–79], Toronto and even in the heroic design of

the Lloyd's Building [Richard Rogers, b.1933; 1979–86], London. Its spirit, meanwhile, resides in attempts to create huge, lightweight buildings, most notably the Eden Project [Nicholas Grimshaw, b.1939; 1999–2001], Cornwall.

Above The Crystal Palace in all its fully-fledged glory on top of Sydenham Hill, in 1855. The building looked truly heroic, but it was never exactly fireproof. When the fire finally came, it raged under acres of old floorboards that ignited like hundreds of thousands of matches.

Opposite The view across one of the lofty transepts of the Crystal Palace, 1853. By this time, the great glazed building had been dismantled and transported across the Thames to a site on Sydenham Hill in south-east London, where it remained a popular attraction until destroyed by fire in 1936.

Right The Torre Windsor, Madrid, shortly before it caught fire in February 2005. No one was hurt even though the building loomed above the popular department store, El Corte Inglés.

Far right Flames engulf the Torre Windsor. Although the fire was intense, the structure remained stable and, despite the drama, the city remained safe. What endangered Madrid at the time was terrorism.

Below The Myer Building (formerly owned by Brownell Bros) in Liverpool Street, Hobart, in 1909. This was never great Victorian architecture, but by the time of the fire that destroyed it in 2007, this was the oldest building in downtown Hobart. If not a house of great design, it was the home of local memories.

Fires are oblivious to the age of buildings. While many old timber buildings are susceptible to destruction by fire, there are timber temples and other historic buildings in Japan and elsewhere, which have survived for over 1,000 years. Equally, there are modern steel and glass towers that have gone up in flames and clouds of smoke. In February 2005 a fire ripped through the Torre Windsor (officially known as Edificio Windsor) in Madrid. The 348-foot (106-metre), 32-storey multi-purpose building in the city centre was so badly damaged, despite the survival of its concrete service core – lift shafts, emergency stairs, cables, pipes and ducts – that it was demolished almost as soon as the fire abated.

This was one of the first high-rise buildings in central Madrid, designed in 1974 by a team of six leading Spanish architects – Genaro Alas, Pedro Casariego, Luis Alemany, Rafael Alemany, Ignacio Ferrero and Manuel del Río – and completed in 1979. The one good thing is that the substantial modern structure stayed upright despite fears of collapse and mercifully there were no injuries. Here is an example of a lost building that few will ever mourn and even fewer will remember as the years roll by.

Many people, though, do miss the Myer Building, a department store in Liverpool Street, Hobart, the capital of Tasmania. This was not just a familiar shop and a place to meet, but one of the oldest buildings in Hobart, dating back to 1836. The shop was engulfed in flames in September 2007. This is an example of a modest building, from an architectural perspective, that with its simple façades and pressed-tin ceilings won the hearts of local people; its loss meant a great deal to them.

These are the stories of individual buildings destroyed by "acts of God", but there is not enough space in this book to record the number and variety of buildings, great and small, destroyed by the tsunami that struck across the Indian Ocean on December 26, 2004. The huge waves that hit coastal settlements across a vast area of south-east Asia were set in fatal motion by an underwater earthquake with its epicentre just off the coast of Sumatra, Indonesia. This was the second most powerful earthquake yet recorded; it measured between 9.1 and 9.3 on the Richter scale (the maximum reading is 10) and caused the whole planet to vibrate. It is estimated that around 225,000 people were killed in 11 countries, while hundreds of villages and towns vanished in an instant.

Entire cities have been destroyed by tsunamis in the past; in 1755 huge waves beat against Lisbon and when fires followed, the city was brought to its foundations. Portugal, a mighty sea-going imperial power, was never to recover from the sudden loss of its opulent capital. While it tried to rally, other mercantile powers took to the high seas and pushed Portuguese influence into remote pockets and corners of the globe. The forces of Nature are never spent; they spare no person or monument, not even the very greatest designs.

Right The principal façade of the Myer Building, Hobart. The building was a rattle-bag of sections, one dating back to 1836, others from later in the nineteenth century. Although ramshackle, in architectural terms, the store was widely considered to be the lynchpin of Hobart's Central Business District.

6 POLITICAL LOSSES

The Euston Arch, a magnificent Greek Revival propylaeum or triumphal gateway, fronted London's Euston station from 1837 to 1961. Designed by Philip Hardwick [1792–1870], it was a glorious conceit, suggesting that the endeavours of the London and Birmingham Railway were the equivalent of the greatest works of the Classical world. Perhaps the directors of the L&B were right; for theirs was the world's first proper main-line railway connecting two of the greatest cities on the planet, London with its money and culture, and Birmingham with its grit and prodigious manufacturing ability. This was the nineteenth-century equivalent of the Roman roads that had once connected key parts of the Empire in imperious straight lines.

The destruction of the Arch was a huge loss to both architecture and London. It also signified that governments who embraced the deeply suspect twin notions of "change" (for change's sake) and "modernization" had won the day and were up to no good. Since the demolition of the Euston Arch, no one with any sense of history, or love of architecture in particular, has trusted politicians who have eked out their cynical craft on the back of such overrated notions.

The "modernization" of British Railways, announced officially in 1955, did not run smoothly from the start. Ostensibly, the aim was to bring Britain's main-line railways, nationalized in 1948, into the age of diesel and electric trains and brighten up their essentially Victorian image. Decades of diligent engineering know-how were to be shunted into sidings, while neophiliac managers invested huge sums of money in buying brand-new and unreliable diesel locomotives that were less powerful and far less glamorous than the steam locomotives they were meant to replace. Euston Station itself was home to the most magnificent and powerful of all British steam locomotives, the "Duchess" or "Coronation" class Pacifics designed in the mid-1930s by Tom Coleman at the Derby Works of the London Midland & Scottish Railway (LMS) under the direction of William Stanier, chief mechanical engineer. I can just remember these superb machines. The diesels that replaced them were a far lesser breed, and symptomatic of the way modernization was shaping up on BR at the very time that many passengers were abandoning the railways in favour of the spurious glamour of new motorways and the first inter-city jets on such routes as London to Manchester, previously best served by express trains from Euston.

The modernization of the railways also brought in its iconoclastic wake the "Beeching Report" of 1963 that led to the axing of so many of Britain's railways, especially its rural branch lines, but also, ultimately, to the electrification of such main lines as Euston to Birmingham, which was a good thing. For the "modernizers" and especially for those like the Tory Prime Minister, Harold Macmillan, doing their worst to hide their Classical education, the Euston Arch was a symbol of the Age of Steam that had to go. The Arch had almost been demolished just a year after the streamlined "Duchess" Pacifics began running from Euston to Scotland. The plan had been for a new, art-deco Classical station designed by Percy Thomas [1883–1969], which would have required the destruction of the Arch. Lord Stamp, president of the LMS, was persuaded by members of the Georgian Group founded in 1937, to consider moving the massive sandstone structure to another site, but the Second World War intervened in 1939 and all such ambitious building projects were put on the back burner.

Right Euston Arch, the majestic and much mourned Greek Revival entrance to Euston station in London, seen here in April 1954, a year before British Railways' Modernization Plan heralded its demise.

Above A fine pen and wash drawing by John Cooke Bourne [1814–96] recording the construction of Philip Webb's Euston Arch in 1837. Curiously, the drawing, if you give it a second, pessimistic look, might just as well be recording its demolition 125 years later.

In 1960 plans for a new station threatened the great Doric arch again. Despite campaigns led by, among others, John Betjeman and the distinguished historian, Nikolaus Pevsner, the government remained unmoved. This was not surprising given that the Minister of Transport, Ernest Marples, was a road construction man with interests in the motorway industry. A group of campaigners, including J M "Grim" Richards, editor of the *Architectural Review*, went to 10 Downing Street to discuss the issue with the Prime Minister. According to Richards, "Macmillan listened, or I suppose he listened… he sat without moving with his eyes apparently closed. He asked no questions; in fact he said nothing except that he would consider the matter." However, Macmillan had already considered the matter and the fate of the Arch had been sealed. It came down, with great difficulty, in 1961. According to the *Architectural Review* at the time:

"Its destruction is wanton and unnecessary – connived at by the British Transport Commission, its guardians, and by the London County Council and the Government, who are jointly responsible for safeguarding London's major architectural monuments, of which this is undoubtedly one. In spite of… being one of the outstanding architectural creations of the early nineteenth century and the most important – and visually satisfying – monument to the railway age which Britain pioneered, the united efforts of many organisations and individuals failed to save it in the face of official apathy and philistinism."

Even those who demolished the Arch [the Leonard Fairclough company] felt a pang of guilt and one of the directors of the firm, Frank Valori, offered to store the stones at his own expense on the understanding that one day soon, these might be re-erected

elsewhere. The government rejected the idea out of hand.

Many of the stones were uncovered in 1994 by the architectural historian Dan Cruickshank in the River Lea in east London. This encouraged Cruickshank to found the Euston Arch Trust two years later, and today, it seems just possible that the Arch might yet be reconstructed where it once stood because the bland, air terminal-style station that replaced the original at Euston in 1968 is itself due to be demolished and replaced by a design worthy of its site and history.

For the record, Hardwick's Arch was 70 feet (21 metres) high and 44 feet (13.5 metres) deep. It was originally flanked by a pair of pavilions and acted as a great entrance, or screen, to a courtyard behind leading into the various offices and railway buildings of Euston Station including the opulent Great Hall of 1849, designed by Hardwick's son, Philip Charles Hardwick [1822–92]. This was where Christmas carols used to be sung by members of the railway staff right up until the

demolition of the building. Today, due to cynical political interference, such delightful services have gone the way of the Euston Arch itself.

If anything good came of the demolition of the Euston Arch, it was the energy and purposeful drive it gave to the conservation and heritage lobbies in Britain. You might be forgiven for thinking that the British have since become a little heritage crazy, but you need to remember that without the vigilance of bodies like the Georgian Group, the Victorian Society, Save Britain's Heritage and the Twentieth Century Society, hundreds of historic buildings from Land's End to John O'Groats would have come tumbling down on the whims of politicians. What a wonderful thing it would be to see the Arch rise again alongside the thunderous roar of London's Euston Road. As for those unsure of the idea of re-erecting lost buildings, surely everyone would raise a cheer at the thought of a victory by the people over philistine and brutal politicians.

Above This is Bourne again, this time celebrating Euston Station in full swing soon after its completion in 1838. The trains were quite dwarfed at this time by the mighty neo-classical buildings that hid them from view. You can just make out a train shed on the far right.

Above A model of the Temple of Jerusalem as rebuilt *c.*520 BC. The Second Temple – the first was destroyed by the Babylonians in 586 BC – was evidently designed in a Grecian manner. Although we cannot be sure of its exact appearance, Greek influence was strong in ancient Jerusalem.

Such brute political behaviour regarding buildings is nothing new. It probably started almost as soon as architecture began; politicians and their generals were well aware from very early on that the destruction of great and respected buildings and cities was a way of driving a spear through the heart of whatever population they were determined to subdue. The wilful destruction of buildings and monuments continues to this day.

For some people or nations, a particular building is a part not just of their heritage, but also of their very character and mindset. One such building is the legendary Temple of Solomon, the great Jewish shrine that towered, in various guises, over the rooftops of Jerusalem. The Temple is so important to traditional Jews that they pray for its

reconstruction three times a day. This is unlikely to happen in the foreseeable future as the Temple stood on what is known today as the Temple Mount, the home for many centuries of two mosques and most importantly the Temple of the Dome of the Rock, one of Islam's holiest places.

The Temple remains as fascinating to non-Jews as it is to Jews themselves. This is where Solomon who completed the first Temple in 953 BC placed the Ark of the Covenant, the chest or shrine that contained the two stone tablets on which God had written the Ten Commandments He had handed down to Moses on Mount Sinai. Ever since it disappeared at the time of the destruction of the first Temple by the Babylonians, led by King Nebuchadnezzar, in 586 BC,

the Ark of the Covenant has been one of the "holy grails" of treasure hunters, archaeologists, the deeply religious and the merely curious. Often granted supernatural powers by fantasists, the Ark and its prized contents were kept in the Holy of Holies, the unadorned spiritual heart of Solomon's Temple.

The Temple was built on the site of what was purported to be the hill where Abraham had offered to sacrifice his son Isaac to God as a test of loyalty. No one knows exactly how the Temple was planned or what it looked like. There are various accounts in the Old Testament, but these cannot be taken as accurate architectural descriptions. Over the centuries, as you can see here, artists and architects have revelled in trying to imagine how the Temple might have looked.

Above A delightful image of King Solomon enthroned in a courtly Italian Renaissance palace being shown plans of his new Italian-style temple. In reality, this – the First Temple – would have been influenced, in all probability, by contemporary Mesopotamian design. No one really knows for sure.

Below This drawing blithely claims to be "An exact representation of Solomon's Temple," although it seems unlikely that a Jewish king living some 2,500 years ago would have commissioned a stately pile quite like this. The idea of the temple being big and important, however, is well conveyed.

It was most probably built of stone, and lined in cedar of Lebanon and various rich fabrics and materials. Its design was probably adopted from various Mesopotamian and Egyptian temples. Two giant columns, named Joachim and Boaz, fronted the Temple and its interior housed two chambers, one adorned with altars and the other hidden behind a curtain, the Holy of Holies. It is unlikely the Temple was anything like as big as it has been depicted in medieval and Renaissance engravings. The Bible suggests it measured 180 ft (55 metres) long, 90 feet (27.5 metres) wide and was 50 feet (15 metres) tall; no one really knows.

What we do know for certain is that the Babylonians marched this way in 586 BC, seized Jerusalem, burned it to the ground and took the Jewish people into captivity. The Jews were effectively imprisoned in Babylonia until the Medes and the Persians conquered Babylon itself in 539 BC. Back in Jerusalem, they rebuilt the Temple between 535 and 515 BC. During the reign of Herod the Great, a local king under imperial Roman control, the Temple was greatly expanded. This is where Jesus preached and drove out merchants trading in its outer courtyard; he would have witnessed Herod's ambitious expansion of the Temple.

An exact representation of SOLOMON'S TEMPLE.

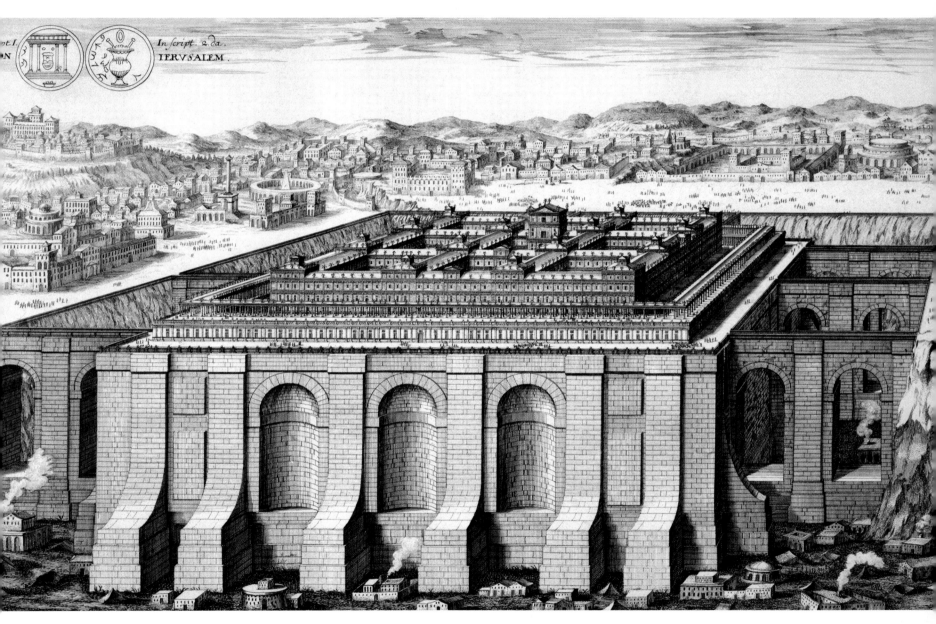

When, some 40 years after what we assume to be Christ's death, the Jews rose up against the Romans, an imperial army led by Titus crushed the rebellion after a long siege and whether accidentally or not – no one is quite sure – set fire to the Temple and destroyed it. The destruction of the Temple has been mourned ever since at the Jewish festival, Tisha B'Av. Meanwhile, tourists in Rome can still gaze at the Arch of Titus, which records – with lively carved illustrations – the Roman general's siege of Jerusalem and its capture in 70 AD. Whether or not Titus ordered the destruction of the Temple, the future of the Jewish people appears to have been cast into the flames for many centuries after this tragic act. The building itself has always haunted the imagination of architects and storytellers throughout the world, and it continues to do so today.

As for the architecture of the Temple, this still informs the design of Masonic and Mormon temples, as it did the plan or layout of Philip II of Spain's magnificent Escorial outside Madrid. This extraordinary monastery-palace, designed by Juan Batista de Toledo [d. 1567] may not look exactly like Solomon's Temple (or Herod's version of the Temple) and yet it gives some idea of just how powerful and mysterious the legendary Jewish building must have been, and why such great buildings have so often been red rags to the bulls of invading armies determined to crush enemies by architectural as well as military means.

Above Here the Temple of Solomon is presented as possibly the biggest and most daunting building of all time. Look at the size of the buildings set around its imposing walls. This wonderful fantasy was drawn by the celebrated Austrian Baroque architect Johann Bernhard Fischer von Erlach [1656–1723].

BASTILE

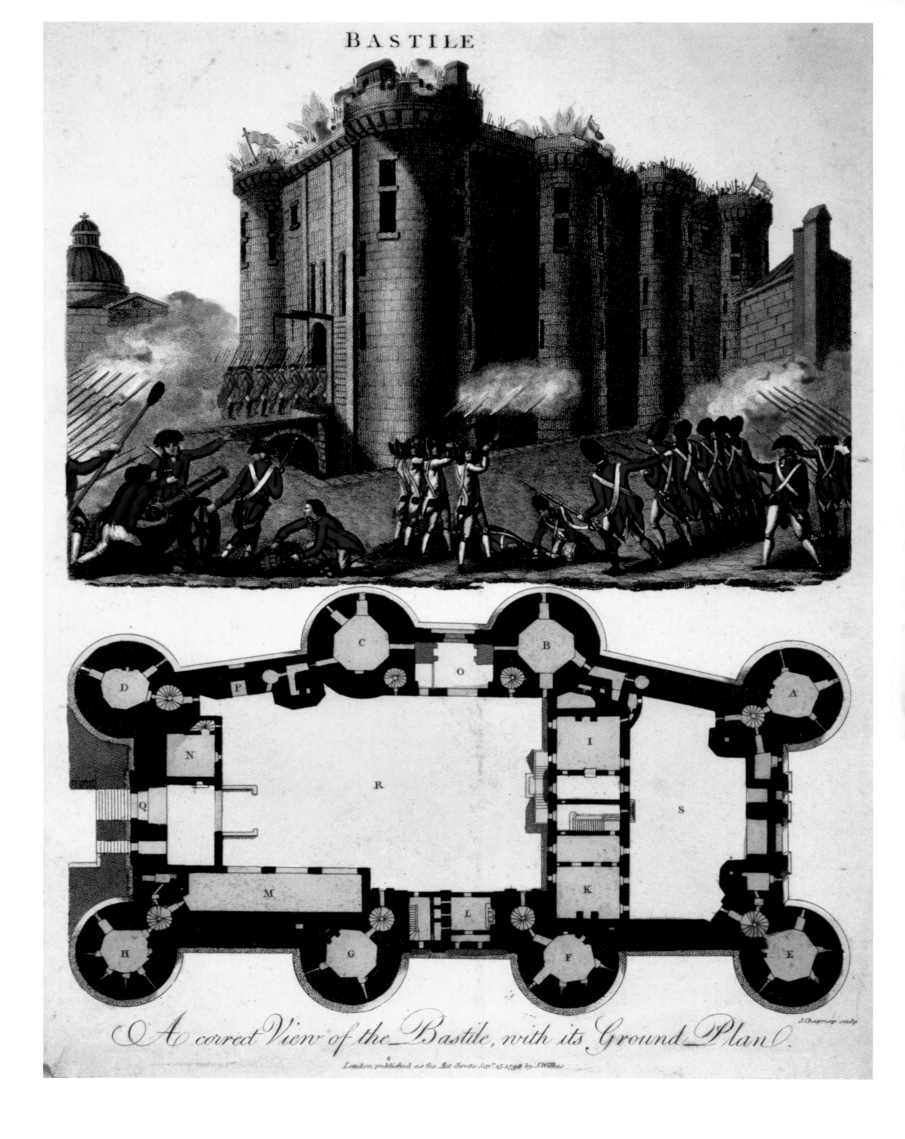

J. Chapman sculp.

A correct View of the Bastile, with its Ground Plan.

London, published as the Act directs Sep.r 15.1798 by J.Wilkes.

Above A romantic, beautifully depicted, image of the Bastille *c.*1420 drawn, in pen and ink, by Theodor Josef Hubert Hoffbauer [1839–1922]. Here, medieval Paris is the perfect model of how a chivalrous city might have looked, or, at least, how nineteenth-century romantics wanted it to have been.

Opposite An accurate plan and picturesque elevation of the Bastille engraved by J Chapman in 1798. The Parisian fortress was made out by domestic and foreign enemies of the French royalists to be a place of horrific tortures and general grimness. This was not true of its last days.

The storming of the Bastille, the grim old Parisian prison, in 1789 raised the spectre of a very different type of political power; not that of empires and mighty armies, but of the mob or common people. The destruction of the Bastille at the time of the French Revolution, was – if only by default – a political act signalling the end of the kingdom's *ancien régime*; the bloody "Terror" that followed the Revolution led to the death of the King of France himself.

The famous events of July 14, 1789, were not quite as they have been portrayed in novels, illustrations and colourful histories. The Bastille, for example, had never been such a dreadful place as it was later presented and at the time of its storming by the mob, it housed just seven prisoners. This was not a place of torture and execution in the eighteenth century, nor was it even a home for political prisoners. Built originally as a gatehouse, but extended into a fortress between 1370 and 1383 at the time of the Hundred Years War, the Bastille was as much a royal palace as it was a castle. It was not particularly big; its 78-foot (24-metre) high stone walls, protected by eight towers of the same height, surrounded an area measuring 223 feet (68

metres) by 88 feet (27 metres). It was not really a menacing building, but for the mob it symbolized the power of the old regime, as well as being a source of arms and gunpowder. It stood on the site of what is the Bastille Opera house today.

On July 14, 1789, 70 French veterans and 32 Swiss grenadiers under the command of the governor, Bernard René de Launay, defended the Bastille. After a brief parlay, the mob – some 1,000 strong – broke into the Bastille and executed de Launay, whose head they marched around Paris on the end of a pike. The Bastille was demolished soon afterwards, not by local people – they would have had a difficult job on their hands – but by a firm of demolition contractors. Even if the true story of the Bastille barely adds up to the drama told in popular novels and films, its destruction was a key part of the genesis of the idea of the power of ordinary people, who might just rise up and overthrow regimes they despised and suffered under. The French Revolution (at least in its early stages) became a model for uprisings in other monarchies and notably that of Russia and its revolution of 1917.

Above left View from the Hotel Moskva of the resurrected Cathedral of Christ the Saviour, Moscow. The original was blown up by Stalin. The site it stood on was reserved for the Palace of the Soviets, but this was never built. A public swimming pool replaced the Orthodox cathedral.

Above right The Cathedral of Christ the Saviour shortly before Stalin destroyed it. The statue in the foreground is a memorial to Tsar Alexander III [1845-1894], a reactionary leader who was also a giant, although the statue, also destroyed by Stalin, was slightly larger than life size.

Above The original caption to this photograph dated November 1, 1931 read "The Light that failed to stem the Soviet tide." Workers are shown taking away one of the great ornamental lamps of the Cathedral of Christ the Saviour immediately before its demolition.

Opposite A handsome oil painting dated 1883 by Fedor Andreevich Klages [1812–90] of the richly decorated interior of the Cathedral of Christ the Saviour. The design was a powerful attempt to reconnect Moscow to its venerable Orthodox Christian, Tsar-fearing past after the Napoleonic war.

The new Soviet leaders were determined to stamp their mark on Russia. Along with the annihilation of millions of their "enemies" at home, they set about demolishing the most prominent buildings symbolizing the last years of Tsarist rule. The grandest of these was the vast Cathedral of Christ the Saviour, designed by Konstantin Thon [1794–1881] and set by the Moskva River near the Kremlin in central Moscow. This giant Orthodox Church, nominally modelled on the Emperor Justinian's magnificent Hagia Sophia in Istanbul, had been commissioned as a sacred memorial commemorating the defeat of the French Emperor Napoleon in 1812. Napoleon had nearly conquered Russia, but like Adolf Hitler 130 years later, his plans were undermined by the extreme depths of the Russian winter and the sheer size of the land he was trying to conquer.

Initially, the cathedral was to have been realized in a grand neoclassical style, but when the profoundly reactionary Nicholas I succeeded to the Russian throne in 1825, Thon was brought in to replace Alexander Vittberg as architect. Thon completed his thumping great design around 1832, although construction work only began in 1839 continuing until 1883. Tchaikovsky's world-famous "1812 Overture" was first performed here in 1882. The following year, on the day of Tsar Alexander III's coronation, the new cathedral was finally consecrated. Its architecture and decoration was a curious mix of national pomp and religious zeal, all glimpsed through layers of gold leaf and lavish marbles under a mighty dome. Not exactly a beautiful building, the cathedral was nevertheless an essential architectural component of the late-flowering Russian monarchy. No wonder Joseph Stalin wanted it removed.

The Soviet dictator's chance came in 1931. Definite plans for building the gigantic Palace of Soviets on the site of the cathedral were finally revealed that year and on December 5, the building was blown apart by a massive charge of dynamite. Such was the rubble, it took another year before the site was cleared in preparation for Stalin's architectural successor. Events and a lack of funds conspired to halt progress on the construction of the Palace of Soviets and for decades the site of the cathedral was dominated by a great gaping hole that was eventually transformed into a gigantic open-air swimming pool. This was a delightful thing; there was something magical in swimming to its surface and gazing around at the Moscow skyline.

In 1990, however, plans were put into action to rebuild the cathedral. As the Soviet Union was falling apart, the authorities chose to go back to some of the old ways and old buildings. The reconstruction of the Cathedral of Christ the Saviour was a giant snub to the imploding Communist regime and an equally major affirmation of Russia's return to Orthodoxy, albeit one dressed in the fashionable garb of a newfound and equally extreme ultra-capitalism. Designed at first by Aleksy Denisov and later by Zurab Tserteteli, the resurrected cathedral is more or less identical to its predecessor. A startling and vulgar thing (the original was much despised by nineteenth-century critics), the marble-clad colossus with its 338-foot (103-metre) high dome was consecrated in 2000.

This was certainly not the only historic Moscow building destroyed by Stalin. In 1936 the early seventeenth-century Church of Our Lady of Kazan was demolished to enable Soviet military parades to pass more easily through Red Square. The destruction of this pretty, domed Orthodox shrine was a real punch in the face as far as Russian history went; it had been built as a celebration of the Russian victory over the Poles in 1612. Prince Dmitry Pozarsky, who built the church, believed his campaign against the Poles had been divinely inspired by the image of the sacred icon of Our Lady of Kazan. A young girl in Kazan had discovered this particular, and very beautiful Russian icon, after the Blessed Virgin appeared to her on the edge of the town in 1579. Later on, the icon was also said to have played its part in the ousting of the Swedish armies of Charles XII in 1709 and the expulsion of Napoleon in 1812. The original icon was lost, although no one knows how or when.

Pozharsky's first wooden church built in honour of the icon was replaced by a brick successor consecrated in 1636. This is the church destroyed by Stalin exactly 300 years later, but not before its plans had been meticulously measured and documented by the Russian architect Peter Baranovsky [1892–1984] who carried out major restoration work here between 1929 and 1932. The drawings were used to reconstruct the bright red and white church between 1990 and 1993, under the direction of Oleg Zhurin.

Top The Church of Our Lady of Kazan, some thirty years before it was demolished by Stalin. Like many old Moscow churches it was very much, as witnessed, a part of the fabric, as well as the life and soul, of the city.

Above Rebuilt between 1990 and 1993, here is the Church of Our Lady of Kazan back where it belongs on the fringe of Moscow's Red Square. Of course it looks a little too new for comfort, but a few Russian winters will soon weather it nicely.

Right Detail of the central ogee arch above the entrance to the Church of Our Lady of Kazan with a reproduction of the much revered icon of the Blessed Virgin, who appeared to a peasant girl in Kazan in 1579, and the infant Christ.

Opposite The rebuilt Resurrection Gate, Moscow, one of the principal entrances to Red Square, with the glorious onion-domed medley of St Basil's in the background and the Kremlin to the right. The original Gate with its ornate twin towers was demolished by Stalin in 1929.

Above Resurrection Gate, Moscow not long before it was blown up to allow Stalin's military parades easy access into Red Square. The entire composition of Red Square was ruined by this act of bloody-minded aggression, but for Stalin might was right and this gate had to go.

On the north-west corner of Red Square stands yet another 1990s reproduction: this is the Resurrection Gate, with its twin arches, twin towers and twin steeples, originally built in 1649 as a holy entrance into the great Moscow square. A chapel on the side of the gate enshrined a copy of the icon of the Mother of God of Iveron (on Mt Athos, Greece). This was said to have great healing powers and was much revered over the centuries. The chapel, rebuilt in 1680 and again modified in the eighteenth century by the artist Matvei Kazakov, was demolished on Stalin's orders in 1929 and replaced by a singularly unbecoming statue of a "heroic" Soviet worker. This was yet another snub to the Orthodox Church and its beliefs, which ran counter to those of the Communist Party of the Soviet Union. When Stalin decided that the rest of the gate itself was an impediment to the progress of Red Army tanks, he had it demolished. Oleg Zhurin rebuilt the Resurrection Gate in 1994–96.

Another distinguished Moscow church that disappeared in the 1930s was the delightful towered and many-domed Chrysostom Monastery. Dating back to 1412, but rebuilt many times following fires or political strife, the monastery adopted its latest form from the 1660s. Burned in 1737 and restored in 1738–40, it was damaged during Napoleon's invasion of 1812 and restored once again. Having

survived so much, it was a great pity that this beautiful monastery was torn down in 1933 for no other reason than that of "delapidation". It is unlikely to be rebuilt.

It is equally unlikely, despite rumours to the contrary, that the Sukharev Tower which once stood on the junction of the Garden Ring Road and Sretenka Street will ever be reconstructed. Designed in a muscular Baroque style by Mikhail Choglokov and built in 1692–95, the tower served as a barracks, as a school for mathematics and navigation, as Russia's first observatory and as the focal point for a lively market around its base. The market, antithetical to Communist beliefs, was closed by 1930 and although the tower was used briefly as a city museum, Stalin disliked it and it was pulled down in 1934.

It may seem that the orgy of mass architectural destruction that took place in Moscow under Stalin in the 1930s was wholly aimed at undermining old faiths, but as in the case of the Sukharev Tower and the Red Gates, Stalin's axe was wielded wherever he saw the processes of his form of "modernization" held back by buildings and monuments from what he regarded as Russia's backward past. What he could not foresee was that all this destruction would leave a gaping hole in Moscow's heart, which would be filled with questionable reproductions of historic buildings only 40 years after his death.

Above The wonderfully romantic roofline of the Chrysostom Monastery, destroyed by Stalin in 1933. The monastery did not impede Stalin's military processions, yet this former trainee Orthodox priest turned Communist dictator enjoyed smashing down churches and undermining the Church at every turn.

Above The impressive Sukharev Tower, Moscow, a heady mix of Russian
Renaissance and medieval design, seen here in a nineteenth-century
engraving, was pulled down on Stalin's orders in 1934. Nothing replaced it;
Stalin objected to it, and that, as far as this delightful monument went, was it.

Above A winter's day in Moscow in the mid-1920s as heroic Soviet commuters set off to fulfil their norms on foot and by tram against a backdrop provided by the superb Red Gate, a Baroque delight, demolished in 1928 for a section of new city ring road.

The Red Gate, an operatic Baroque gateway designed by Prince Dmitry Ukhtomsky [1719–74], chief architect of Moscow under Tsarina Elizabeth, was destroyed in 1928 to make way for a section of the Garden Ring Road around central Moscow. Originally made of wood and erected as a monument to the Battle of Poltava (1709), the red and white archway was rebuilt in stone in 1753. It must have been a fine entrance into the city, but sadly, despite the reconstruction of so many old Moscow buildings, the Red Gate will not be coming back; this monumental gateway would get in the way of the city's streaming traffic.

Yekaterinburg, a town founded by Peter the Great in 1727 and named after his wife, lies far from Moscow. This is the town notorious for hosting the captive Russian royal family after the 1917 Revolution and witnessing their brutal deaths in the Ipatiev House. The house, a comfortable Baroque-style two-storey affair with all modern

conveniences, was built in 1897 for Andrei Redikortsev, a local mining engineer. In 1908 it was bought by a local merchant, Nicholas Ipatiev. It was Ipatiev's misfortune to have had his home confiscated by the Bolsheviks in 1918. Surrounded by a high wooden fence and guarded by Red Army soldiers, Ipatiev's dream home was now referred to as "the house of special purpose."

The nature of that special purpose became gruesomely clear early in the morning of July 17, 1918, when the royal family was ordered down into the basement of the house. A party of 10 soldiers marched in and the Tsar and his family were gunned down, and then bayoneted for good measure. Their bodies were crudely buried in a pit beyond the town, until they were uncovered and identified in the late 1980s. The physical remains of the last of the Romanovs have since been buried in St Petersburg and the family canonized by the Orthodox Church.

As for the Ipatiev House, this was given back to its owner after the murders. Ipatiev himself emigrated soon afterwards and died abroad. The house survived until 1977 when the First Communist Party Secretary of the region ordered its demolition. Why this was done so long after the events of July 1918 is something of a mystery, although perhaps the discovery of the Romanov remains was on the cards and the Communist Party was concerned that the fate of royal family might be a rallying call again for ordinary people after so many years.

Although the Ipatiev House has gone, its site has been built over by a vast, traditional medieval style Russian Orthodox Church designed by Grigory Mazaev and completed in 2003. With its gilded domes, and dazzing white walls, it is known as the Cathedral of the Blood, a grandiloquent memorial to the murder of the Romanovs and an instantly popular attraction for both the faithful and those tourists who make it this far into Mother Russia. In the crypt of the church you will find a replica of the basement of the ill-fated Ipatiev House.

Above left Here is the Ipatiev House, Yekaterinburg in 1917. Surrounded by a crude and tall wooden fence, this late nineteenth-century provincial villa was the last home to the Russian royal family; they were held here until their murder by the Bolsheviks the following year.

Above right The wall inside one of the rooms of the Ipatiev House against which the Tsar and his family were lined up, shot and bayoneted to death. Not surprisingly, the house was later demolished in an attempt to wipe its bloody history from the Soviet slate.

Right The new Cathedral of the Blood, Yekaterinburg, rising from the site of the Ipatiev House. This mighty memorial to the Russian royal family, designed in a determinedly traditional Orthodox style, is a place of pilgrimage in today's ultra-capitalist, yet heavily governed Russia.

From a distance, this church and that of the Cathedral of Christ the Saviour, Moscow, might be mistaken for one another. In fact, Alexander Nevsky Cathedral in Warsaw was a gift from the Soviet government to the Polish people. This Russian interloper was demolished in the mid-1920s when it was less than 15 years old. Again, politics played their part in both the construction and demolition of the building.

Russia occupied much of Poland from 1815 and by the 1890s Warsaw, traditionally one of the most intensely Roman Catholic European capital cities, was home to an Orthodox population of more than 42,000. There was little room for these worshippers in Warsaw's few Orthodox churches and so in 1894 work began on the enormous Alexander Nevsky Cathedral. Designed by the Russian architect Leon Benois [1856–1928], the church, lavishly decorated with mosaics, marbles and precious stones, was completed in 1912. It stood on the site where patriotic Polish officers had executed Polish soldiers loyal to Russia. This was evidently a highly charged political act.

When the Russians abandoned Poland in 1915, the cathedral became St Henry's, a Catholic church for German soldiers, but it was handed back to Polish authorities at the end of the First World War in 1918. The Poles had to decide what to do with the building. For most, it represented Russian domination and so, despite the pleas of a minority dubbed "Cathedralists" and looked upon as lacking in patriotism, the church was blown up between 1924 and 1926. It took at least 15,000 blasts of dynamite before the building finally collapsed. Today all that remains of it are a number of mosaics that can be seen in the Mary Magdalene Orthodox Cathedral in the Warsaw suburb of Praga.

Shrines of a specifically political nature in Eastern Europe were also to meet sudden ends when regimes, either foreign or else perceived to be alien, imploded from the late 1980s. The Georgi Dimitrov mausoleum in the centre of Sofia survived for a remarkably long

Opposite This might be a street scene from Moscow before the October Revolution. But this is Warsaw in the early twentieth century and the onion-domed church is the Alexander Nevsky Cathedral, an unwanted gift from the Russians to the Poles, or to Russians occupying Poland.

Right The nave and apse of the Alexander Nevksy Cathedral in Warsaw. The Poles were, by and large, Roman Catholics, and this lavish Orthodox church was seen as a symbol of Russian imperialism and an unwanted form of Christian rite. It was demolished, gleefully, when the Russians left Poland.

Top Mausoleum of Georgi Dimitrov, Sofia seen here in "former times" – the
1970s in this case – as the days of Communist rule are known throughout
Eastern Europe and the ex-Soviet Union. The style of the building was intended
to please Stalin.

Above The demolition of the Georgi Dimitrov Mausoleum. The building was
not universally disliked in Sofia. It had become a familiar part of the streetscape
and many argued for its retention, but its association with the former
Communist regime ensured its downfall.

time. The white marble and black granite-clad monument housed the
embalmed body of the Bulgarian Communist leader who died in 1949.
Designs were made overnight at the time by a team of local architects
and the tomb was built in just six days.

Until 1990 it was possible to queue to see Dimitrov's corpse.
This lay inside a glass shrine that could be lowered at night into a
laboratory where the cadaver could be dressed in a new suit or else
freshly pumped with conserving liquids. A "secret" corridor led from
here to the Communist Party headquarters. Local people told me that
the mausoleum had been designed to withstand a nuclear attack.
This seems unlikely, although in 1999 when Ivan Kostov's UDF-led
government finally managed to rid Sofia of the building, it took four
massive controlled explosions to bring it down.

The corpse had been removed from the mausoleum and cremated
in 1990, but an argument raged over what should happen to a building
that many thought had become an accepted part of the cityscape
despite its political history. Some suggested it could be turned into
a museum or gallery. A poll showed that two-thirds of local people
were in favour of retaining the mausoleum as late as local government
elections held in Sofia in 1999, but Kostov took the matter into his
own hands and that was the end of the Communist mausoleum. It was
also nearly the end of one of the oddest types of twentieth-century
buildings – those shrines devoted to the pickled remains of Communist
leaders. Just two survive in 2008: one is the mausoleum of Ho
Chi Min in Hanoi; the other is that of the first of these embalmed
politicians, Vladimir Ilych Lenin in Moscow's Red Square.

Communist architecture has also been swept away in what was,
until the collapse of the city's infamous Wall in 1989, East Berlin. The
most notable recent victim is the Palast der Republik [1973–76], the
enormous steel, glass and concrete home of the parliament of the
former German Democratic Republic. Commissioned soon after Erich
Honecker came to power in 1972, the Palast der Republik was built

Above Palast der Republik, Berlin,
seen here on a January morning
in 2006. A symbol of East Berlin's
Communist government, and of the
entire political construct of the former
German Democratic Republic, this
"people's palace" was doomed
as soon as the Berlin Wall came
tumbling down in 1989.

Right An East German Trabant
car burbles past the Palast der
Republik. Behind is the East Berlin
TV tower on Alexanderplatz, a
showcase of Communist design.
The Palast der Republik is to be
replaced by a façade-thin replica of
the former Prussian Stadtschloss that
once stood here.

Above The brand new foyer of the Palast der Republik in 1976. Today, this could easily be a very fashionable interior – 1970s chic – but it stood no chance because of its decidedly unfashionable political associations; and the building was laced through with asbestos.

on the site of what had been, until it was demolished in 1950–51, the old Stadtschloss, a medieval castle given an extensive Baroque makeover and the Berlin home of the Prussian Kaisers. The castle had been demolished as an act of political spite and to rid Berlin of associations with its imperial past. Construction of the new Palast, originally to have been designed in a Stalinist neoclassical style, was much delayed. By the time the project was given the go-ahead from Honecker, its architects, Heinz Graffunder and Karl-Ernst Swora, had a very different idea of what it should look like. The built design would have made a superb stage set for Stanley Kubrick's film *A Clockwork Orange* (1971); pure Seventies, its double-height reception hall was filled with fashionable, white round lamps – prompting East Berliners to dub the completed building "Erich's Lamp Shop".

This public building was no monster; it housed not just the Volkskammer (the East German "People's Chamber"), but also a public conference hall together with public bars and restaurants. However, the change in politics heralded by the fall of the Berlin Wall signalled the end for the Palast der Republik. It represented all too clearly the former Communist regime; as such its fate was sealed. Condemned by the last East German government, because of the asbestos used in its construction, the building was abandoned in 1990, stripped to its structural shell and finally demolished in 2006–7.

Even so, many Berliners liked the building and believed that new uses could be found for it; they viewed it as part of a distinctive cityscape created in East Berlin from the 1950s to the 1970s. Berliners from across the city were also infuriated by plans to replace the Palast with a reproduction of the Stadtschloss at immense cost to be used as a theme-park-style tourist-magnet, and probably as a home to yet more art galleries and restaurants.

There has been far less debate about the likely reconstruction of another historic Prussian building demolished by Communist authorities. This is because the former Königsberg Castle, built by the Teutonic knights in 1255 as a stepping off point for Crusades to the Holy Land, is in Kaliningrad, a Russian "*oblast*" (a region or district that was a part of Germany until 1945). Since then, Kaliningrad has been a forgotten backwater of both Prussia and Russia. However, now that the Russian Prime Minister and former president, Vladimir Putin, is building a family home there, along with a number of Russian oligarchs, Kaliningrad is about to be transformed. Half of the city was destroyed by Allied bombing in 1944 and much of the rest by the Red Army in 1945, and it is in dire need of renovation. Under the direction of its new architect, Alexander Bazhin, it looks as if much of the old city will be rebuilt as it was, including the castle.

This is a real change of heart by the Russians. In 1977 what had survived of the castle was razed to the ground on the orders of the Soviet leader, Leonid Brezhnev. Remnants of the Prussian imperial past were to be obliterated. Dominated by its 263-foot (80-metre) high Gothic tower, the castle was a triumphant design and is much missed. Reconstruction, which will cost something like £50 million, is scheduled for completion in 2010. What was once lost has been found again, with one exception: the Amber Room. This magical room, lined with more than 1,000 pieces of amber, a natural product of this stretch of the Baltic coast, was originally presented as a gift from Prussia to Peter the Great of Russia and was installed in the Tsarskoye Selo palace near St Petersburg. In 1941 it was seized by the German military and installed in what was then Königsburg Castle, but by the end of the Second World War it had disappeared and no one knows exactly what happened to it. The room has since been recreated in Tsarskoye Selo, but not in Königsberg where, even if sufficient funds were available, such a project would only re-open old political sores.

Above right Königsberg Castle in 1935, when this port town, once home of the great eighteenth-century German philosopher Immanuel Kant, was still very much Prussian in spirit as well as name. Since 1945 Königsberg, badly damaged by Allied and Soviet bombing, has been Kaliningrad, a Russian territory.

Right A coloured photograph from the 1890s, showing the principal courtyard of Königsberg Castle. Some of the buildings dated back to the medieval era, although most were from the late sixteenth and early eighteeth centuries. Destroyed by the Communists, this former stronghold of the Teutonic Knights is now to be recreated.

A building many local people have no regret for, and one that is very unlikely ever to be "found" again, is what was known as the Korean National Capitol in Seoul. This Baroque-looking granite pile was originally built by the Japanese between 1916 and 1926, to designs by the German architect Georg de Lalande (succeeded after his death by Nomura Ichiro), as the Japanese General Government Building. Japan had annexed Korea in 1910.

To spite the Koreans, construction of the General Government Building demanded the demolition of 10 historic buildings and it was deliberately sited so as to block views of the old Korean royal palace, the Gyeongbokgung, from the city centre. In 1945, however, this is where the Japanese surrendered Korea to the US military, which then encouraged the birth of the Republic of Korea or South Korea, as we know it today. Until 1975 the building was used as the Korean Capitol. It later became home to the National Museum, but when Kim Young-sam came to power in 1993 an announcement was made to the effect that the building was a symbol of Japanese political power and would be demolished in 1995 in time to mark the 50th anniversary of the liberation of Korea from Japanese rule. The building had a number

of supporters who pointed out that no one had wanted to demolish either the City Hall or the principal city railway station, both of which were imperial Japanese buildings. Such arguments were to no avail and demolition began on August 15, 1995.

The ebb and flow of politics will continue to see buildings vanish in the future. Architecture is the most political of the arts and politicians have and will continue to use it, for better or worse, as an instrument of prestige, power and even the humiliation of those they purport to serve.

Above The General Government Building, Seoul, seen here in 1947 shortly after the Japanese had been ousted from Korea by US forces. A heavy-handed imperial baroque design, the building was disliked on two counts: the fact that it was a symbol of Japanese oppression, and the way it looked.

Opposite Displaying the flags of Korea and its allies, the General Government Building is seen here in 1946 with various big-wigs stepping inside to determine the fate of a country once brutally occupied by the Japanese. The building was demolished, despite local protest, in 1995.

7 LOST IN DREAMS

M any of the buildings lost to us in the sense that they are fictional, are nevertheless very much alive and real in their own terms – in books, films, poems and science-fiction fantasies. As a teenager, there were few places I dreamed of visiting more than Kublai Khan's "pleasure dome". The great Mongolian Khan never owned or lived in such a building and yet it was lyrically evoked by the English Romantic poet Samuel Taylor Coleridge [1772–1834] in one of his most famous poems. It begins:

"In Xanadu did Kubla Khan
A stately pleasure-dome decree:
Where Alph, the sacred river, ran
Through caverns measureless to man
Down to a sunless sea.
So twice five miles of fertile ground
With walls and towers were girdled round:
And there were gardens bright with sinuous rills,
Where blossomed many an incense-bearing tree;
And here were forests ancient as the hills,
Enfolding sunny spots of greenery."

And ends:

"The shadow of the dome of pleasure
Floated midway on the waves;
Where was heard the mingled measure
From the fountain and the caves.
It was a miracle of rare device,

A sunny pleasure-dome with caves of ice!
A damsel with a dulcimer
In a vision once I saw:
It was an Abyssinian maid,
And on her dulcimer she played,
Singing of Mount Abora.
Could I revive within me
Her symphony and song,
To such a deep delight 'twould win me,
That with music loud and long,
I would build that dome in air,
That sunny dome! those caves of ice!
And all who heard should see them there,
And all should cry, Beware! Beware!
His flashing eyes, his floating hair!
Weave a circle round him thrice,
And close your eyes with holy dread,
For he on honey-dew hath fed,
And drunk the milk of Paradise."

Coleridge claimed that this beautifully crafted poem was a mere fragment of a vision that had rushed into his head one day, and that the spell had been broken by a visitor from Porlock knocking at his cottage door before he had time to set the whole poem down on paper.

Whatever the truth behind its making, "Kubla Khan" is a work of genius and magic, evoking a place, a building and a mood that are mystical, sensual and credible. Ever since, artists have made illustrations to interpret Coleridge's poem, but they have never quite managed to capture the exotic nature of his vision of Kublai Khan's pleasure dome. Perhaps this is because, as you can see from the accompanying illustrations, they have been hidebound not by artistic, but by architectural tradition. Coleridge's poem might suggest something like Brighton Pavilion (yet to be built when the poem was written) mixed up with the Alhambra, the Taj Mahal and gardens like Bodnant at Taly-y-Cafn overlooking Colywn Bay in North Wales, and yet "Kubla Khan" is a pure fantasy, as hard to pin down or substantiate as moods expressed in wordless music.

Right The arrival of the Venetian adventurer Marco Polo – which one is he? – at the court of Kublai Khan [1215-94], in a fanciful nineteenth-century illustration that tells us precious little of the real event.

From the earliest written works, authors have imagined and described fantastic buildings, gardens, towns and cities. One of the very first literary works we know of – *The Epic of Gilgamesh*, written sometime around 2000 BC, and possibly earlier – describes the gestation and birth of Eridu in ancient Sumeria (p.18), arguably the world's first city. And one of the most powerful books ever written, the Bible, contains some magnificent descriptions of buildings and cities. The most famous of these is probably the Heavenly City evoked by St John the Divine in the Book of Revelation, or the Apocalypse (Chapter 21, 2), written somewhere between 70 and 100 AD:

"And I John saw the holy city, new Jerusalem, coming down from God out of heaven, prepared as a bride adorned for her husband."

John goes on to describe the city in great detail. It lay "foursquare". Its walls were made of jasper, its buildings from pure gold "like unto clear glass." Its 12 gates were made of pearl, while even the foundations of the city "were garnished with all manner of precious stones." Most notably, though, John saw no temple in the city. Why? Because "the Lord God Almighty and the Lamb are the temple of it." And we learn that the gates were always open because it was always day in the City of God, and that the city "had no need of the sun, neither of the moon, to shine in it: for the glory of God did lighten it, and the Lamb is the light thereof."

Revelation is the last book in the Bible. The first is Genesis. Significantly, here the ideal home created by God is not a city, but a garden: the Garden of Eden. In many ancient and venerable religious writings – Sumerian, Judaic, Christian, Islamic – the happiest place for humans to live, and to be close to God, is a garden.

" In Xanadu did Kubla Khan
A stately pleasure-dome decree."

Above A delightful drawing of "Kubla Khan's" Xanadu, from Coleridge's poem, by Patten Wilson [1868–1928]. This is from an illustrated edition of Coleridge published by Longmans Green in 1898. Xanadu appears to be a marriage of the Alhambra, Granada, and the Hagia Sophia, Istanbul.

Right Coleridge's Xanadu seen, appropriately, as if through a haze of opium smoke in an illustration said to be by Walter Crane [1845–1915]. Xanadu emerges as a mix of Istanbul, a medieval castle, daunting rocks and wreaths of clouds. The real Xanadu is nothing like this whatsoever.

KUBLA KHAN
A VISION IN A DREAM ··

"And the Lord God planted a garden eastward in Eden; and there He put the man whom He had formed.

And out of the ground made the Lord God to grow every tree that is pleasant to the sight, and good for food; the tree of life also in the midst of the garden, and the tree of knowledge of good and evil." (Genesis, Chapter 2, 8–9)

It was from this garden, of course, that Adam and Eve were expelled for eating the fruit of the Tree of Knowledge. Ever since – when humankind first became self-aware – many of us have been looking for a garden of sorts to live and thrive in, but as we need buildings and have a knack for creating these as architecture, there is a happy balance to be struck somewhere between gardens and buildings, a

Above God expels Adam and Eve from Paradise after they have been tempted to eat from the forbidden Tree of Knowledge. This painted panel is by Giovanni di Paolo di Grazia [1403–83]. God points to the world where they will delve and spin and build.

balance you can feel and almost see in Coleridge's "Kubla Khan".

One of the greatest and most beautiful of all buildings is the Alhambra in Granada in southern Spain. Here is the best of both worlds, a playfully irrigated Arabic garden that meanders in and out of dream-like palace rooms and grottoes, all tucked safely behind fairy-tale castle walls and set against a backdrop of the snow-capped peaks of the Sierra Nevada. Here is an earthly semblance of paradise.

Children's stories are often set in idyllic landscapes, far and away from our ordinary workaday worlds: *Winnie the Pooh*, *Thomas the Tank Engine* and *The Wind in the Willows*. The last of these, written by Kenneth Grahame [1859–1932] was published in 1908 without illustrations. The first illustrated edition appeared in 1931, adorned with memorable drawings by E H Shepherd [1879–1976]. These

evoke a pastoral vision of the Edwardian countryside along the banks of the River Thames, west of London. The modern world is not allowed to intrude; if it does, as in the case of Toad's new-fangled motor car, the results are disastrous.

The most notable work of architecture in the book is Toad Hall, the grand ancestral home of the conceited and foolish Toad who is rescued by the decent Rat, Mole and Badger. Toad Hall is an Elizabethan or Jacobean (or even Jacobethan) mansion built before the fashion for Italian or Classical design came to dominate the British architectural scene. For many of the English upper middle class or gentry brought up in late Victorian England, this type of house came to typify the national ideal; it was seen to be as indigenous as Badger, one of the most ancient of English beasts – an English yeoman in animal guise.

Above Rat and Mole row past Toad Hall, an idyllic Jacobethan English country house on the banks of the River Thames. The scene was illustrated by E H Shephard [1879–1976] for the hugely popular 1931 edition of Kenneth Grahame's *The Wind in the Willows.*

Above left Stoats and weasels occupying Toad Hall shoot at Toad himself as he attempts to regain his home. E H Shephard was no stranger to violence; he had won the Military Cross in France in the First World War. Toad, his chums and his home belonged to a pre-War world.

This idea of such a thoroughly English architectural setting has been nurtured over the decades in books, films and television programmes. Whether in *Rupert the Bear* annuals, the mid-Sixties' sets for the television series *The Avengers*, Merchant Ivory films such as *A Room with a View* (1985) and *Howards End* (1992), or any number of novels, this English rural dream is still celebrated. All of these invoke or involve a sense of loss; ways of life, cultures and buildings that, as far as they existed, have vanished in our graceless, insatiable consumer-led culture. The more we hear newsreaders and government apparatchiks using the word "communities" today, the more we are aware that in the twenty-first century there is no such thing as a cohesive society or a shared vision of how we might live, or even what our cities, towns and villages should look like.

Above right Rat, Mole and Badger confront Toad as he comes proudly down the steps of Toad Hall making for the driving wheel of his big, fast, new-fangled motor-car. The car was a symbol of an unwelcome modern world set against the age-old comfort of the handsome house.

There has long been a darker side to English writing, dreaming and drawing. Some of the only "dungeons and dragons" school of books I have ever managed to read are those by Mervyn Peake [1911–68], a brilliant, if eccentric, artist and writer. His "Gormenghast" trilogy – *Titus Groan* (1946), *Gormenghast* (1950) and *Titus Alone* (1959) – was partly, and most famously, set in Gormenghast Castle, a terrifying and all but impenetrable building that, although the stuff of nightmares, is utterly compelling. This haunting building set under precipitous roofs is where the unsettling comings and goings of the Groan family take place. Here, among other delightfully named characters, are Lord Sepulgrave, Flay his manservant, Dr Prunesquallor, Swelter the chef, Nanny Slag, Sourdust, the master of ritual, and Pentecost, the head gardener. Here is the Hall of Bright Carvings, the terrifying kitchens run by the sadistic Swelter and the Tower of Flints that soars above even the highest of Gormenghast's countless roofs. These characters and spaces add up to a magnificent work of modern Gothic imagination.

Peake was born and partly brought up in China; it seems that Gormenghast was inspired by his youthful sense and understanding of the Forbidden City in Beijing, the imperial palace designed like a series of vast boxes within boxes, set about with ineffable, age-old rituals, and hiding somewhere in its mysterious core was the distant figure of the Emperor himself. Gormenghast is not quite English.

Peake himself tried to draw Gormenghast. His most successful illustrations conjure a mood – brooding, aloof, massive, dank, improbable, labyrinthine, ivy-clad, ultimately unknowable – rather than depict a lovingly detailed design. Even Peake was better at writing about Gormenghast than trying to visualize it on paper.

Above Another Peake sketch of Gormenghast and the houses at the base of
its mountainous walls. Here, and close by, are the Twisted Woods, the Mud
Dwellers' Village, the home of the Death Owls, a deep, dark lake, and other
buildings and places drawn from nightmares and dreams.

Top A space station orbits the Moon. Inside is the Space Hilton Hotel. A scene from Stanley Kubrick's *2001: A Space Odyssey* (1968). The film suggests that whatever cleverness mankind enjoys – enough to colonize space – this is owed to powers, and minds, beyond human imagination.

Above An awkward meeting of US and Russian scientists in the lobby of the Space Hilton, complete with lightweight space age chairs by the French designer Olivier Morgue, inside the orbiting space station, from *2001: A Space Odyssey*. The Moon can be seen riding past the window.

It is the art of the film-maker that has really brought to life so many fantasy buildings. Everyone will have their favourite architectural moments in films spanning a century. One of the films that still thrills me – mostly for its special effects and its sly, underplayed satire – is Stanley Kubrick's epic *2001: A Space Odyssey* (1968). In this extraordinary film, in which human characters are mere ciphers given to uttering glib platitudes and banal corporate speak, the special effects played a dominant role. A team of highly talented designers – Anthony Masters, Harry Lange and Ernest Archer – created the look of the film and its detailed design. Expert camera work by Geoffrey Unsworth led to an astonishingly crisp print. Forty years on, *2001* still looks very convincing; this may not be the way the real world (and worlds beyond it) have moved on, but Kubrick created his own space age world that had a sense of both sincerity and authenticity.

I find images of the "Space Hilton" inside the vast space station orbiting the earth, a delight. Where could you find such a smoothly futuristic interior in 2008? Even the lightweight red "Djinn" chairs dating from 1965, by the French designer Olivier Morgue, seem as ultra-modern as ever. Kubrick's genius was to evoke a wholly convincing look, derived in part from a detailed knowledge of contemporary design at NASA (National Aeronautics and Space Administration, USA) and in equal measure from a highly disciplined imagination.

The space stations and vehicles that star in *2001* were largely the work of the artist Harry Lange [b.1930]. Lange left his native Germany in 1949 and soon found work at the US Army Ballistic Mission Agency in Huntsville, Alabama, where many of Nazi Germany's leading scientists, under Hitler's rocketeer Werner von Braun, had been gathered together to develop a part of the American space programme. Later on, Lange went to work at NASA when von Braun was transferred there with a mission to land a man on the moon by the end of the 1960s. Lange's job was to illustrate future spacecraft and in doing so create blueprints for real machines. When he left NASA Lange brought to the film industry, via Arthur C Clarke, author of *The Sentinel* (the sci-fi story that drove the script of *2001*), a detailed knowledge of what space vehicles of the future would look like. What you see in Kubrick's majestic film are machines that actually might have been if only the space programme had continued as it was meant to have done. Lange's is a world of lost future design.

Watching the film again recently, I still felt that I would like to visit some of the places and machines depicted in it. But this can never be; cinema is more about smoke and mirrors or special effects, than it is about concrete, stone and steel.

Above Here the Russian and US scientists exchange polite banalities sat in Olivier Morgue's Djinn chairs. The set designs and special effects shown throughout Kubrick's *2001* were based on the latest visualizations from NASA. They still look remarkably convincing even forty years on.

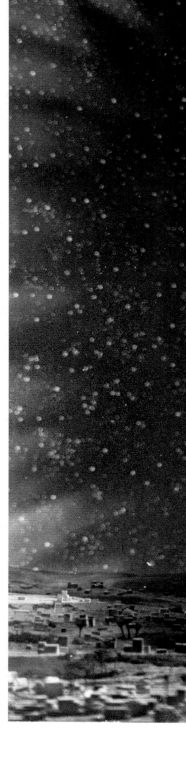

Having said this, no one should forget the extraordinary set designs of the Oscar-winning Ken Adam [b.1921]. Famous for his designs for several of the James Bond films, including *Goldfinger* (1964), *You Only Live Twice* (1967) and *The Spy Who Loved Me* (1977), Adam also worked with Kubrick on *Dr Strangelove* (1964), the Cold War satire featuring Adam's design for the US president's War Room. The story goes that his design was so convincing that when Ronald Reagan was elected US president in 1981, he asked to see the War Room, and was disappointed to find that it didn't look like the one he had seen in *Dr Strangelove*…

On another occasion, Adam was asked how the Bond team had been allowed to film inside Fort Knox during the making of *Goldfinger*. We didn't, he said, before realizing that the set design he had dreamed up as a stand-in for Fort Knox was widely considered to be the real thing. Adam has since explained that his version of the vaults of Fort

Above A fight scene between Oddjob (Harold Sakata) and James Bond (Sean Connery) in *Goldfinger* (Guy Hamilton, 1964) inside Fort Knox. The interiors shown in the film, although convincing, were drawn entirely from the lively, architecturally-trained imagination of the legendary set designer, Ken Adam.

Above A hypnotic twentieth-century version of the Tower of Babel from Fritz Lang's *Metropolis*. Clearly based on Pieter Breughel the Elder's famous painting of the Biblical tower, the celluloid version suggested that the sinister city of the film's title was destined to fall.

Knox was unrealistic in that gold could not be stored in the way he had shown; if it were stacked up, *Goldfinger*-style, it would be impossibly heavy. What Adam wanted to create was the visual idea of there being huge amounts of glistering gold in Fort Knox, a temptation beyond all temptations for greedy Bond villains.

Like many set designers, Adam trained as an architect. This background explains, to an extent, just why his film interiors are so convincing even when deliberately exaggerated. They have also been, as an architect's work should be, in one way or another, functional. Several of his sets in the Bond movies, as well as for *Chitty Chitty Bang Bang* (Ken Hughes, 1968), were galleries designed especially for chase or dance sequences; and in the case of the Bond films, they formed a kind of giant playpen for goodies and baddies to climb up and down, and to be shot down and fall from.

Adam was born in Berlin and grew up there before his family moved to London to escape the Nazis. As a small boy, he was aware of the powerful architectural images being used in contemporary German cinema. Fritz Lang [1890–1976] made the most effective use of a dream-like architecture, extrapolated from the latest avant-garde design, in his legendary silent epic *Metropolis* (1927). Lang's art directors were Erich Kettelhut [1893–1979] and Otto Hunte [1883–1960]. Together, they ensured that their imaginary city would look as realistic as possible. It remains a magnificent achievement: looming art deco and German Expressionist skyscrapers, buildings so tall that aircraft fly below and between them, vast and soulless corporate headquarters, streams of traffic racing along wide streets and daring bridges linking buildings across cavernous avenues.

The biggest of all the buildings in *Metropolis* was cleverly modelled on Breughel's sixteenth-century painting of the Tower of Babel (p.16): *Metropolis* was clearly meant to be a new Babel. Lang's film was

Above Awe-inspiring architecture and streetscape from Fritz Lang's *Metropolis*. Lang and his set designers drew freely from the architecture of legend as well as the canyon-like streets of contemporary New York to conjure this brilliantly realized dream of an all-controlling city of the future.

hugely influential. Ridley Scott [b.1937] paid tribute to *Metropolis* in his much admired film *Blade Runner* (1982), a film-noir detective thriller set in the future, 2019, in a profoundly dystopian yet strangely beautiful Los Angeles, heavily influenced by modern Tokyo and Hong Kong.

The sets were by the American artist Syd Mead [b.1933] and realized by Lawrence G Paull, the film's production designer, and David Snyder, art director; they were simply stunning. Scott said that the brooding panorama of the city that opens the film with its terrifying 700-storey office blocks set against a backdrop of fiery chimneys belching smoke in a sky perpetually darkened by acid rain, was rooted as much in Los Angeles as it was in the fiery steelworks and other fierce industrial plants he knew as a child in Teesside, in the North East of England.

As for the scenes in brooding cafes down on the city's streets, Scott says that he much influenced by Edward Hopper's painting "Nighthawks" (1942); "I was constantly waving a reproduction of this painting under the noses of the production team to illustrate the look and mood I was after." Hopper was a hugely popular American artist

and was also influenced by the cinema. Whatever the mix and brew of visual ideas, Scott and his team created a vision of a truly haunting city, cleverly realized, beautifully lit and impossible to forget.

There are so many imaginary buildings that stir or tease the imagination. Generations of children will recall designs for exciting buildings, from the funny Hanna-Barbera television cartoon show *The Jetsons*, to the serious design work in the Dan Dare strip in the English comic, the *Eagle*, drawn by Frank Hampson, Don Harley, Frank Bellamy and Keith Watson, all of whom seemed to have had a fascination with modern and futuristic architecture. Equally, there are the exquisitely romantic houses and buildings evoked in the water-colours of Beatrix Potter, or the beautifully drawn and often highly accurate buildings and interiors depicted in Herge's *Tintin* comic books. The list is endless and I hope you will be encouraged to sit down and make up your own; you might be awake all night trying to remember just where you imagined you saw that dream building – in a comic, a book, a film, a novel, or perhaps somewhere in the depths of your own imagination.

Above top A police craft races through a deeply polluted sky above the 700-storey skyscrapers of the Los Angeles of the future created for Ridley Scott's haunting film *Blade Runner*. Scott was clearly making visual references to Lang's *Metropolis*; these buildings are Towers of Babel, too.

Above A terrifying cityscape, all mysterious flames, furnaces, smog, spotlights and massive buildings rising above urban blight. The disturbing architecture, streets and interiors brought to brooding, half-lit life in *Blade Runner* remain a cinematic triumph over a quarter of a century on from the film's release.

8 SELF-DESTRUCTION

Fonthill Abbey collapsed for the final time on December 21, 1825. John Farquhar, an ammunitions dealer, who had paid £330,000 for the vast and dreamy Gothic house just two years earlier, decided that enough was enough. He swept away 90 per cent of the ruins, sold up and moved away. As for the man who had built the house in the first place, William Beckford [1760–1844], he had wisely got rid of this awe-inspiring folly and built an impressive, if less ambitious tower near Bath, which still stands today.

Beckford's dream house was an extraordinary labour of wealthy eccentricity. Started in 1796 and more or less completed in 1813, it was far too big and flimsy for its own good. The tower collapsed early on and was rebuilt, and Beckford spent a fortune patching up the building during its brief life. When I say a fortune, I mean it. Beckford himself said Fonthill Abbey had cost him £30,000 a year to run. Even for a man who had inherited what was rumoured to be a million pounds shortly before his 11th birthday, this was only just affordable. His income from the immense legacy his father left him from the prodigious economic spoils garnered from sugar plantations in the West Indies, was about £70,000 a year. He was possibly Britain's richest man at the time, but he had also spent more than anyone else in the country on his greatest indulgence: architecture.

Though lampooned at the time, how thrilling the long-lost Fonthill Abbey must have been for anyone who managed to see it. Although this was one of the biggest of all English country houses, crowned with a 300-foot (91-metre) tower, it was hidden behind miles of 12-foot (3.65-metre) high walls near Hindon in the depths of rural Wiltshire. For all its architectural bombast, Fonthill Abbey remained something of a secret until Beckford sold up and left in 1823.

His timing had been good. The house was too large and the tower was a problem. Built of cheap stone and cement, it rose from a high vaulted crossing, much like the tower of nearby Salisbury Cathedral, and was so designed because Beckford wanted to be able to see from one end of the house to the other – all 318 feet (93 metres) of it – without the base of the tower interrupting his view. This great vista ended in an oratory devoted to St Anthony, Beckford's patron saint. From the main entrance, the oratory could be seen at the far end of the great corridor, which was lit by just 24 candles, while Beckford's prized alabaster statue of his saint was set around with three-dozen lit tapers. This spectacular and gloriously gloomy interior vista meant that the tower was balanced rather precariously above the rest of the house. It was hardly surprising that it soon collapsed. Beckford, a complete aesthete, might have been pleased to learn that the tower's going was, in its own particular way, rather delightful. An eyewitness recalled:

"The manner of it falling was very beautiful, it first sank perpendicularly, and slowly, then burst and spread out over the roofs adjoining on every side."

Beckford said that he was only sorry he could not see it fall for himself.

Opposite St Michael's Gallery, a fan-vaulted Gothic corridor lined with precious books and choice antiques inside Fonthill Abbey, Wiltshire, the magical faux-medieval building designed by James Wyatt for William Beckford. Aquatint by D Wolstenholme Jr, engraved by John Cleghorn, 1823, for a book on the house by John Britton.

Left The decorative design for a room in Fonthill Abbey by the architect John Buonarotti Papworth [1775–1847]. Papworth worked on the interiors of a number of exotic contemporary buildings including the long-lost Egyptian Halls, Piccadilly, London. Beckford, meanwhile, could afford whatever special effects he desired.

Fonthill Abbey was designed by James Wyatt (p.61), the prolific and fashionable society architect. It was built a few hundred yards away from Fonthill Splendens, the Palladian house Beckford's father had built after a fire had destroyed the Elizabethan house that had stood on the site in 1755. In 1807 Beckford Jr demolished Fonthill Splendens. The new house was rushed up with as many as 500 labourers working around the clock at any one time. Beckford wanted to produce in a matter of a few years what had taken the medieval cathedral builders decades to achieve.

The result was certainly imposing. Four tall, long wings spread out in a cruciform plan from the central tower. The rooms were gained through 37-foot (11-metre) high doors opened and closed by a dwarf to make them seem even bigger, an ambitious stair and a corridor that ran the length of the main entrance axis. The grand rooms were filled with Beckford's collection of some 20,000 books and his equally demanding cache of antiques. Of the paintings that hung on the Abbey walls, including works by Raphael, Titian, Rembrandt, Rubens, Canaletto and Velasquez, no fewer than 20 hang in the National Gallery in London today.

Yet for all its grandeur, its great kitchen and its ample accommodation, Beckford lived here more or less as a recluse. He had been at the centre of a homosexual scandal (theoretically, homosexuality was a capital crime at the time), and had spent much time travelling abroad to escape attention as well as to enjoy the pleasures and treasures of the wider world. He had been married briefly to Lady Margaret Gordon with whom he had two daughters, but she died in childbirth, a tragic event that only encouraged Beckford to travel all the more.

Lord Nelson and the Hamiltons came for Christmas Day, 1800, and the event was written up in some detail in the April 1801 issue of *The Gentleman's Magazine*. Clearly, Beckford's hospitality was as lavish and as imaginative, as it was rare. The house was dramatically lit for the occasion and the entrance lobby and stairway lined with soldiers.

"From thence they were received into the great saloon called the Cardinal's Parlour, furnished with rich tapestries, long curtains of purple damask before the arched windows, ebony tables and chairs studded with ivory, of various but antique fashion; the whole room in the noblest style of monastic ornament, and illuminated by lights on silver sconces."

Dinner was served at once in the company of fellow guests including Wyatt and leading literary figures of the day, at a table measuring nearly 50 feet (15 metres) long in front of a blazing fire. After dinner, the party moved upstairs, "the staircase… lighted by certain mysterious living figures at different intervals, dressed in hooded gowns, and standing with large wax-torches in their hands", and so into the Library, "which when finished will be 270-feet long". Solemn Catholic music played from hidden sources while "a collation was presented… consisting of various sorts of confectionery served in gold baskets, with spiced wines, & etc."

Lady Hamilton, who must have made a quick change, appeared "in the character of Agrippina, bearing the ashes of Germanicus in a golden urn", and struck various dramatic attitudes, before the entertainment ended and the coaches left. The correspondent of *The Gentleman's Magazine* concluded:

Above A view of Fonthill Abbey from the south west, drawn by J Rutter and engraved by T Higham, 1823. It seems astonishing that the house really looked like this, but it did. Often mocked at the time, it would be a national treasure today.

"On leaving this strange nocturnal scene of vast buildings and extensive forest, now rendered dimly and partially visible by the declining light of lamps and torches, and the twinkling of a few scattered stars in a clouded sky, the company seemed, as soon as they had passed the sacred boundary of the great wall, as if waking from a dream, or just freed from the influence of some magic spell."

Fonthill Abbey was all but a dream; it came and went so quickly, but still haunts our collective imagination – if only we could have been invited to Christmas dinner in this make-believe Georgian abbey.

Some writers have suggested that Fonthill Abbey was populated by a harem of young boys for Beckford's delight. I have no idea whether this is true, but I do know that the house was surrounded and even bedevilled by gossip and rumours. A coach and horses, it was said, could be driven up to the top of the tower.

What survives of this private estate today? A mile-long (1.5-kilometre) avenue leading to a rather nice surprise: a section of the Abbey's north wing in a good state of repair. This comprises a 76-foot (23-metre) Gothic tower, a sanctuary, an oratory, a suite of rooms and a long, single-storey kitchen wing. Sadly, there are no signs of decoration and the buildings are used to store agricultural equipment. Beckford's picturesque landscape remains, although much is in a state of what the great writer, traveller, politician and collector, might have enjoyed calling "pleasing decay". It's certainly rather Gothic, in a Hammer House of Horror style.

The contents of the house, rivalling those of the world's great museums, were partly sold off when Beckford abandoned Fonthill. The brilliant essayist William Hazlitt [1778–1830] went to have a look at the sale. Of his visit, he wrote:

Left A cross-sectional drawing of Fonthill Abbey from 1823, showing the extreme height and the construction of the central tower. Much of the space inside the house was given over to improbably long corridors leading the eye along quaint and mysterious vistas to chapels and other faux-religious spaces.

"Fonthill Abbey, after being enveloped in impenetrable mystery for a length of years, has been unexpectedly thrown open to the vulgar gaze, and has lost none of its reputation for magnificence – though, perhaps, its visionary glory, its classic renown, have vanished from the public mind for ever. It is, in a word, a desert of magnificence, a glittering waste of laborious idleness, a cathedral turned into a toy-shop, an immense Museum of all that is most curious and costly, and, at the same time, most worthless, in the productions of art and nature. Ships of pearl and seas of amber are scarce a fable here – a nautilus's shell surmounted with a gilt triumph of Neptune – tables of agate, cabinets of ebony, and precious stones, painted windows 'shedding a gaudy, crimson light,' satin borders, marble floors, and lamps of solid gold – Chinese pagodas and Persian tapestry - all the splendour of Solomon's Temple is displayed to the view – in miniature whatever is far-fetched and dear-bought, rich in the materials, or rare and difficult in the workmanship – but scarce one genuine work of art, one solid proof of taste, one lofty relic of sentiment or imagination!

The difficult, the unattainable, the exclusive, are to be found here in profusion, in perfection, all else is wanting, or is brought in merely as a foil or as a stop-gap.

In this respect the collection is as satisfactory as it is unique. The specimens exhibited are the best, the most highly finished, the most costly and curious, of that kind of ostentatious magnificence which is calculated to gratify the sense of property in the owner, and to excite the wondering curiosity of the stranger, who is permitted to see or (as a choice privilege and favour) even to touch baubles so dazzling and of such exquisite nicety of execution; and which, if broken or defaced, it would be next to impossible to replace. Mr. Beckford has undoubtedly shown himself an industrious bijoutier, a prodigious virtuoso, an accomplished patron of unproductive labour, an enthusiastic collector of expensive trifles – the only proof of taste (to our thinking) he has shown in this collection is his getting rid of it."

Even then, Hazlitt rather enjoyed his trip to Fonthill; it must have been a dazzling treasure chest as well as a breathtaking building. However, several basic flaws with Fonthill Abbey ultimately caused this hasty, ambitious pile to fall. The fashionable word today for Beckford's overweaning ambition and folly is "hubris". This is a condition that undermined reckless politicians as well as ambitious architects, patrons and builders for thousands of years. Beckford wanted to build as high as the medieval cathedral masons had, but in a dangerous rush. And although we like to think of medieval cathedrals as some of the greatest and most flawless of all buildings – which to an extent they are – they also suffered from the fateful flaw of hubris.

Above The daringly high choir of Beauvais Cathedral. In fact, the choir is the Cathedral as the rest of the church was either never built, or else collapsed under the strain of its vaulting ambition. This remnant, propped up today, is Gothic design taken to an exquisite extreme.

Beauvais Cathedral remains one of the most spectacular examples of medieval architectural arrogance. Commissioned in 1225 by Bishop Miles of Nanteuil, this was supposed to be a symbol of French national unity, although client, architects and masons were all clearly determined to build the tallest cathedral in Europe. What they achieved was truly spectacular, a choir soaring into the sky, its stone vaults supported by the slenderest flying buttresses. Completed in 1272, the choir collapsed in high winds just 12 years later. Nevertheless, Miles' successors, Bishops Robert of Cressonsac and William of Grez, pursued this highly ambitious project. Stronger buttresses allowed the choir to stand, as it does, more or less, today.

The choir has been described as "the Parthenon of French Gothic", implying that it is as perfect as that defining Greek Temple from the Golden Age of Athens. Look up at those vaults; they appear to hover above the choir at the astonishing height of 157$\frac{1}{2}$ feet (48 metres). How do they stand up? The answer is, with some difficulty and with the support of faith as much as stones. Because of the collapse of 1284 and other social and economic factors, including the spread of the Black Death, work on Beauvais slowed down. Although transepts were built, a sky-scraping central tower collapsed in 1573 – it was just nine years old – and the nave was never built. What you see today is a mere fragment of what was to have been the greatest Gothic cathedral of all. But without a nave to shore them up, the transepts have long begun to wobble and these are currently held in place by a number of unsightly wooden trusses. If the transepts were to move much more than they already have, the eye-boggling choir might begin to collapse as it did over than 700 years ago. Every time I have gone to see Beauvais – one of the most spectacular and memorable of all architectural experiences – I fear that it may be my last because the building might yet keel over, as it has before.

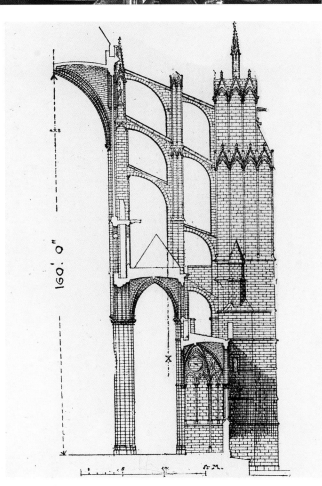

Above A nineteenth-century drawing explaining the system of flying buttresses used in the construction of Beauvais Cathedral. This was a clever way of spreading the weight of the stone vaults across the widest possible area. Beauvais, though, was stretched to limits beyond the boundaries of medieval ingenuity.

Above The choir of Beauvais Cathdedral in all its sublime Gothic glory. The aim had been not just to create a building of unrivalled height, but a building that would appear to be more glass than stone, a temple of coloured light and music, echoing the wonders of Heaven.

This has happened to a number of historic buildings we take for granted. I remember being surprised to learn that the famous campanile of St Mark's Cathedral in Venice is a reproduction and little more than 100 years old. What happened? In the morning of July 14, 1902, the bell tower imploded. It was an extraordinary event for those who witnessed it; one moment the campanile was there, the next it was nothing more than a huge pile of brick and marble rubble. It fell so neatly that the rubble was confined to a surprisingly small area of Piazza San Marco and the only casualty was the caretaker's cat. A large crack had appeared in the tower over the previous fortnight, but by the time anyone thought of doing anything about this, the bell tower had fallen.

A decision was made almost immediately to rebuild the campanile exactly as it had been. It was, after all, the symbol of Venice in much the same way as the Eiffel Tower has been of Paris since 1889; it was too important to lose. This time, though, the tall brick shaft of the 315-foot (96-metre) tower was reinforced with steel. The original tower, completed in 1513, had been designed by Giorgio Spavento and Bartolomeo Bon [d.1464]. It rose from a base that had been a barracks for soldiers guarding the Doge's Palace; this was rebuilt in a Renaissance style by Jacopo Sansovino [1486–1570] in 1549 and remodelled in 1663. The tower itself had been rocked by tremors and damaged by fire several times over the centuries, but Venetians must have regarded it as a lofty and immutable symbol of their undoubted imperial might. When it collapsed Venice was reduced to what it remains today, a compulsive tourist destination and the most subtle of architectural theme parks.

Above Venetians turn out to gawp at the rubble that just a few hours earlier had been the campanile of St Mark's. The tower imploded and its stones fell into a remarkably tidy heap, sparing Piazza San Marco and the basilica itself. Rarely has a building collapsed so politely.

Right The cover of the July 27, 1902 edition of La Domenica del Corriere telling the story of the sudden collapse of the campanile.

Opposite Can you spot the cracks? The original campanile of St Mark's not long before its fall in July 1902. The world famous piazza seems strangely empty to our eyes. Perhaps this was just as well; when it came tumbling down no one was hurt.

LA DOMENICA DEL CORRIERE

SI PUBBLICA A MILANO OGNI DOMENICA
Dono agli Abbonati del " Corriere della Sera,,
27 Luglio 1902

CIO' CHE È RIMASTO DEL CAMPANILE DI SAN MARCO, A VENEZIA, DOPO IL CROLLO AVVENUTO IL 14 CORRENTE.

While it might be tempting to think that modern buildings, conditioned by any number of safety regulations, must be more reliable structures than their predecessors, there is no guarantee that even the most carefully designed might not suddenly collapse. On July 17, 1981, two of the three overhead concrete walkways crossing the airy atrium lobby of the Hyatt Regency Hotel in Kansas City, Missouri, came tumbling down, killing 114 people and injuring 200. As fate would have it, the lobby was crowded that evening as the glamorous new 40-storey hotel, opened the year before, was hosting a popular dance contest. The fourth level walkway, suspended by steel tie-rods, gave way under the weight of the crowd looking over its parapets down to the dance floor. Mistakes made in the engineering and construction of the walkway meant that it had barely been able to support itself, much less a crowd of people. It crashed onto the walkway directly below it, bringing both down onto the lobby floor. The hotel had been the tallest building in Missouri and, rather spookily, it seemed as if fate had taken against such soaring ambition. Several months before the hotel opened, a 2,700-square foot (250-square metre) section of the atrium ceiling had collapsed in October 1979. The architects – Edward Larrable Barnes [1915–2004] and PBNDML Associates – were found innocent of any professional misconduct or failure, and the blame was placed firmly on the structural engineers, Jack D Gillum and Associates. The hotel was reopened in October 1981; a terrace, replacing the three walkways, was supported on 10 concrete columns sunk two storeys down into the rock-bed below. No one was taking any chances.

Above left The man on the left is checking out. Who could blame him? This is the lobby of the Hyatt Regency Hotel, Kansas City, photographed on July 19, 1981, two days after two high-level concrete catwalks came crashing down, killing 114 people and injuring 200.

Left This is the same lobby on September 30, 1981. Debris was cleared and the Hyatt Regency was back in full swing within weeks of the tragic events of July. The ultra-modern design of the original space was toned down. It has been safe ever since.

Someone certainly took chances with the design of the ill-fated Sampoong department store in downtown Seoul. Originally commissioned as a four-storey shop, with construction work starting in 1987, the building was converted into a department store before its completion in 1989. The steelwork employed was flimsy from the outset, but the strength of the completed building was hugely compromised during construction when a central atrium with escalators was created by the simple expedient of cutting through its structural frame. To add to the problem, a fifth floor set on a heavy concrete raft was added to the store in 1990 together with a weighty air-conditioning plant on the roof. Something had to give… and it did.

On the evening of June 29, 1995, when the popular store was as busy as ever, huge cracks appeared as the top floor began to buckle. Within an hour, virtually the entire building imploded, killing 501 people. The last survivor, a 19-year old man, was pulled from the tangled steel wreckage 16 days later. The fate of the Sampoong store was both a tragedy and a national scandal. The ensuing court case uncovered a web of corruption, lax building practices, unreliable foundations and a callous attitude to those who used the building. It was as if the script of the Hollywood shocker *The Towering Inferno* (John Guillermin, 1974) had been for real. Engineers calculated that the building needed to have been twice as strong as it was to fully support itself. The wonder of it was that it had lasted as long as five years. The building's chairman and the man who had commissioned it, Lee Joon, was sentenced to over 10 years in prison.

Left Rescue workers comb the ruins of the Sampoong department store, Seoul, shortly after it collapsed, with terrible consequences, on June 29, 1995. The building had been overstretched during an ill-conceived attempt to extend it; more than 500 shoppers lost their lives as a result.

Above The Sampoong department store immediately after its spectacular collapse. This was not a terrorist attack, as it had at first seemed to onlookers. Customers had continued to shop even as the building began to crack under the strain of its fundamental structural weakness.

TAY BRIDGE, FROM N

Left This is the brand new and astonishingly spindly looking Tay Bridge, Dundee, built to the designs of Thomas Bouch in 1878. Hindsight tells us just how weak, and poorly made, this bridge was. Even so, surely any self-respecting Victorian engineer might have questioned its design.

Weak structures have long been a cause of sudden structural collapse. And when ambitious design and inadequate structure combine, the results are almost inevitably catastrophic. Bridges are daring things by their very nature: crossing ravines, valleys and rivers and subject to the brute force of nature. On windy days, many bridges worldwide are closed as a safety precaution, but not the Tay Railway Bridge, Dundee, on the stormy night of December 28, 1879. A northbound, six-coach express from Edinburgh set out across the two-mile bridge at 7.15pm in the teeth of a force 10 or 11 gale. As it steamed cautiously over the high central section of the bridge, raised so that ships could pass beneath it, the ironwork gave way and the train fell into the river below, with the loss of 75 lives and the collapse of the reputation of Sir Thomas Bouch [1822–80], the engineer responsible for the bridge's inadequate design.

Seven years in the making, the spindly looking Tay Bridge was the longest in the world when it opened to great acclaim in 1878.

Queen Victoria rode across it and knighted the engineer, yet it was only to stand for some 18 months. The inspectors found the bridge had been "poorly designed, poorly built and poorly maintained". It had. The central section was too high and flimsy. Foundry work for the wrought and cast iron components had been well below standard. The lattice grids along the length of the bridge were improperly fixed. The iron columns the bridge stood on were too narrow. Bouch had failed to include calculations for wind resistance in his design despite the savage gales that roar along the Tay all year round.

Even before the disaster, there had been concerns about the safety of the bridge. Its maintenance inspector, Henry Noble, said that he had heard wrought-iron tie-bars "chattering" in the wind, and with the "hammer blows" of passing locomotives and trains shortly after the royal opening. Painters saw the central section swaying and passengers complained of an uncomfortable ride across the bridge. A

Above A rescue team, complete with faithful collie dog, goes into action looking for survivors from the North British Railway express that fell from the Tay Bridge on the howling evening of December 28, 1879. The scene is captured in an engraving by W H Overend for the *Illustrated London News*, January 10, 1880.

OLD TAY BRIDGE DISASTER, FALLEN GIRDERS.

01864

Above Calm after the storm. Slimline steel girders from the central section of the Tay Bridge seen lying in the Scottish firth in January 1880. The bridge had been an ambitious two miles long, but had never been tested for the effect of powerful side winds.

speed limit of 25mph was imposed, but it was not enough to prevent the inevitable collapse. The poet William McGonagall recorded the event in his famous, and wonderfully funny, "Tay Bridge Disaster":

"Beautiful Railway Bridge of the Silv'ry Tay,
Alas! I am very sorry to say
That ninety lives have been taken away
On the last Sabbath Day of 1879,
Which will be remember'd for a very long time."

Sir Thomas retired immediately after the inquiry that found him responsible for the bridge's failure; he died very shortly after the inquiry was wound up. His commission to build a new and even more ambitious suspension bridge across the Firth of Forth was cancelled, although the foundation stone had been laid. The work was handed

over to Sir Benjamin Baker and Sir John Fowler who shaped the peerless and much-admired Forth Railway Bridge, completed in 1890, that we know and hold dear today. Many of the bodies of the passengers who died in the accident were never recovered, although the train's locomotive – No 79, a North British Railway Wheatley 4-4-0 – was; it was put back into service and ran until 1919, when it was still known by Scottish enginemen as "the diver".

As you cross today's Tay Bridge [William Henry Barlow and William Arroll, 1883–87], you can still see the stumps of the iron pillars that once failed to support the original bridge. In his inimitable manner, William McGonagall recommended buttresses to support the new bridge:

"For the stronger we our houses do build
The less chance we have of being killed."

Souvenir of
TACOMA NARROWS BRIDGE

Tacoma, Washington

OCTOBER FOURTEENTH *1950* **FIFTY CENTS**

Opposite Calm before the storm. This is a souvenir publication celebrating the opening of the Tacoma Narrows Bridge, Washington in July 1940. Someone, though, had got their calculations wrong and this very modern looking, and very thin, bridge was to be very short-lived indeed.

Left The Tacoma Narrows Bridge begins to swing, before rocking and rolling its way to self-destruction. This extraordinary event was captured on film on November 7, 1940. This all but incredible amateur movie must have been studied exhaustively by structural engineers around the world ever since.

Bottom left The roadway of the Tacoma Narrows Bridge finally gives way and plunges into Puget Sound below. The film taken of the bridge was a structural "*dance macabre*". Suspension bridges continue to sway and, today, are very often closed when winds get up to storm force.

No one could argue with that, but it didn't stop bridge-builders continuing to dream up ways of creating elegant lightweight bridges that would push structural design to new limits in the twentieth century. One of the lightest was the narrow suspension bridge spanning the Tacoma Narrows across Puget Sound in Tacoma, Washington State. This short-lived bridge became famous thanks to the fact that its sensational collapse on November 7, 1940, was caught on film. The bridge opened to great acclaim on July 1, 1940, to designs modified by Leon Moisseiff [1872–1943], engineer of San Francisco's Golden Gate Bridge. From the start, the bridge bucked and swayed in strong winds; it was nicknamed "Gallopin' Gertie" by locals brave enough to cross her. The bridge finally shook itself to pieces. One driver who cheated death that November day, although he lost his dog, Tubby, was Leonard Coatsworth, who recalled:

"Just as I drove past the towers, the bridge began to sway violently from side to side. Before I realised it, the tilt became so violent that I lost control of the car…. I jammed on the brakes and got out, only to be thrown onto my face against the curb…. Around me I could hear concrete cracking…. The car itself began to slide from side to side of the roadway.

On hands and knees most of the time, I crawled 500 yards or more to the towers …. My breath was coming in gasps; my knees were raw and bleeding, my hands bruised and swollen from gripping the concrete curb…. Toward the last, I risked rising to my feet and running a few yards at a time…. Safely back at the toll plaza, I saw the bridge in its final collapse and saw my car plunge into the Narrows."

Moisseiff was ruined by the incident and died of a heart attack not long afterwards. The story of the bridge is still told as one of arrogant design. As for the Tacoma Narrows, Route 16 crosses it today across twin suspension bridges, one built in 1950 and another in 2007, which sway as little as necessary when the wind whips down Puget Sound.

The wind was barely blowing on September 26, 1996, when the Koror-Babeldaob road bridge in Palau, an island republic in the Pacific Ocean, collapsed killing two and injuring four people. The weather was calm and there was virtually no traffic passing across the 1,265-foot (385.6-metre) long bridge when it collapsed out of the blue. It had certainly looked sturdy enough when it opened in 1977. The pre-stressed concrete box-girder design was by Dyckerhoff and Widman AG, while the contractor was Socio Construction. The one thing that might have worried the island authorities was the fact that the contractors had won the bid by promising to build the bridge at half the cost of its rivals. Repairs needed to be carried out early on and local people took to driving slowly across the bridge with their car windows open in case they need to bail out quickly.

It's not clear exactly what went wrong, but the bridge was cheaply built and a major repair of its tarmac carriageway carried out in 1995 seems to have weakened it. Such disasters, as this example proves, can happen even in the most remote corners of the world where the weather is fine and typhoons rare. The Koror-Babeldaob bridge was replaced by a Japanese design in 2002.

Above The Koror-Babeldaob Bridge, Palau, when newly opened in 1977. The bridge looked strong, yet appearances were clearly deceptive. Local people had their suspicions from the beginning and many were too scared to drive across it. Sadly, their intuition proved to be right.

Right The remains of the original Koror-Babeldaob Bridge seen from its Japanese designed and built replacement, opened in 2002. The fundamental problem with the first bridge was that it had been built far too cheaply. Cost cutting in architecture and structural engineering has never been wise.

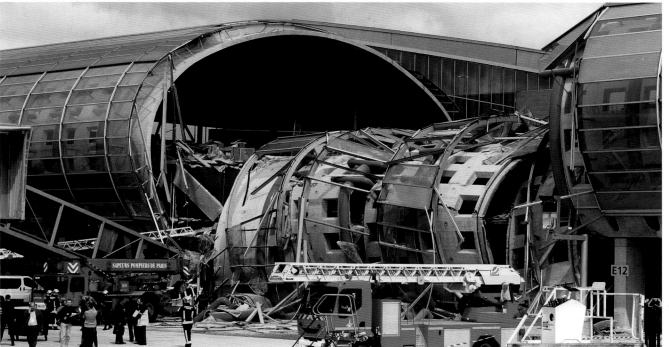

Above The daring, Space Age-style design of the latest section of Charles de Gaulle Airport, Terminal 2E, Paris. From the outset, the airport was meant to represent the very latest in optimistic, government-directed French "*technocratie*". Here, though, the future was to look rather bleak.

Left Policemen spotted cracks in the concrete of the ceiling structure of Terminal 2E at Charles de Gaulle airport on May 23, 2004, but by the time they had alerted colleagues in the emergency services, an entire section of one of the new walkways came crashing down.

The sudden implosion of daring buildings, meanwhile, continues to be a sorry feature of world news. On May 23, 2004, the roof of the departure lounge of the brand new Terminal 2E at Charles de Gaulle airport collapsed, trapping passengers waiting for flights and killing five people. In France, a country that prides itself on its modern technocratic tradition and its imaginative engineering, this came as a tremendous blow. The design of the 2,100-foot (640-metre) long, 100-foot (30-metre) wide terminal was certainly daring. To ensure that the interior was entirely free of columns, its architect, Paul Andreu [b.1938] designed it in the form of a giant extruded tunnel built of a concrete shell and held together, section by section, with interlocking steel hoops and carbon-fibre reinforcements.

Andreu's adventurous design was not blamed for the accident. An inquiry found that costs had been cut and the construction work had been handed out to a number of sub-contractors who were not necessarily professionally in tune with one another. To try to cut costs on such a project was extremely stupid, but as what used to be in the public realm in so many countries, is today run by accountants, cheap means good, until cheap spells disaster. The rebuilt terminal, due to be reopened in 2008, is a far more conventional steel and glass design. France did not want a twenty-first century Beauvais on its hands.

As someone who cares greatly about architecture, I think it is fitting to relate the tale of my own near destruction by an historic building. This took place in June 1993 when I was in Havana. I was going to visit an early nineteenth-century merchant's house in Plaza Vieja with an architect from the National Centre for Conservation, Restoration, and Museum Science (CENCRM), when I stopped to take a photograph of the building. I pressed the shutter and the building fell down. The episode might have been from a latter-day Buster Keaton film, but it was quite real. Luckily no one was hurt. The building, eaten away by tropical humidity and ravenous termites, imploded. No one was inside, although I would have been if I had not stopped to take that photograph. Perhaps this might have been an appropriate end – like the comedian Tommy Cooper falling dead on stage with the sound of the audience's laughter in his ears – but I'm glad to still be here and pleased to say that Plaza Vieja, including that merchant's house, has since been restored.

Right An early nineteenth-century merchant's house in Plaza Vieja, Havana, in June 1993, snapped seconds after it collapsed. The incident was partly instrumental in the launch of a major Cuban government initiative to extend its programme of urban restoration.

9 LEFT ON THE DRAWING BOARD

A building a mile high – now, that was ambitious. Not surprisingly, Frank Lloyd Wright [1867–1959], the brilliant and theatrically egotistical American architect never did find a client to go along with his plans for The Illinois, a 528-storey, 5,280-foot (1,690-metre) high skyscraper which he imagined soaring over Chicago, the state capital of Illinois.

Wright held a press conference on October 16, 1956, to show off his outlandish design. The vertiginous drawings he made of the cloud-piercing building were thrilling, beautiful and rather wistful. An architect with a poet's mind, Wright told the assembled members of the American press that the tapering tower would be like a mighty sword driven into the ground; for all its prodigious height, it would be rooted as firmly as the sword in the stone of the Arthurian romance. But it would have taken the strength of more than a dozen young King Arthurs to pull this steel sword from its Illinois rock-bed.

Wright was 89 when he unveiled this startling proposal; he was a man of seemingly infinite energy who thrived on imaginative design and controversy. His extraordinary Solomon R Guggenheim Museum was already under construction in New York, a building that was to be visited more over the ensuing decades for its provocative architecture than for the art shows displayed inside it. The Guggenheim is an awkward building for art exhibitions as Wright's design forces visitors to look at paintings while standing on the great ramp that spirals from top to bottom of the building's central courtyard; this means that you have to stand at an angle. No matter; what everyone looks at is the ramp and the view above and below of the interior of the building itself. Nor has the Guggenheim been a cheap building to look after; it has just undergone a second major restoration to stop its seamless, sprayed concrete walls from cracking apart.

Wright was a brilliant designer, but sometimes it was hard not to get the feeling that he didn't much care how practical his buildings were for day-to-day use. The Illinois, sadly, would have been very impractical indeed. While the construction of such a tall building was not beyond the bounds of what was possible at the time, the problem of getting people in and out and up and down the tower was almost insurmountable. The steel structure would have taken the form of a giant tripod and been fairly stable, but as visitors to the tops of skyscrapers know, either to their delight or concern, these buildings do sway in the wind. I was intrigued to see my dry martini, served in the cocktail bar at the top of Chicago's John Hancock Tower [SOM, architects, and Fazlur Kahn, engineer, 1969], swish gently from side to side of the glass as the building rode out a winter storm. The John Hancock Tower is just 1,127 feet (344 metres) tall, less than a quarter of the height Wright proposed for The Illinois. A giant pendulum installed inside the core of the tower would have been necessary to keep its swaying in check, but although such devices have been fitted in skyscrapers since the 1980s, this technology was unavailable to Wright.

Right A very tall story indeed. Frank Lloyd Wright addresses journalists at a press conference on October 16, 1956 to announce his design for a mile-high skyscraper – The Illinois – to be built, some day in the far off future, in Chicago.

Above Frank Lloyd Wright was a monumentally talented and prolific architect who was also a great and often poetic dreamer. Here, like some medieval herald, he holds a scroll-like drawing for The Illinois as if presenting it to some king of infinite space.

Right Presentation drawing, from 1956, of The Illinois, four times as high as the Empire State Building. The design was undeniably elegant and, in theory, there was no reason why it could not have been built. Wright was always interested in pushing boundaries, and his clients.

The problem of stability aside, how would the many thousands of people who might have lived and worked in The Illinois have travelled up and down inside the building? Wright calculated that The Illinois needed 76 elevators. If these were to have been placed inside the tower, they would have taken up the entire space; Wright suggested, although I have never seen a drawing to show this, five-storey elevators climbing up and down the outside of the building. Fascinating, but what about the view out from the office floors?

These concerns, though, are mere quibbles. I am sure that Wright never expected The Illinois to be built. It was a brilliant provocation from an architectural showman who kept pulling marvels out of his hat until the day he died. The Illinois was a part of the age-old quest to build, as with the Tower of the Babel, as high as technically possible, to reach for the sky and beyond to the heavens. Building so high might seem a little old-fashioned, environmentally unsound and plain mad in the early twenty-first century and yet The Illinois retains the power to excite and delight more than half a century on from Wright's press conference. It is one of those many buildings that architects dream up every so often to stir us up.

What such designs tend to have in common is their improbable scale – either enormously large or extremely tall. This may be a reflection of the ego of their designers, but more often, of their insanely ambitious clients. Giant buildings have existed from the outset; if you have ever seen the Great Pyramid of Cheops at Giza, you will know just how big ancient buildings could be; it was originally 481 feet (146 metres) tall and completed more than 4,500 years ago.

For some politicians, scale is everything and no politician dreamed of bigger buildings or came closer to realizing them than Adolf Hitler [1889–1945]. Hitler had grown up on the Austrian-German borders and rose to power in Munich, the beautiful Bavarian city he came to love. When the Nazi party was elected into power in 1933, Hitler was, by the nature of German politics, forced to spend much time in Berlin. He never liked the city. It was far too liberal, generally lax and dirty for the fastidious Chancellor. Hitler devoted an inordinate amount of time in the late 1930s to working on plans for a completely remodelled Berlin. Once Germany had won the Second World War, by 1945 according to Hitler's own plans, the centre of the city would be transformed into a heroic new capital of "Greater Germany" built on a Herculean scale, to be known as Germania. Its architect, and planner, was the young and intensely ambitious architect, Albert Speer [1905–81].

The plan, created in a grand model built in 1938–39, was centred on an imperious three-mile long avenue running north to south through the heart of Berlin. It was to have been topped and tailed by two grand railway stations. In between, there were to have been enormous stripped-classical palaces, embassies, ministries and the headquarters of the armed forces, along with giant monuments, hotels, cinemas and apartment blocks for the party faithful. Speer calculated that 80,000 homes would have to be demolished to make way for Germania. With the abundance of slave labour Germany would have access to by 1945, much of the work was planned to be complete by 1950.

Of all the massive buildings shown in the Speer model, none came close to the sheer size of the proposed "Volkshalle", or

Below Albert Speer's 1938 model of Germania, or Berlin as it was to have been rebuilt after the Second World War. This is a detail of the great north-south axis, or avenue, with the Victory Monument in the foreground and the Südbahnhof [south railway station] behind it.

Above A model of the colossal domed Volkshalle, by Albert Speer, 1938. The dome was to have been seventeen times bigger than that of St Peter's, Rome. The Brandenberg Gate – there long before Hitler, and still very much with us – stands proudly, if completely dwarfed, in the foreground.

Opposite Looking along the entire length of the north-south axis planned for Germania, in Albert Speer's model of 1938. Seen here, the axis begins with the Volkshalle and ends up at the Südbahnhof. Note the parade of guns, rather than trees, between the station and the Victory monument.

People's Hall. This improbable assembly hall was to have been 951 feet (290 metres) high. Its ribbed, copper-clad dome crowned by a lantern surmounted by an eagle clutching the world in its talons, would have been by far the biggest the world had ever known. It would have been 17 times the size of the dome of St Peter's in Rome – 700 feet (213 metres) high and 800 feet (244 metres) wide. The design was based on the Roman Pantheon, although blown up to a scale that not even film-makers such as Fritz Lang might have imagined.

Inside, the domed hall was so vast that, as Speer himself came to believe, when filled with an 180,000 capacity audience, hot air rising into the heights of the dome might well have formed clouds. What an appropriately Wagnerian setting this would have been for a victorious Hitler to deliver his ranting speeches to his race of Aryan *übermenschen* (or super humans). The thought is also deliciously funny that if clouds really could have formed inside the dome, the rain falling from them would have made such occasions little more than damp political squibs.

The design of the Volkshalle was worked out in loving detail; the plans, which survived, are complete. Speer had taken up the design from a sketch by Hitler. Speer later recalled that the Führer had been excited by a private visit to the Pantheon in May 1938, but in fact Hitler's

enthusiasm for the building dated back to at least the mid-1920s. As he told Hermann Giesler [1898–1987], another of his pet architects:

"from the time I experienced this building – no description, picture or photograph did it justice… I became interested in its history… for a short while I stood in this space – what majesty! I gazed at the large open oculus and saw the universe and sensed what had given this space the name Pantheon – God and the world are one."

Hitler had certainly read the Pantheon correctly; this was Hadrian's architectural model of the universe, a brilliant conceit and a truly magnificent building. The Volkshalle was to be the architectural embodiment of the Greater German universe, an unavoidable symbol of what Hitler himself saw as the quasi-religious link between his mission, his people and the universal spirit. In an interview with *Playboy* magazine (June 1971), Speer said: "Hitler believed that as centuries passed, his huge domed assembly hall would acquire great holy significance and become a hallowed shrine as important to National Socialism as St Peter's in Rome is to Roman Catholicism. Such cultism was the root of the entire plan." The steel, concrete and stone Volkshalle was to have risen from a giant square granite base, and to be entered beneath a vast portico lined with red granite

columns topped with Egyptian palm-leaf capitals. The auditorium itself comprised three tiers of seating above which a hundred 80-foot (24-metre) marble pillars reached up to support the base of the coffered ceiling, suspended by hidden steel girders. On the north side of the hall, a vast niche, lined with gold mosaic and presided over by a gigantic eagle, was to have contained Hitler's tribunal.

Germania was destined never to come about. By launching Operation Barbarossa, the invasion of the Soviet Union on June 22, 1941, Hitler overstretched the resources of Nazi Germany; the tide of the war slowly began to turn against Germany and the regime was to implode. Does anything survive of Speer and Hitler's plans for Germania? There are drawings and models, a number of Speer-designed lampposts along the *Tiergarten* (there was to have been a grand east-west as well as a north-south avenue) and sections of the underground freeway designed to channel traffic beneath the north-south avenue that would have been busy on many days of the

Nazi calendar, with marches and rallies. Hitler planned to complete Germania, hold an enormous World Fair in Berlin in 1950 and then retire to Linz, his favourite Austrian town, although this was to have been given a monumental make-over, too.

Strangely, Hitler appeared to have no plans to erect a giant statue of himself in Germania, Linz or anywhere else in his ill-fated Reich. That could not be said of his most hated enemies, the Bolsheviks, or the Communist regime led by Joseph Stalin [1879–1953] from the mid-1920s. Stalin had every intention of building on just as madcap a scale as Hitler and the biggest of all the buildings he planned was the Palace of the Soviets. This was to have risen grotesquely from the site of the demolished Cathedral of Christ the Saviour (p.164).

Originally, the plan had been to design a Modern Movement *tour de force*; some of the most adventurous and rigorous Modernists, including Le Corbusier [1887–1965] were invited to submit proposals for this Soviet centrepiece, but Stalin had a change of heart. In the late 1920s he began to speak of Modernism as being un-Russian and that what was needed from then on in all the arts was a new Russian form of cultural expression. In 1932 he issued the decree "On the Reconstruction of Literary and Art Organisations". It was hard to know exactly what this meant for architecture, but anyone who disagreed either in public or private was likely to end up in a Siberian *gulag* (labour camp). In the event, the new style or styles known as Socialist Realism, was an odd marriage of bombastic neoclassicism, art deco and folksy Russian kitsch. As for the Palace of the Soviets, the 272 Modern designs submitted in 1931 were rejected out of hand and replaced by plans for a monumental building developed from an original proposal by Boris Iofan [1891–1976], which was chilling and rather funny at the same time. A colossal stepped tower rising from the base of a Classical temple of sorts was to be topped with an enormous statue of Lenin.

Stalin played a key part in the development of the design. Iofan was teamed up with the neoclassical architects Vladimir Schuko and Vladimir Gelfreik, while the original idea for a statue of a heroic Soviet worker on top of the tower was abandoned. Iofan's proletarian palace was to have been 853 feet (260 metres) high, but this was hardly enough for Stalin who insisted that it should be higher than the Eiffel Tower and the Empire State Building. The height was stretched to 1,316 feet (415 metres). The statue of Lenin alone was to be 328 feet (100 metres) high.

Construction work finally began after the foundations were completed in 1939, but the war intervened and what steelwork had been erected was quickly cut down to be used as defences against the invading German armies rapidly making their way to Moscow. Although the architects continued working on the designs into the 1950s, and much useful development work took place in the fields of structural engineering, mechanical services technology and building materials, it seems Stalin must have lost interest in the project, as no new work was carried out on the ground. Three years after the Soviet dictator's death, his successor, Nikita Khrushchev [1894–1971], First Secretary of the Communist Party, denounced Stalin and his cult of personality. In 1958 the construction site was turned into a public swimming pool and the Cathedral of Christ the Saviour was rebuilt where Stalin's palace of a cowed people was once to have risen above the tallest rooftops of Moscow. This is one architectural project that no one is likely to want to revive.

Left A model of the Palace of Soviets as revised in 1934. Now it appears to have taken the form of a latter day Tower of Babel, and although a touch more graceful than the competition-winning design of 1931, it was still a monstrous conceit.

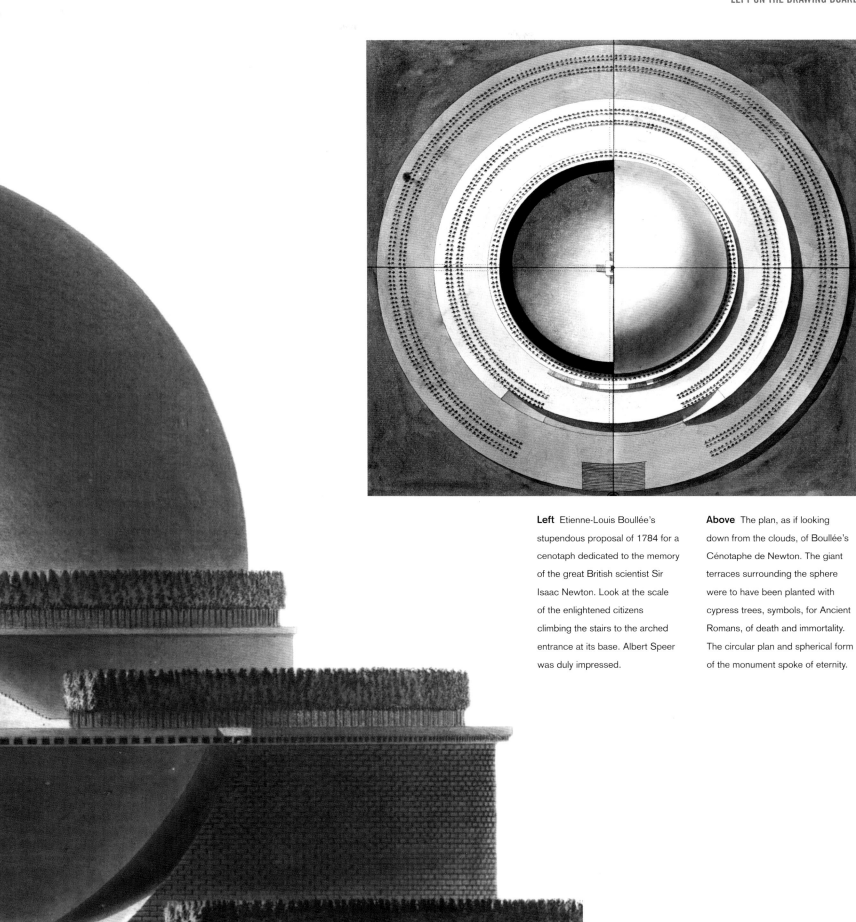

Left Etienne-Louis Boullée's stupendous proposal of 1784 for a cenotaph dedicated to the memory of the great British scientist Sir Isaac Newton. Look at the scale of the enlightened citizens climbing the stairs to the arched entrance at its base. Albert Speer was duly impressed.

Above The plan, as if looking down from the clouds, of Boullée's Cénotaphe de Newton. The giant terraces surrounding the sphere were to have been planted with cypress trees, symbols, for Ancient Romans, of death and immortality. The circular plan and spherical form of the monument spoke of eternity.

Below A cross-section of Boullée's Cénotaphe de Newton as it would have been during the day. Circular holes cut into the enveloping sphere would have sent shafts of sunlight into the core of the building; others would have shone like stars. Newton's tomb rests among a bank of clouds below.

Nazi and Soviet architects alike, with their love of grandiose neoclassical architecture, were greatly indebted either in fact or subliminally to the work of one of the greatest of all architectural fantasists, Etienne-Louis Boullée [1728–99] and particularly by two of his grandest proposals – designs for a Cenotaph for Newton and a new Bibliothèque Nationale (National Library) in Paris. Both projects, realized in exquisite drawings, still have the power to take one's breath away today; the former by its sheer daring, the latter because of its vast scale that, like Speer's Volkshalle, reduces humans to the size of ants. Speer was greatly influenced by Boullée and aimed to outdo the eighteenth-century Frenchman in scale and extravagance.

Boullée himself, a Parisian, was from 1762 the chief architect to Frederick II of Prussia and built little more than a number of fine villas,

most of which have since vanished. It was as a teacher and theorist at the Ecole Nationale des Ponts Chaussées between 1778 and 1788, that he made his greatest and lasting impact. Even so, his brilliant book *Architecture, Essai sur l'Art (Essay on the Art of Architecture)* was published as late as 1953. Boullée's sensational style had many detractors at the time, but the book of his designs for extraordinary public buildings is truly thrilling. He drew brilliantly even if his projects were slightly mad. A firm favourite of neoclassical architects, illustrators and film-makers is his Cenotaph for Newton.

Isaac Newton [1643–1727], the great English scientist, had died some 60 years before Boullée drew up his proposal for a funerary monument to this key figure of the eighteenth-century Enlightenment. To Boullée, Newton was a hero and only the most heroic architecture

could possibly be appropriate to nurture the memory of the great man. The resulting drawings were awe-inspiring. Boullée depicts a huge hollow sphere, 500 feet (150 metres) high, set in a circular base and surrounded with concentric rings of cypress trees. An arched doorway at the base of the structure led to the terrifying interior of the sphere. At night this was to have been lit by a vast lantern hanging in the centre of the space; by day, the sphere would be dark, yet pinpricked with lights representing the night sky. Down below, a sarcophagus would cherish the remains of Newton. All this is pure fantasy, but just look at Boullée's drawings; they are wondrous things. It is said Boullée had wanted to be a painter and became an architect more to please his father than himself.

Below The Cénotaphe de Newton by night. The interior of the sphere was to have been lit by a giant lantern shaped like a model of the solar system. Presumably, this would have vanished into the dark at the centre of the sphere during the day.

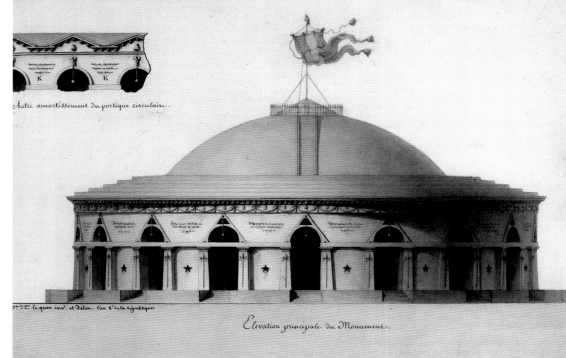

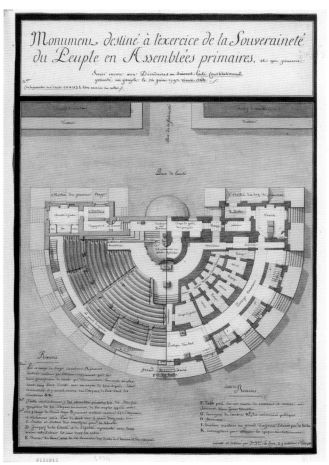

Above A plan of a proposed Monument to the Sovereignty of the People by Jean-Jacques Lequeu, 1793–94. Although designed to appeal to members of the revolutionary French government, this circus-like design (top right) looked too much like a Big Top to win the affections of deadly serious politicians.

Right A section through the Monument to the Sovereignty of the People . This was more like an opera house than a parliamentary chamber. Perhaps if Lequeu had aimed this design at the art world rather than the political lobby, he might have got it built.

Opposite top A dazzling colour-wash drawing by Etienne-Louis Boullée of a proposal for a renovated and expanded Bibliothèque Nationale, Paris, 1785. This is the Reading Room, for which a "Silence" notice would have been essential: if anyone spoke in here, their voice would have boomed like thunder around this massive space.

Opposite below Proposed entrance for the remodelled Bibliothèque Nationale, Paris by Etienne-Louis Boullée, 1785, set between a brace of Atlases supporting the World's knowledge.

The project for the National Library, although more conventional, is equally daunting. Here, Boullée relied on sheer scale for effect, but he also showed that an enormous interior might be built free of columns to support its roof. The most famous of these drawings is the vista showing the length and terrific ceiling of a room designed to "aggrandise" the King's Library, a part of the library complex the architect imagined rebuilding. Boullée's sense of scale and neoclassical drama were taken up in Revolutionary and Napoleonic France, although sadly it was architects like Speer who had the best shot at realizing them and in doing so, unfairly gave a bad name to almost all monumental neoclassical architecture. Such design has its place.

As for Boullée's buildings, you can see an example in *rue de la Ville l'Evêque*, Paris. This is the Hôtel Alexandre [1763–66], a private house designed for the banker Andre-Claude-Nicholas Alexandre. The courtyard garden in front of this handsome townhouse boasts a colossal order of Ionic pilasters and gives just a hint of what Boullée could do to create heroic drama even on a relatively small scale.

One of Boullée's contemporaries was Jean-Jacques Lequeu [1757–1826], whose career as an architect never quite took off, even with designs as evidently intended to appeal to the new Revolutionary French regime as his Monument to the Sovereignty of the People [1793–94]. Perhaps such work was considered too flighty and theatrical. Lequeu devoted much of his time to drawing wildly imaginative buildings that could never be, or else pornography, and ingeniously, a combination of the two. You can find these in the Bibliothèque Nationale de France, or through the Library's website.

Right Mr John Thorp, architectural model maker, sits on the giant wooden model he made of the proposed design for the domed Metropolitan Cathedral of Christ the King, Liverpool, designed by Edwin Lutyens. Only the crypt was built but, happily, the model survives.

Below A rapid pencil sketch by Edwin Lutyens of the west front of his proposed Liverpool Roman Catholic Cathedral. St Paul's Cathedral would have fitted inside this ambitious church with room to spare. The west front was based on the design of a particularly monumental Roman victory arch.

Left A restored model of Lutyens's Liverpool Cathedral: Rome, Byzantium, Romanesque, Renaissance and twentieth-century English Baroque all rolled, with assurance and utter conviction, into one truly magnificent building. There had been nothing quite like it before, and there has certainly been nothing like it since.

Boullée, meanwhile, also made designs for a Metropolitan Cathedral. Inevitably, this was a colossal affair topped with a stupendous dome. This was very much what Sir Edwin Lutyens [1869–1944] was trying to create in Liverpool from the 1930s. Lutyens and his client, the new Roman Catholic archbishop of Liverpool, Richard Downey, aimed to build the biggest cathedral in Britain. Not only would be it much greater in scale than the rival Anglican cathedral, designed by Giles Gilbert Scott [1880–1960], currently rising at the opposite end of Liverpool's Hope Street, but it was to be one of the greatest buildings of all time. Lutyens's design has often been described by British writers as "the greatest building never built", and it was certainly a magnificent design. A large-scale wooden model of Lutyens's design was built by Messrs John B Thorp for fund-raising purposes and although neglected for many years, this has recently been lovingly restored. It gives a fine and detailed impression of what this ambitious place of worship might have been. Liverpool was home to a rapidly expanding Catholic population at the time Lutyens was charged with Downey's commission. Most were from Ireland and despite their poverty, or perhaps because of it, the archbishop wanted them to have the greatest of all cathedrals. Although unsure of designing for the Catholic Church, Lutyens was reassured when he met Downey in Liverpool; the first thing Downey asked him was, "Will you have a cocktail?" Archbishop and architect were to get on famously. Downey went to Rome with Lutyens in 1933 and plans for the mighty domed cathedral received a Papal blessing.

And what plans they were. The cathedral was to rise in great interlocking blocks of pinkish-brown bricks interspersed with bands of silver-grey granite. The west front resembles a massive triumphal gateway that, if you could imagine a cross-sectional drawing through the building, pushes its way all the way to the crossing, under the dome and resumes it afterwards to inform the plan and internal modelling of the entire building. The west fronts of St Paul's and St Peter's are pure façades.

As its magisterial bulk rose, the design of the cathedral became more complex, culminating in massive belfry towers surrounding a dome clearly based on that of Wren's St Paul's Cathedral. Lutyens worshipped Wren and described the work of his own English Baroque phase as "Wrenaissance". Even so, his design for Liverpool owed as much to Justinian's Santa Sophia in Istanbul as it did to St Paul's. St Paul's is a clever building and wonderful in its own complex and compromised way; Lutyens's cathedral, to be dedicated to Christ the King, was profound.

It was also a much bigger and altogether more monumental work than St Paul's; in fact it was so big that Wren's cathedral would have fitted inside it with room to spare. It was to stand fully 510 feet (155 metres) high, 60 feet (18 metres) taller than St Peter's, Rome, and, given that the church was to be set on top of Brownlow Hill and 530 feet (162 metres) long, it would have dominated Liverpool.

The interior, with its soaring 138-foot (42-metre) high nave, saucer domes, small lunette windows and 53 candle-lit side altars, was to be a solemn and noble affair, lined throughout in granite. There had been nothing this like in Britain before; where St Paul's was designed to be a bright civic temple, Liverpool's cathedral was planned to enshrine the mysteries of the Catholic faith. The foundation stone was laid on June 5, 1933, less than three months after Hitler had appropriated his dictatorial powers in Germany. By 1941 when work ceased, and some four million bricks and 40,000 cubic feet (1,132 cubic metres) of Penrith granite had been laid, the crypt was almost complete. It was used as an air-raid shelter during the Blitz.

Although building work resumed after the war, Lutyens was dead and the cost of the building had risen from £3 million to over £27 million. The crypt and the great paved podium slab above it were completed in 1958 under the direction of Adrian Gilbert Scott [1882–1963], younger brother of Giles, still busy with the neo-Gothic Anglican cathedral at the other end of the street. Adrian Scott was also asked to redesign the cathedral on a less ambitious scale, but this was a poisoned chalice; which architect would really want to prepare watered-down designs for Lutyens's divine scheme? In the event, Scott's plans were abandoned and in their place Sir Frederick Gibberd built his intriguing Gemini space-capsule-like cathedral. Consecrated in 1967 and known locally as "Paddy's Wigwam", this ultra-modern, yet numinous, church occupies a tiny area of the podium Lutyens' cathedral would have filled. It cost about £4 million to build.

The loss of Lutyens's cathedral was, given the era it was commissioned in, almost inevitable. The design, though, is sublime and utterly brilliant. At the time of the fine Lutyens exhibition held in 1981 at the Hayward Gallery in London, the eminent English architectural historian, Sir John Summerson [1904–92] had this to say:

"The question whether a building can assume a place of authority in the world of architecture without actually being built is a curious one; but the answer is not in doubt. Bramante's design for St Peter's dome and Wren's great model for St Paul's still pull their weight in the history books and a whole treatise could be written on Bernini's rejected design for the Louvre. Lutyens's cathedral, no less than these, is a landmark in the architectural history of its time. It will survive as an architectural creation of the highest

order, perhaps as the last and supreme attempt to embrace Rome, Byzantium, the Romanesque and the Renaissance in one triumphal and triumphant synthesis."

Unlike Lutyens, Sir Christopher Wren had been able to build a cathedral within his own lifetime, yet the St Paul's you see today is not the church Wren had wanted to build. The design he favoured most was his third – a superb domed Greek Cross design with beautifully curved walls and fronted by a magnificent Corinthian portico. To show what he intended, Wren commissioned a 13-foot (3.9-metre) high oak model of the design, made for £500 by the carpenters William and Richard Cleere. The restored model now resides in the crypt of the fourth design of St Paul's, the cathedral finally commissioned. Sadly for Wren and perhaps for London too, the reaction to the model was the opposite of what he had hoped for. The clergy and authorities disapproved its Greek Cross plan. Too Catholic, they said. Wren was sent back to the drawing board to produce the brilliant compromise we know today, a Gothic cathedral of sorts, wrapped around in a concealing Baroque wall and crowned with one of the world's finest domes.

After the rejection of his preferred design, Wren said that he would "make no more models, or publicly expose his drawings, which did but lose time, and subjected his business many times to

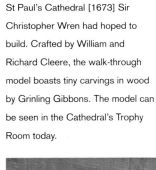

Below The oak model of the St Paul's Cathedral [1673] Sir Christopher Wren had hoped to build. Crafted by William and Richard Cleere, the walk-through model boasts tiny carvings in wood by Grinling Gibbons. The model can be seen in the Cathedral's Trophy Room today.

Right A sensationally over-the-top, and hugely enjoyable drawing of 1918 by Philip Armstrong Tilden of a towering extension for Selfridge's department store in Oxford Street, London. It is thought that this was dreamed up by the architect in rather more than several idle moments. What fun.

incompetent judges." He worked secretly on the final design of St Paul's and in doing so, was able to greatly improve on the design actually commissioned. Luckily, we still have the Great Model of his earlier design.

Britain is not a country known for architectural bombast, but this has never stopped architects and clients, including Lutyens and Downey, from imagining and even trying to realize buildings on a heroic scale. Most such designs remain in the bottom drawer of rejected work, but they are often entertaining. I have no idea what was going through the head of Philip Armstrong Tilden

[1887–1956], for example, when he drew up designs in 1918 for an insanely huge tower to rise above Selfridges's department store on London's Oxford Street. Tilden was Gordon Selfridge's in-house architect and although his American boss clearly had a taste for ambitious neoclassical *beaux-arts* design (the style of the shop), this towering colossus was a step too far. I suppose that this was a bit of fun, a way for the architect to entertain his employer. It was never a serious proposition, but it remains one of those drawings that catches the eye even in today's age of anything-goes "iconic" architecture.

The master of disturbing, unbuilt fantasy designs was a much earlier Classical architect – Giovanni Battista Piranesi [1720–78]. I have not discussed him until here, after the other great architectural fantasists, because I think in some ways he underpinned all their work. This was perhaps not consciously and yet all great architects since Piranesi first published his famous engravings know the Venetian artist's works, and once you have looked again at his nightmare-like prison drawings – *Carceri d'Invenzione* (Imaginary Prisons) – you will see premonitions of the works of many architects who traded in and understood the sublime undercurrents of great architecture.

Piranesi studied as an architect under his uncle, Matteo Lucchesi, who just happened to be an engineer in charge of excavation works. While he went on to make commercially successful engravings of the ruins of ancient Rome and to work on the restoration of the church of Santa Maria del Priorato where he is buried in Rome, Piranesi's most expressive works are undoubtedly his prison drawings and engravings issued as series of prints in 1745 and in revised form in 1761. These depict strange and massive ancient subterranean Roman buildings, all forbidding stairs and galleries, with gloomy vistas extending into hellish corners of a chiaroscuro world. To an extent, their titles speak for themselves: "The Man on the Rack", "The Smoking Fire", "The Giant Wheel", "The Sawhorse" and "The Pier with Chains".

Although their subject matter is macabre, Piranesi's imaginative use of perspectives along with his sudden changes of scale, from minute detail to massive architectural elements, can all be found in the buildings not just of later eighteenth-century architects, including George Dance Jr who designed Newgate gaol (p.51), but also in the monumental drawings of Boullée and the titanic architecture of Albert Speer (p.221).

Left, above and opposite The imaginary "Prison" drawings of the Roman architect and illustrator Giovanni Battista Piranesi have haunted the imagination of artists and architects ever since. Dating from 1745, these include "Carceri XII" (above), with its daunting arches, "Carceri IV" (left) with its disturbing ropes and dizzying changes of levels, and "Carceri II" (opposite), a scene of implied horror, and yet abounding in clever architectural devices and plays on light, shade and unexplained vistas.

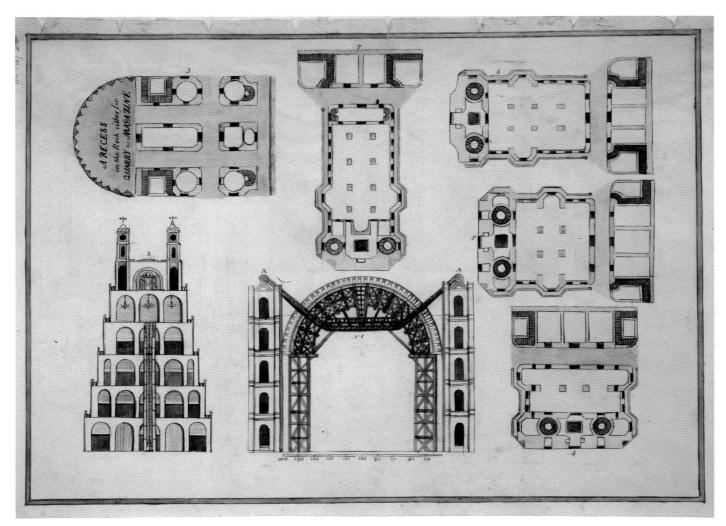

Not that all architectural fantasies from the Classical era were overbearing. Far from it – and just to reassure you, here is an utterly charming design from 1793, by the appropriately named William Bridges [dates unknown] for a bridge over the River Avon between Sion Row, Clifton and Leigh Down, near Bristol Hotwells. The proposal seems to have been a serious one, although it would have been expensive. The carriageway rode over an arch high enough for tall ships to sail beneath it, while on either side of the arch, the spaces between it and the embankments on either side of the river were filled with five storeys of rooms. These included a public granary, a corn exchange, wharves, a coal store, a market, a museum, a library, a marine school, offices, stables, warehouses and 20 dwellings. There was to be a chapel, a toll house, a belfry with a lighthouse on top of the bridge and a pair of windmills. The bridge, cleverly designed for the needs of the river trade, would not only have been useful, but would also have been a wonderful eye-catcher. The Clifton Gorge was eventually spanned, between 1829 and 1836, by Isambard Kingdom Brunel's magical suspension bridge.

As the modern era dawned, artists and architects began to make ever more elaborate images and buildings, as if pulling together all the styles created throughout history, before traditionalism seemed to give way to the apparent purity of Modernism after the carnage of that great historic melting pot, the First World War. It was as if an artistic bubble had burst. In the 30 years leading up to the war, buildings were raised around the world that appeared to meld together every possible

architectural style – Free Style as this has often been labelled. It was against this backdrop that Antoni Gaudí [1852–1926] created buildings that looked like pure fantasy, but were very real.

In the Springfield Museum of Fine Arts, Massachusetts, hangs the extraordinary painting "The Historical Monument of the American Republic" (1867–88) by the folk artist Erastus Salisbury Field [1805–1900]. Field chose to distil 250 years of American history leading up to the centenary of the founding of the Republic, in 10 Babylonian towers. Look closely and you will see that although the towers rise from an Egyptian base, of sorts, they end up in steel-girded catwalks linking the towers together and criss-crossed by steam trains. This was a strange way of getting across the epic story Field wanted to tell and it demonstrates how the story of architecture is as important as any other way of framing history. And in a curious way, if you stand back far enough, Field's painting might just be a visionary representation of the twentieth-century New York skyline.

Above Plans, section and elevation for a Bridge over the River Avon, by William Bridges, 1793.

Right The Historical Monument of the American Republic, by Erastus Salisbury Field, 1877–88.

HISTORICAL MONUMENT OF THE AMERICAN REPUBLIC.

Opposite Metropolis, 1923, a
photo-lithograph by Paul Citroen, a
Bauhaus trained artist, celebrating,
or simply playing with, architectural
notions of how the city – any modern
city – was changing in the twentieth
century; a glimpse, too, into a
collage-like future.

Now look at "Metropolis, 1923", a photo-litho by Paul Citroen [1896–1983] now in the Israel Museum, Jerusalem. This is a collage of architecture from the Modern age depicting it as a great, fragmented jumble – in other words, everything that the great and idealistic architects of the Modern Movement didn't want the Modern world to be. The French-Swiss architect Le Corbusier's 1922 plan for a "Ville Contemporaine" proposed the polar alternative to the randomness of Free Style design or of the noisy world suggested by Paul Citroen. The Contemporary City was to be a model of a new and determinedly Modern order. Le Corbusier imagined sweeping away a great tract of cluttered, dirty old Paris and replacing it with an extensive urban parkland set about with 64 cruciform high-rise steel and glass apartment and office blocks. Here in a Brave New World, the refined bourgeoisie would work and play, cars would speed along freeways and aircraft would land on the roofs of the new towers. The proletariat would live in lower blocks around the edge of this parkland. Everything would be neat, clean, efficient, life ticking away like the mechanism of a Swiss clock.

Even though it was just a fantasy, Le Corbusier's dream of a zoned contemporary city composed of high-rise towers has been seen as the blueprint of hideous post-Second World War housing estates in cities across the world, blighted by new roads and cars. This is sad, because even if wrong-headed, Le Corbusier was attempting to dream up a New Jerusalem, not a hell of third-rate architects' and we-know-what's-best-for-you politicians' making.

Above Perspective of La Ville
Contemporaine, by Le Corbusier,
1922. This was an idea of how Paris
might look if rebuilt for a modern way
of life. It seems unlikely that even Le
Corbusier would have demolished
half of the city that adopted him to
execute such a proposal.

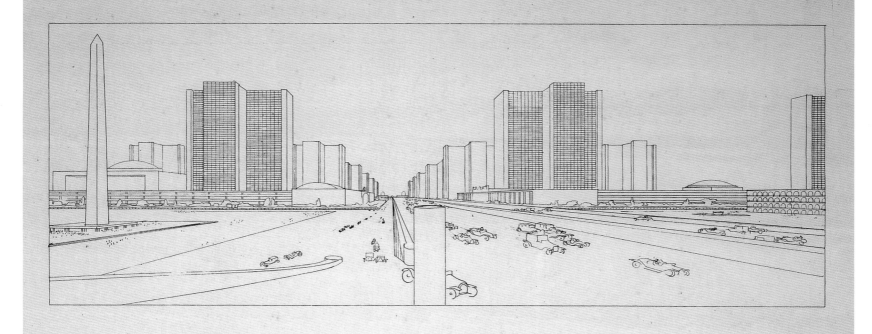

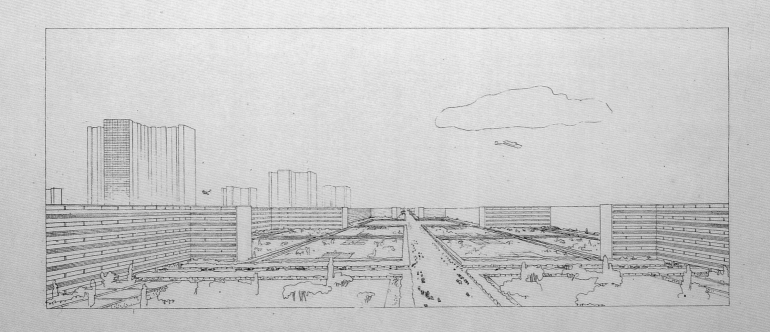

Despite the negative reception of La Ville Contemporaine, dream images of a new architecture began to weave their spell. The fantasy drawings of Antonio Sant'Elia [1888–1916], an Italian architect killed in the First World War, have woven their way into books (Aldous Huxley's *Brave New World*, 1932), films (*Metropolis*, p.193 and *Blade Runner*, p.194) and into the real fabric of modern cities themselves. A key member of the Futurist group of artists, Sant'Elia imagined a modern city composed of vast, brightly coloured mega-structures in which urban life could be played out. You would barely need to leave one of Sant'Elia's towers at any time of the day, week or month. What made the Futurists unattractive to many people outside their artistic circle, however, was their collective obsession with speed, machinery and, unfortunately, Fascism.

Opposite Visionary drawings by Le Corbusier of La Ville Contemporaine, 1922. They depict a city of comfortable, generous residential towers set in urban parkland and connected by fast, elevated roads. When these ideas were applied in crude reality – not by Le Corbusier – the results tended to be horrific.

Above A coloured drawing by Antonio Sant'Elia of La Città Nuova [1913], a city more monumental than that proposed a decade, and a World War, later by Le Corbusier. Like all Italian Futurists, Sant'Elia was in love with speed; look at the cars racing along his multi-laned freeway.

Right The original model of Tatlin's Tower, or the Monument to the Third International [1919-20], on show to party cadres, heroic soldiers and ladies looking too bourgeois for their future comfort, in Moscow when new. Although never built, the proposal echoed down through the decades into the architecture of the 1990s and onwards.

Opposite A proposal made by Alexander Vesnin and his brothers in 1923 for offices for the *Pravda* newspaper, Leningrad. A brilliant conceit, it imagines the building as an advertising and broadcasting platform for the publication, an idea that, strangely, has yet to catch on with today's global media companies.

The most radical architects in Communist Russia tried their best, until Stalin's decree of 1932, to imagine a new world in which symbolism played a large part. A wave of new monuments and buildings would announce to the newly liberated Russian proletariat and to the decadent capitalist world beyond the Soviet borders, just how inspiring life under the Revolution might be. Soon the state itself would wither away and everyone (except the hated middle classes, who would be annihilated) would live in a workers' paradise.

In 1920 Vladimir Tatlin [1885–1953] designed his famous Monument to the Third International, the organization founded the year before dedicated to the overthrow of all capitalist regimes. The slanting design was certainly sensational. Its double spiral steel structure was to have risen to 1,300 feet (396 metres), a third as high again as the

Eiffel Tower, while inside, three steel and glass buildings would house auditoriums and presumably restaurants and other places to meet and discuss the dismantling of the state over a few socialist vodkas. One of these, a cube, would revolve once a year. A second, a pyramid, would do the same once a month, while a third, a cylinder, would turn on its axis daily. This fascinating design continues to excite architects nearly 90 years later – long after the fall of the Soviet Union and the rise of an ultra-capitalist new Russia.

There were other radical Soviet Russian projects including, for example, the "Project for the Leningrad *Pravda*", a design for the Russian newspaper's offices by Alexander Vesnin [1883–1959] and his brothers, but the political tide was turning against the self-styled "Constructivists" and when it swung towards Stalin's Socialist Realism, Vesnin found himself unemployable as an architect.

Opposite Model of a glass and steel skyscraper intended for a site in Berlin designed by Ludwig Mies van der Rohe, 1922. The model no longer exists; although its design has inspired architects ever since, few have ever come up with anything either as pure or as elegant.

Right Charcoal drawing by Mies van der Rohe of the 1922 proposal for a glass and steel skyscraper. The form of the building, as this drawing shows, was to be fluid, a sophisticated play of undulating curves. Only recently has building technology been up to such a challenging task.

Below A typical floor plan of Mies's 1922 glass and steel skyscraper proposal. When Mies got the opportunity to build skyscrapers in the 1950s, he opted for relentlessly straight lines. If only he had lived longer, he might have turned back to this design to go forwards.

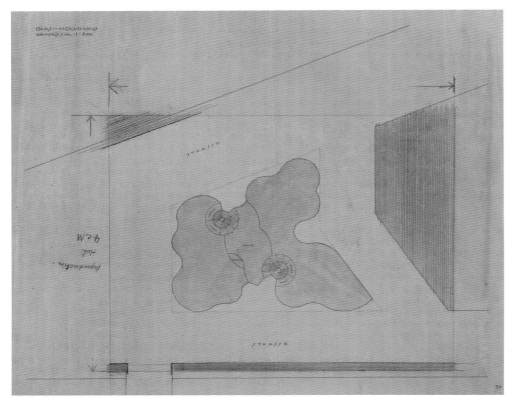

This was unlike the long career enjoyed by Ludwig Mies van der Rohe [1886–1969], a German architect who toyed with revolutionary socialism when young, but went on to become one of the most successful and admired Modern professionals in the United States. With his design of the Seagram Building [1954–58] on Manhattan's Park Avenue, Mies was to set the style for opulent corporate headquarters around the world for the next quarter of a century and probably beyond.

Mies had been playing with the design of a sleek steel and glass skyscraper – more glass than steel – as early as 1920. The glass skyscraper model, since lost, which he presented in Berlin in 1922 was a pioneering work, both elegant and perceptive. This indeed was the shape of things to come, although at the time, building technology was not up to the demands of a real building based on the model. This was no straight up-and-down steel and glass box. The walls, if you look at the plan, followed an organic, amoeba-like form. It was daring stuff and only realizable with the assistance of computers in recent years. Mies was never, I think, as radical as this again; here is one office tower from nearly 90 years ago that would be worth trying to build today.

Above An illustration depicting the scale of the civic hospital for Venice proposed by Le Corbusier. The architect was working on this design at the time of his death in 1965.

Left A model showing a cross-section through patients' rooms in Le Corbusier's Venice hospital. Note the secluded garden terraces, with views over the city and lagoon, set between the sloping roofs.

Le Corbusier, meanwhile, went on to design imaginative white Modern Movement villas and many other hugely influential designs, if not the Palace of the Soviets, until the Second World War when he retreated into the unlovable depths of Vichy France. He later reinvented himself for what must have been the third time. In the 1950s Le Corbusier worked on designs for powerfully sculpted apartment blocks, villas, churches, a monastery and even the new town of Chandigarh on the baking plains of the Punjab. The buildings from this period in his complex career are emotionally charged and quite brilliant.

His last design, a public hospital for the Canareggio district of the city of Venice, promised to be a masterpiece. It would have taken the form of a sequence of internal courtyards, each offering privacy and calm to patients; there would be views from beds across the lagoon. Here was a kind of modern city-within-a-city based on the precedent of medieval monasteries and modern design, infused with the spirit of a city built on water. Models and drawings of the project are not particularly easy to understand and I hope that one day someone will make a large model of the design so that its quality can shine through again today. After Le Corbusier's death in 1965, the project was handed on to the Chilean architect Guillermo Jullian de la Fuente [b.1931] who had worked with the Swiss-French master since 1959. A change of city government, however, put an end to this intriguing project.

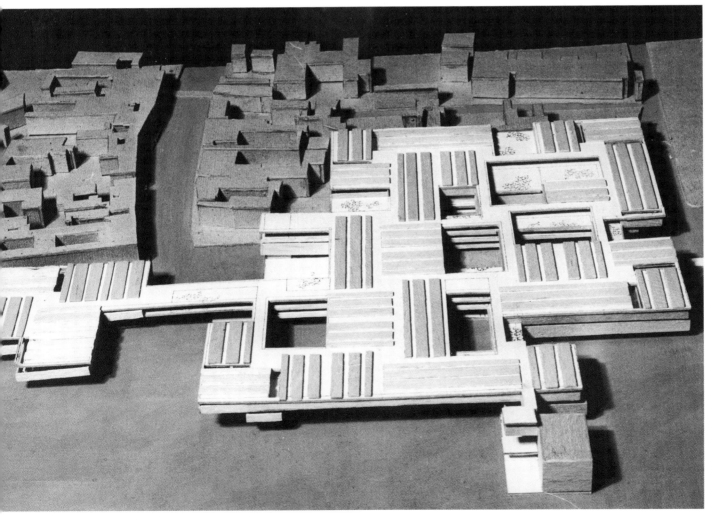

Left This model shows that the design of the hospital comprises a sequence of courtyards. The sloping roofs and garden terraces dominate the hospital skyline. This would have been an intriguing and a humane building, but funds were unforthcoming and the architect died.

Not even today's most successful architects manage to build all of their most cherished designs. One of the world's most dynamic and famous architects, Norman Foster [b.1935], has lost a number of projects over the past 25 years. His office, Foster+Partners, is always hugely busy. Most recently it has completed work on the new terminal at Beijing International Airport, the biggest of its kind in the world. Yet Foster would have loved to have realized the studio's 1982 design for a new BBC Radio headquarters opposite the art-deco style Broadcasting House in Portland Place, London.

This was a subtle and well-planned building – Fosters at their best – occupying the site of the Langham Hotel (since restored). Its entrance, leading into a street-like atrium, faced John Nash's Regency-style All Souls Church. The building was designed only after extensive consultation with BBC staff, and the drawings and models still look good and relevant more than 25 years on. The BBC abandoned the scheme. The Langham Hotel was renovated and after many years the BBC decided to build a new central London headquarters across the street alongside Broadcasting House. This started well with bold designs by MacCormac Jamieson Prichard [led by Richard MacCormac, b.1938], but since the architects were pushed aside, this has been an unhappy story.

Foster's design for a 2,000-foot (600-metre) high Millennium Tower in Tokyo was perhaps even less likely to happen than the BBC Radio headquarters, although the slightly faux excitement generated by the impending Millennium encouraged any number of ambitious architectural schemes around the world which failed to get off drawing boards and computer screens.

The 170-storey Millennium Tower was an exciting challenge. Commissioned by the Obayashi Corporation, it was to take the form of a helical steel tower designed to withstand typhoons and earthquakes. It was to have stood 1 1/4 miles (2 kilometres) offshore in the Bay of Tokyo. Home to 60,000 residents and workers, it was intended to be self-sufficient in energy, while the problem of how to move people efficiently up and down the tower was to have been resolved by the installation of a kind of internal metro railway climbing up, around and across the structure of the building. A sleek and elegant version of

Left The entrance to a new BBC Radio headquarters in Portland Place, London, designed by Foster+Partners, 1982. The giant windows frame John Nash's All Souls' church. If the Foster proposal had been built, the old Langham Hotel, where Albert Speer died, would have been demolished; instead, it has since been renovated.

Below A model of the proposal for the new BBC Radio headquarters opposite the Art Deco Broadcasting House (bottom right), and All Soul's Church, Langham Place (bottom, centre). This was Foster+Partners at their best. The BBC opted for a mean-minded modern tin shed at White City instead.

what Sant'Elia had been trying to do before the Second World War or of what Frank Lloyd Wright was aiming to achieve with his mile-high Illinois building, the Millennium Tower was a perfectly realistic proposition. Money, or a fear of money, put an end to the project, but at least we knew that it was possible to build responsibly at least half a mile into the sky. Whether or not a building will ever really reach that height remains a matter of speculation.

Above A false dawn for Foster's 170-storey-high Millennium Tower, Tokyo. This needle-like skyscraper was one of many idealistic millennial projects dreamed up by architects and their clients as the calendar neared 2000.

Right A detail from a model of the Millennium Tower. The Tower was to have risen from an artificial island or marina off the Japanese coast, complete with helipad and fast road and rail connections to the city.

INDEX

PICTURE CREDITS

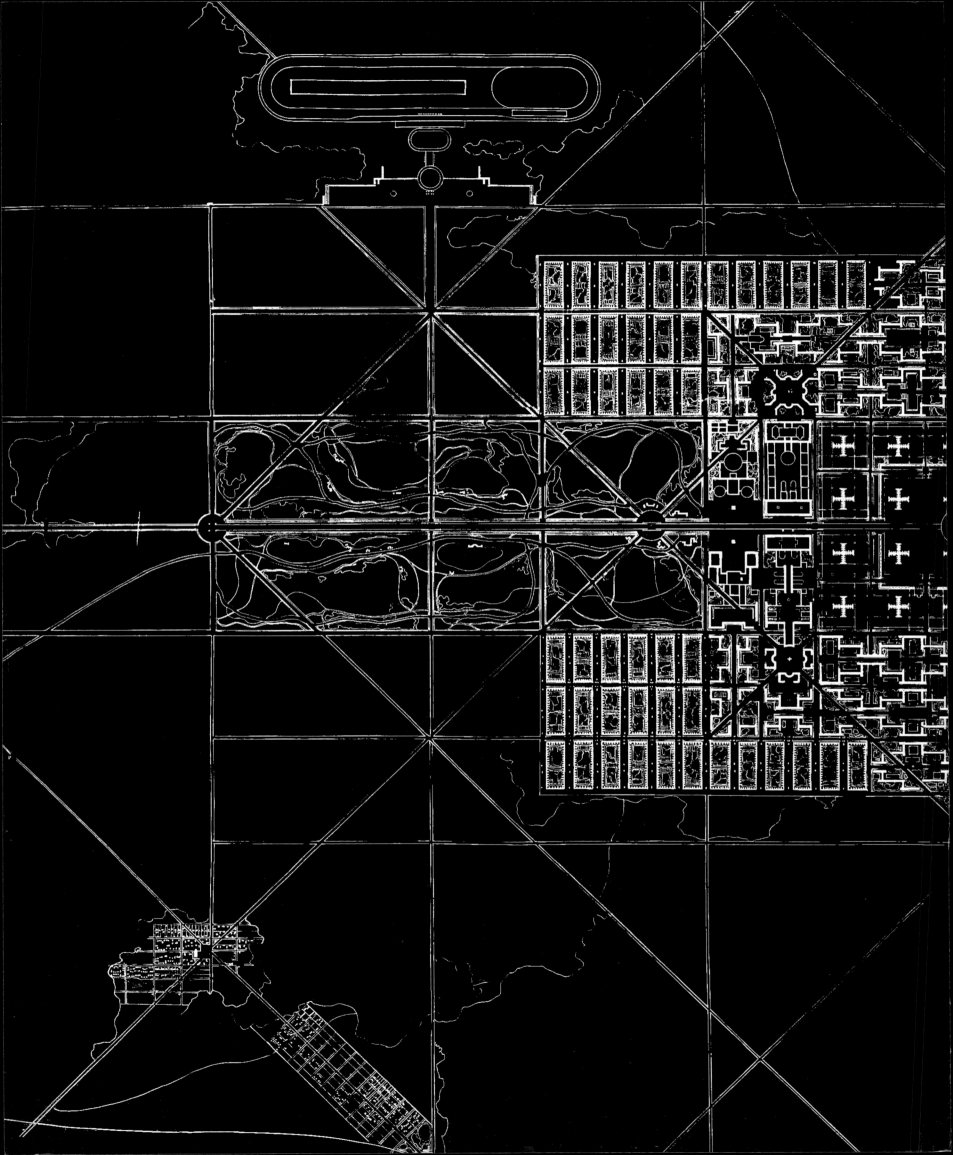